GW00676509

Glenn McCrory is a former IBF Cruiserweight World Champion who fought Lennox Lewis and sparred with Mike Tyson during a ten-year professional boxing career. He is now a broadcaster for Sky Television and has over twenty-five years of continuous service with the network. He still lives in his native North East.

# CARRYING DAVID
## MY AUTOBIOGRAPHY

# GLENN McCRORY

*Chequered Flag*
PUBLISHING

First published in the UK by Chequered Flag Publishing 2016
PO Box 4669, Sheffield, S6 9ET
www.chequeredflagpublishing.co.uk

A CIP record for this book is available from the British Library

Printed in the EU by Print Group Sp. z o.o.

ISBN 9780993215278

To my brother, David.
'The wind beneath my wings.'

# FOREWORD

By John Gibson, *Newcastle Evening Chronicle*
Six-times Regional Sportswriter of Great Britain

Glenn McCrory stands apart from mortals. In a world of bloody conflict Glenn rose from hardship to heights achieved only by a few.

For a long time he was the only boxing world champion ever produced by the North East where fighting men have walked for a century and more.

Glenn survived the murky world of rip-off merchants, of politics and greed, being boiled like a chicken to make a weight no longer his by nature, and forced to train in his own living room with his missus on the pads.

Yet after winning the British and Commonwealth cruiserweight crowns Glenn became the IBF World Champion on a wonderful night of gripping emotion on 3 June 1989.

He did it, too, on his very own patch before his own folk in a style which immediately elevated him into folklore. Another fine mess, Stanley? Not on your life. McCrory strode the Louisa Centre like a king waiting to be crowned and Patrick Lumumba, imported to meet the challenge, was doomed to failure.

Glenn McCrory, the kid from no place, was in the only place worth inhabiting and both Newcastle United and Sunderland were knocked off the back pages which is quite a feat in the soccer mad North East. A triumphant fighter rode through the streets of north-west Durham on an open topped bus. He had fame but certainly not fortune.

I was privileged to witness not only Glenn's four world title fights from ringside but his British and Commonwealth successes as well. And, yes, I admit to a definite bias supposedly not in the make-up of a boxing hack.

Glenn was and has remained the very best of friends. A man generous of spirit, warm and all-embracing despite the way he once earned his meagre living. We have travelled the globe together making TV documentaries, interviewing celebrities and generally ripping the backside out of life.

We shot *The Meanest Men on the Planet* about Sonny Liston and Mike Tyson in Las Vegas, filmed the nostalgic return to Tyneside of legendary rocker Jerry Lee Lewis and retraced the famed but troubled steps of Newcastle United number 9 legend Hughie Gallacher.

Glenn of course has gone on to have a fine career as the voice of Sky Television boxing. Always one with the gift of the gab, he has spent twenty-five unbroken years reaching for the Sky.

Never has a man had such a diverse life, done so much and yet thirsted to do more. For Glenn the glass is always half full and tomorrow is the start of a brand new adventure.

I have known and mixed with enough sporting celebrities and a few others to satisfy any stargazer but none has matched up to the Big Man. And we've only just got started!

# PROLOGUE

'The one duty we owe to history is to rewrite it.'
Oscar Wilde

Saturday 3 June 1989, Louisa Centre, Stanley.

The bell rang and the whole place exploded into a cacophony of sound. I didn't walk to the centre of the ring, I sprinted – and smacked Patrick Lumumba flush on the nose. This was my moment, my destiny. I was fighting in front of my own folk. Another chance like this would never come around again. It was time to grab life by the throat. Time to claim my prize. Shy bairns get nowt. I know because I'm from a family of seven.

The Louisa Centre was packed; wall to wall people. You couldn't wedge a cigarette paper between the folk, all bellowing their support in unison.

All my neighbours were there. I had walked from our house past them to go up the road and fight for the

Cruiserweight Championship of the World. It was a surreal experience. I was carrying my bag, wondering where everyone was going. Then I realised. To see me! Not many warriors have entered the coliseum by strolling up and slipping through the back door.

That morning I had woken to six-foot high headlines in *The Sun* proclaiming 'Glenn's A Goner'. And the prediction was made by a pal of mine, Colin Hart! That's how much of an outsider I was. Lumumba was a beast – he had an impeccable record as an amateur and was the fighter who sane men ducked. I hadn't a choice, it was him or nowt. So it was him.

Alone, with destiny beckoning, I looked in the mirror and asked myself one question: how much did I really want it? The answer was stark and crystal clear: I'm prepared to die tonight.

What Lumumba didn't know was that I had a secret weapon. My brother and inspiration. David. I might have been the fighting man but he possessed an unbreakable spirit and a sheer force of will that gave him the strength to battle every day for survival. David was the brave one, not me. So, so brave. He fought for life, not titles.

Mam and Dad had fostered David as a little lad. I remember us all going to Sandyford in Newcastle to pick him up from the orphanage. At first he was just like any other little boy – cheery and cheeky. Competing for everything. David and I were the closest in age and became the closest of all us brothers.

Yet tragedy lay ahead. It soon became apparent that David was suffering from a muscle-wasting disease. He used to lag behind when we were walking to school. Come on, I used to say, hurry up or we'll be late. Eventually I took him on my back and carried him to school.

Eventually David was left powerless to move or speak by this unforgiving disease, yet he brought incredible love and joy into the lives of everyone he touched.

We both had a dream. His was to live beyond the four-teen years he had been allotted by doctors. Mine was to become a world champion. Together, two brothers with a single determination could both be victorious. This was to be *our* night. Lumumba didn't know it, but the outcome was written in the stars.

I decided the best way to become world champion was to attack. Not to stand around waiting to be picked off by snaking fists into my face. Death or glory. I've always been like that. A chancer; a believer that my glass is half full, never half empty.

Lumumba was so cocky on entering the ring. He obvi-ously felt superior. He had come to claim what rightfully was his. All right, we would see about that.

I was a whirling dervish and the crowd was electric. They sensed it was a special night as my opponent shipped leather. He was brave, I'll give him that, but I had David as my inspiration. I was a man possessed.

I established who was boss from the very first round and when Lumumba had his purple patch, as all boxers must over the course of twelve rounds, I had the strength and determination to hold on. I remember being on the ropes under a bombardment when I looked out into the crowd. There was Tim Healy and the *Auf Wiedersehen* crowd bawling their support. I knew that pop singer PJ Proby, who had infamously split his pants during a particularly raunchy act, was also in the hall somewhere. And then there was Tom, Dick, and Harry, all urging me to stand tall.

My mother had taken our David to stay at my Auntie Delia's house, a mile or so from the venue. Suddenly there was a sharp knock on the door. My mother answered to be met by a policeman with blue lights flashing. He told her to get in. Fearing something awful might have happened, she bundled David and his wheelchair into the police car as quickly as she could. They sped off towards the Louisa Centre.

Upon arrival, the copper forced open the fire doors, piled into the stadium past security guards with Mam pushing David behind him. He took her down to ringside, parked the wheelchair and told her to enjoy the moment her son was crowned champion.

To this day, we don't know how the police knew where my mother and David were. Who alerted them or how. It's still a mystery twenty-seven years later. I would like to thank whoever was responsible because they completed our night, they really did.

As the final bell sounded I walked away with arms aloft. Legendary ITV commentator Reg Gutteridge stated confidently, 'The crowd knows it, certainly McCrory knows it. He's the new world champion.'

As I was being carried shoulder-high, my gaze alighted on a young man sitting ringside, his eyes burning with pride and welling with tears. It was David. I was in pieces. My joy was complete. We looked at one another and knew what we were thinking: brother, we made it!

We had. David was there in the nick of time to see my dreams come true; our dreams come true. I thought back to carrying him to school and realised we had achieved everything we set out to achieve back then. We had worked together and triumphed together. Two brothers, one fight. Life was never going to get sweeter.

David was twenty-nine when he died. I think of him every day and love him more. 3 June 1989 was our day and I'm grateful to God for that.

# ACT ONE

# DREAMS

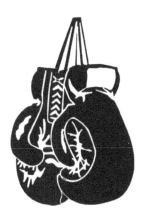

# 1

'Success is the ability to go from one failure to another
with no loss of enthusiasm.'
Winston Churchill

As a kid growing up in the iron and coal-scarred County
Durham of Annfield Plain, I could never have imagined
the switchback life which lay before me. World champion
and full-time Sky Television career? That's only half of it.
I've starred in a West End play, appeared in films, auditioned for James Bond, been a pro chef hosting my own
Ten Club, made telly documentaries, worked with the un-
employed, ran a pub, trained boxers both professional and
amateur. Have I left anything out? Yeah, no doubt.

But then I've always believed that life is best lived as
though it's a theatre and I've had more than my fair share
of drama, both tragic and comic. Maybe it's the theatrical nature of my personality, but I've always been hard to
pin down. I've had my moments of despair but, by and

large, I consider myself an optimistic person. If you want to see and do absolutely everything as I do then you have to be prepared for the kick back. As Oscar Wilde put it so beautifully: 'The wild regrets and bloody sweats, none knew so well as I; for he who lives more lives than one, more deaths than one must die.'

I believe that wholeheartedly. If you're going to live a fearless and full existence then you're going to have a few deaths along the way. That has been the story of my life.

I've never wanted to *be* something. I hate being pigeon-holed. People may come up to me and say 'you're that commentator', 'that boxer' or even 'aren't you that actor who was in such and such?' but I've never been easy to sum up like that. My life's been so diverse because I didn't set out to *be* anything. I set out to *do* everything. I wanted to see things and experience life, to visit places and have adventures. I still do. Consequently, people know me for differing reasons but they tend not to know me for me.

So many things have seemed stacked against me as I've charged through life at full tilt but my attitude has always been to overcome all obstacles in my way. From being a kid I decided that just living life was not enough for me. I was going to kick the arse out of it. I wanted to live for me, for my family, for my brother David. I wanted, and still do, to experience as much as I could of what my time on earth has to offer.

I heard a quote recently that sums up my philosophy perfectly: 'Life is like an ice cream. You have got to enjoy it before it melts.' I like that. Nothing is going to lick me!

*

I was born, Glenn George McCrory, on 23 September 1964, the third of six children, in Annfield Plain, near Stanley in County Durham, which is a nothing sort of village in the middle of nowhere. My dad was a steelworker at the Consett Iron Company and my upbringing was very much in the way of a traditional North East, working-class family. But the family roots, perhaps unsurprisingly given the name McCrory, were Irish. My great-grandfather, Hugh McCrory, was a Catholic born in County Tyrone in 1873. I'm not sure precisely when Hugh came to England with his large family, which included my grandfather, Joseph McCrory, who had been born in 1905. I do know that Joseph became a professional soldier and married my grandmother, Florence Thompson in 1936.

Granddad Joe was a real tough, grumpy old guy. As kids we were scared to death of him. He was in the army for a number of years but still came out a private, so I don't think he was necessarily the best-behaved soldier around. He was a big drinker and I remember, even as a tot, that all you ever got from him was a growl. He would wander in half-drunk, roll up his tie and take off his cufflinks with military precision, growl at us then go to bed. That was it as far as my early memories of my granddad go.

Granddad Joe is partly responsible for my becoming a world champion in a round-about way, for he was the man who brought boxing into the family. He was a bodybuilding champion in the army; a squat, muscular, fit guy about 5'6" in height who boxed while on duty in India with the Ghurkhas. He sent some gloves home to his younger brother Jim, my great-uncle, who took up the sport and went on to record over a hundred wins, fight for a European title and box a draw with Spider Jim Kelly in Belfast.

For various reasons Great-Uncle Jim fought under the name of Jim Palmer and remained known as Palmer to a great many people long after his career had finished. He never seemed to mind this until I became world champion. He still lived in Consett at the time and whenever anybody called him Palmer after I won the title he'd say, 'No – it's McCrory!' He was a lovely old bloke and so proud of me.

After Joseph returned from India he met my grandmother, Florence, who worked as a servant in a house in London. They married, moved to Consett in County Durham and had three children. My dad, Brian, was the eldest, born on 15 September 1937. His brother, Tony, arrived two years later and finally his sister, Patricia, in 1942. Tony followed his father in becoming a professional soldier, which he remained for around twenty years. My father did his National Service with the Royal Artillery, initially training in Oswestry with the remainder of his time spent in Germany. Other than that two-year period he spent much of his working life in the plate mills at the Consett Iron Company from the age of sixteen until the mills closed when he was forty-one. He subsequently spent several years as a Forestry Worker for Tyne and Wear Council.

My dad told us stories of how, as a young boy, his father would put up sacks filled with sawdust and teach him how to box. He did train with the boxing squad in the army but he never had a proper bout. Nevertheless, he maintained his love of the sport and would later introduce his own sons to it, with major consequences!

My mother's family too has an Irish background; her maternal grandfather, William Morrison, having been born in the south of the country. William's daughter, Lavinia, married Scotsman Robert Barrass and proceeded to have six children, of whom my mother, Gloria Barrass, was the fifth to arrive, on 28 April 1939. They lived in Burnhope, a small village near Stanley in County Durham. Burnhope is a mining community and my mother's father and brothers all earned their livings down the pit. My Granddad Bob was the loveliest, nicest, sweetest man you could imagine. As toddlers we would sit on his knee and he'd let us smoke his pipe. I'm not sure he would be allowed to get away with that these days!

My mother left school at fifteen and the following week began working at Shimelds Drapery Shop in Stanley, where she stayed for two years, before moving to Ransome and Marles Ballbearing Factory in Greencroft for a better wage. She did not stay there long, however, as she was about to start a family.

My parents had met for the first time at Castle's Ballroom, Annfield Plain, in September 1958. So they tell me, it was love at first sight.

As my mother tells it she was sitting with her friend near the entrance when Brian came in with his pal, turned and stared right at her. Their eyes were fixed on each other across the room and, after handing in his coat, he came straight over and asked her to dance. At the end of the night they agreed to meet again at the cinema the following evening.

Unfortunately for the two young lovebirds, they had reckoned without my grandmother. My mum was a Protestant and when her mother discovered that her daughter was planning on dating a Catholic she nearly had a fit. She forbade Gloria from going and so poor Brian was stood up and the Glenn McCrory story was nearly over before it began!

Luckily for me, my mother was both smitten and resourceful. She had a friend who knew someone who knew Brian and through this route she managed to get a message to him. They arranged to meet again despite my mother knowing that she would be in no end of trouble if she was discovered. The romance flourished from there.

Eventually, Brian became accepted by my mother's father, Granddad Bob, and, although my nana remained unhappy, the relationship progressed and Brian soon asked for permission to marry their daughter. My mother converted to Catholicism and they were married at All Saints Roman Catholic Church in Lanchester on 27 February 1960. My dad was twenty-two, my mum twenty.

I'm pleased to say that my grandmother's attitude towards my father did mellow over the years. The assumption had been that my mother's mother had a problem with Catholics down to the whole Protestant/Catholic issue that existed, but it turned out that my grandmother's family were originally Catholic themselves. Her father, William Morrison, came to England, had a family of six children and then disappeared back to Ireland leaving his wife to bring up the children on her own. This led my grandmother to develop a dislike and mistrust of all Catholics simply because she could not forget the experience of her family being abandoned by their Irish Catholic father.

Following my parents' marriage they rented a room from an older couple in Dorset Crescent in the Moorside area of Consett. My brother Gary was already on the way and was born, a month prematurely, in October 1960. He would have been conceived on the wedding night knowing my parents! Anyway, a single room was no place to begin life with a baby so my mum and dad began renting a house in Mitchell Street, Annfield Plain, for fifteen shillings a week. It was this house that I was to call home throughout my childhood.

Little more than a year after Gary's arrival came Karen, and then I arrived in September 1964. I was followed by another brother, Neil, in September 1966 and later by twins, Kelly and Shaun, born in June 1969. The six siblings were later joined by our foster-brother David, but that is another story in itself.

Ours was very much a traditional family with my father working and my mother staying at home bringing up the children. As kids we were all very close. Gary was always a bit ahead of us, although there was no real seniority as such. Gary though, as the eldest and after having had my parents to himself, I think he always harboured a slight resentment towards the rest of us simply for coming along, which older siblings tend to do. I certainly don't blame him because it wasn't just one that came along; it was a whole tribe!

Gary was always doing his own thing. He was very much into animals and kept hens, ducks and goats in the allotments at the end of Mitchell Street. My dad liked to race pigeons and took Gary along to help out, which he really liked. He loved the pigeons and thoroughly enjoyed being involved with the whole scene. As far as I was concerned, animals like birds and rabbits were only good for eating.

Karen, being the first daughter, has always been close to my mum, and Kelly is too. The three girls have always had a fabulous relationship.

Neil arrived after me and from an early age it became apparent that he was struggling to speak properly. He underwent an operation on his adenoids and to have fluid drained from his ears. From the age of six he was issued with a hearing aid and had to leave St Patrick's School to attend Craghead School in Stanley, which had a specialist unit for deaf children. He later attended a school in Durham. All of this no doubt added to my parents' burden, as they now had children attending three different schools at the same time, with Gary having moved on to St Bede's Grammar School. To make it worse for them, none of the three schools in question were in Annfield Plain itself.

Funnily enough, I was the only one who could understand Neil when he was little. Before he left St Patrick's, people at school would often ask me to translate what he was saying. Luckily, Neil was only partially deaf. He learned sign language and lip-reading but, thankfully, somehow his hearing gradually improved. At eleven years of age he could dispense with his hearing aid and he returned to a mainstream school, eventually joining the rest of us at St Bede's. .

From an early age I think my position within the family added to my sense of it being me against the world at times. These days my brothers and sisters joke that I am the 'golden boy', but that was not how it felt to me growing up. I felt that Gary had come first and was therefore the apple of my father's eye. After Gary came Karen and she is also special, being the oldest girl. Neil was given special attention due to his hearing difficulties, then the twins arrived and, of course, twins are always special. This left me with a sense that I was the only one who didn't have anything unique about me. I honestly felt at times as though I was invisible, almost wanting to shout, 'Hello! Can anybody see me? I'm here! Hello!'

Today I have no insecurities with regards to my parents; I know they loved me to bits. I remain convinced, however, that they would rather have upset me than any of the others because they knew it wouldn't *really* upset me, if that makes sense. They were more likely to leave me out of something rather than Gary or Shaun, because they knew I'd be okay. It was as though people assumed that I would be fine, because I was tall, big and physically strong. It may sound ridiculous, and people may disagree, but I really felt it at the time and I genuinely think it is one of the reasons that I went out of my way to be noticed from the start and was determined that, one day, I would achieve something in life that would make people pay attention to me.

# 2

'I have known Glenn for half my life. Let's just say that half has been far more entertaining, far more fascinating, far more memorable and much more fun.'

Adam Smith, Sky Sports Head of Boxing

When I was a child, the whole of the North East region was coal mines, shipyards and steel. My dad's family mainly lived in Consett, where the iron and steelworks were based, and my mother's in Burnhope, with Burnhope, Maiden Law and Morrison Busty Collieries all nearby. As a young kid I briefly thought all my mother's relatives were black because all I ever saw were black faces when the men came home from work!

Growing up I used to have nightmares about Consett Iron Company and the mine shafts because they made the future seem so bleak. Back in those days, for so many kids growing up in County Durham, it seemed like the future was already mapped out. You're born, you go down the pit, you get married, you have kids, you spend the whole time working yourself to a standstill and then you die earlier than you really should. And that's what it seemed my future was lined up to be. However, that was reckoning without my inbuilt rebellious streak. My attitude to the life which seemed to be looming for me was very much one of 'well fuck that!' I have always had a sense that nobody was going to tell me what to do. I think it came from a childhood spent thinking: Why us? Why me? Why this? I was pissed off with what we had been given in life. It seemed unfair. As my childhood progressed so my rebellious streak grew and I developed a disdain for any sort of authority whatsoever. This became even more apparent once I started school.

Like every kid I suppose, I used my imagination to escape from the drudgery of day-to-day life. I would watch TV and dream of being a cowboy, an astronaut or a pirate. Back then I really just wanted to be another Errol Flynn and rescue some maiden from a desert island. I wanted to escape because reality was pretty bleak and awful. As a result, my imagination and a desire to become or to achieve something special was always there, and this stayed with me into adulthood. When I look back at some of the wild things I've done I think it is clear that, for one reason or another, it felt as though I was still trying to escape in some way. I think I made a bit of a breakthrough in that respect recently, if I'm honest. It dawned on me that, actually, life's pretty good now. I quite like where I'm at, I've done okay. I've got my family, my friends and my work colleagues and things are not so bad after all. But it's taken a long time to shift the feelings that were planted at an early age.

Both my parents came from poor families and started out together with nothing. They really had to struggle to put food on the table, especially as the family grew ever larger.

Then, in 1967, and with four young children to support, my dad suffered a serious accident. He fell into the furnace at work and shattered the bones in both his feet and ankles. He was only twenty-nine and was in a wheelchair for several months. Happily, he eventually got stronger and was able to walk again, but he suffered considerable pain over the years. This was, of course, a terrible blow for my parents in many ways, but the one saving grace was that he was awarded compensation which enabled him to buy the house in Mitchell Street for £600 in 1968.

The house in which I grew up was a simple three-bedroom terraced property, so typical of the houses found in County Durham mining communities. It is hard to imagine that at one point there were nine of us living there.

Only recently I was talking to a friend of mine, Mike Allen, on his wedding day. Mike was in his fifties and his dad was there for the occasion at an impressive ninety-four years of age. Mike began discussing his father and explained how he came from a different era entirely. He stated, 'you know, my dad comes from a time when there were outside toilets and when the coalman came and filled the bunker because it was all coal fires in those days.' Well, far from being a different era, that was very much part of my own childhood. We had an outside toilet and I clearly remember the coal wagon coming round to fill up the outhouse. That was still part of everyday life in north-west Durham during the seventies, not to mention having to take it in turns to get in the tin bath in front of the fireplace. I'm just glad I wasn't one of the twins because they used to have to take their turn last. Heaven only knows what the water was like by that stage!

The three bedrooms were split so that there was a boys' bedroom, a girls' bedroom and my parents' bedroom. Kelly and Karen shared a single bed in a tiny room. In the boys' room, David had the bottom bunk once he had arrived. Neil was in the top bunk and Gary, Shaun and I had to share a huge, old, second-hand, wooden double bed until I was eighteen and Gary was twenty-two. At different points we would get a new mattress, but the amount of times I cut my leg on some old spring that had burst through was nobody's business. After a spring had emerged we would merely resort to putting sticky tape or a pillow over it to enable us to have a night's sleep without fear of being stabbed.

I've always worn underpants in bed as a result of that early sleeping arrangement. In many a subsequent relationship my partner has asked me why I keep my underwear on in bed but if you've slept with your two brothers until you were eighteen then you're not going to be in the habit of taking them off!

I also still sleep with the bed covers right up around my ears as a result of how cold it could be during the winter. We had no central heating or double glazing back then and the bedroom had a cracked window for a while, so the cold could be almost unbearable. The three of us had to huddle together to keep warm and we could hardly breathe with the weight of the blankets upon us.

One morning we even woke to find a snowdrift at the bottom of the bed. I kid you not! Our roof had a couple of slates either broken or missing and there had been a heavy snowfall during the night. The snow had come in through the roof and the weight of it had caused one of the light-weight ceiling boards to give way, meaning we woke up with a two-foot drift at the foot of the bed. And to show how cold it used to be in our bedroom, it hadn't even melted. At the time we thought it was fantastic. There were five lads having a snowball fight in their bedroom, how could it not be fun?

Despite some of the fun we had, and despite my being aware that my parents had done their very best to find us a house in Annfield Plain in the first place, even as a child I was desperate to get out. That was my motivation for what followed. My thinking was: this is not for me. I am *not* going down the pit. There's got to be more to life than this. Although we were very happy as kids playing together and we had fabulous, loving parents it still seemed a really dark and bleak existence.

I also had a sense of feeling as though I didn't really come from anywhere. It was never a question of being Irish or English, or of being from a city like Newcastle or Sunderland. I felt like I was from nowhere. There's a little village called No Place on the opposite side of Stanley to Annfield Plain, in which you can find my favourite pub, the Beamish Mary. It is fairly ironic that as a child I felt as though I came from No Place and there it was on my doorstep.

I worry that it will sound as though I have no love for Annfield Plain, Stanley or Consett, but the truth is that, although they seemed like dead-end places at the time, I am still fiercely proud of where I came from. We are, all of us, shaped by our surroundings and upbringing. Part of what I achieved and who I am today was formed back in those terraced streets. When I was young and staring at the abyss of a working life down a pit I was determined to break away and thought that if I managed to do so that I would never go back; but in the end I've never really left. Today I live in Newcastle upon Tyne, no more than a dozen miles from where I was raised.

When I return to Stanley the people are still friendly and I'm always just 'Glenn'. They will ask how my parents are doing, tell me if they saw me on TV and are always down to earth and welcoming. They make me feel proud to have come from County Durham. I love the North East and it's where I will always call home.

I will admit though that while I was growing up there was a fair amount of trouble and a number of rough characters around. There was a lot of vandalism, fighting and theft. However, for some reason, people always seemed to look after us. I don't know if people felt sorry for us, or whether it was that my parents were so popular, but we always seemed to be shielded from the trouble that surrounded us.

Although my dad was a really nice man, he always seemed to know the nutters! For some reason the genuine hard guys all seemed to respect my dad. There used to be burglaries all the time where we lived and our house would have been an easy target. You wouldn't have had to force the lock because the door didn't work. You'd need not have broken a window because half the windows were open or broken already. But nobody ever broke into our house. My parents could literally leave the door wide open. Mind you, we had nothing to nick which might have had something to do with it!

I was aware from a young age that we were poor and that people used to look after my parents and try to help them out from time to time. They were good Catholics and used to get a lot of help from Father Noel Phelan, the priest from St Teresa's Church in Annfield Plain. He was a big, almost John Wayne-like, man, around 6'4" tall, who loved my mum and dad and did what he could to help out. If somebody had died he'd bring the clothes round to see if they would fit any of us. This sometimes meant that I would go out looking like one of the Kray twins when everybody else was looking like the Bay City Rollers in their flares!

Some things stick in my mind so vividly. There was an old guy down the street who died and, sure enough, his clothes were brought round for me. I must have only been about eleven because it was my last year at junior school and it was the night of the school Christmas party. My mum packed me off all lovely and clean, looking, to her mind, like a million dollars, but in fact I looked like I had just come off the set of a gangster movie! Everybody else was in jeans and flares and the fashionable clothing of the mid-1970s. I remember being so embarrassed that I had secretly taken an old pair of jeans I used to play in, stitched the backside back into them and ironed them to take with me. As an aside, let me point out that you had to learn very quickly how to iron your own clothes in a big family like ours or you would end up going out with about four pleats in your pants!

I didn't want to upset my mother by telling her I wasn't happy about going to the Christmas party in the clothing she had acquired for me. I remember getting changed at school and dancing around thinking I looked great when, after a matter of minutes, the whole arse fell out of my jeans! I had no choice but to dash out and put my other gear back on. I was absolutely gutted. Naturally all the other kids took the piss and I just had to take it. I kept that sort of thing to myself as a child because, although I was embarrassed that I didn't have the stuff that everybody else had, I also knew how hard my parents were trying. That's why I could never let on to them; I just learned to accept it.

Despite the money worries, one time that was always magical in our family was Christmas. Every year it was just fantastic. The excitement of Christmas with so many kids in the house was just unbelievable and each year my parents managed to pull out all the stops. My mum would use the Empire Stores catalogue to buy all the presents and pay for them over the rest of the year. It must have been hard for them, but every year our rooms were like Santa's Grotto. I suppose if you haven't got a lot, and then all of a sudden there are presents for all, it just makes everything seem all the more fabulous.

We always had stockings full of fruit thanks to Sammy Castle, the local greengrocer. He would come every Saturday night with apples and oranges and the vegetables for Sunday dinner and he'd make a big trip when it was

Christmas, so we'd have loads of tangerines and apples in our stockings, which was great. Everybody played with each other's toys; we would all help each other build stuff and it was just a wonderful time.

I've always been somebody that likes to plan things in detail. As a child I would combine this love of planning with my love of Christmas and would draw up a detailed strategy of what we would do on Christmas morning. It seemed as though I sometimes started doing this around September. It was crazy. I'd draw maps of the house and I'd go over it with my brothers, explaining how we'd come downstairs. I mean… what? There was only one way down. How else were we going to do it? Come down the chimney?! But that formed part of my enjoyment at Christmas time. And I was so excitable that I often wouldn't wait until the morning. I would wake everyone up at a ridiculous hour. One year we went downstairs and my parents hadn't even gone to bed yet! They chased us back up and locked us in our bedroom. Our bedroom door handle had come off on the inside so if my parents pulled the door shut we were locked in. We'd have all manner of implements in there such as knives and Meccano to try to prise it open in such circumstances.

I can recall only ever having two disappointments at Christmas. The first was when I dreamt and prayed for a Chopper bike. I just wanted one so badly but, realistically, I was never going to get a bike. My parents simply couldn't afford one. We got lots of presents but there was no way they could stretch to anything like that. My mum wouldn't say that though. Her explanation would always be, 'No – they're too dangerous; far too dangerous', before adding, 'why don't you go to the boxing instead?!'

So I never got my Chopper which was my first big Christmas disappointment. The second was my brother Gary. He would usually go along with my Christmas plans. He'd still fit in and we'd all go down in order until one year, he must have been about seventeen, I went to wake him up and he said, 'No. I'm not going downstairs like that. It's stupid.' He'd grown up. That was a huge disappointment because from then on Christmases were never the same, but until then they were magical times.

That's one of the reasons why I always wanted to have a big family myself. I wanted the same because it was just such a happy experience to have a gang of excited children coming downstairs together. When there were five boys, all with different toys, all different ages, and I could play with both the younger and the older ones, it was just brilliant.

Compared to Christmas it has to be said that our family holidays were not quite so exciting. We would always spend them at a nearby caravan site. I think we once travelled as far as Blackpool, but other than that the furthest we ever went was Scarborough. We certainly never went abroad. Normally, despite us thinking we seemed to be going miles, we would end up little more than half an hour up the road at Sandy Bay near Newbiggin. I remember it was usually cold and bleak and there was seemingly nobody else there. For one reason or another we seemed to go the week before the school holidays began. I don't quite know why, but we'd often go a week early and there would be no other kids around.

With seven of us around, it was impossible to get much one-on-one time with either of my parents. I didn't see a lot of my dad as he was at work for much of the time, but he would always try to be there at school football matches and the like. My mum was at home all day, but she was always busy doing something for one of us. We may have been kids but we understood from very early on that you had to take a back seat from time to time and just get on with stuff.

I think that if you're from a big family, especially one which is seen to be a bit poorer than everybody else, then you do tend to stick together and we were certainly like that. We did look out for each other and were very close. I adore both my parents, they've always been fantastic, but I will confess that I was always a bit of a mummy's boy when I was young. I had a special relationship with my mum and I'd always want to do stuff for her.

There was a lovely period when my dad used to go to the club regularly. He was never a heavy drinker, but he would always like a night down the club. He'd have his tea, watch TV with us for a bit and then be off out from around nine o'clock until eleven. My older siblings would be doing their own thing and the younger ones would be in bed so I had my mum to myself for a little while. We developed this routine where, every Friday, she would go and have a bath and I'd make her supper. It would only be something like a box of chicken chow mein and involved nothing more than boiling the pan, heating the noodles and preparing the fried rice, but my mum would come downstairs and tell me it was lovely and eat her supper. It was a wonderful bonding moment between us.

To this day I still thoroughly enjoy cooking for people; it's a real passion of mine. However, it isn't just the cooking itself that I relish, I simply love looking after people. I think that love started back then, preparing my mum's supper while she had her bath. Special memories.

I remain very close to my mum, not that I'm constantly on the phone to her or round visiting all the time or anything like that; we're just very close to one another. My mum's quite an artistic person and that has definitely influenced me. I have grown to develop a similar love of theatre, poetry and classical music. My mum regularly has poems featured in the *Newcastle Evening Chronicle*. I may be biased but I believe she's very good and she has won various competitions. I was delighted when, in 2012, I was able to surprise her by publishing an anthology of her poems as a proper book, entitled *My Life in Verse*.

I don't know whether my mum's influence alone brought about my fascination with the written word, but it certainly must have had an effect. It's not that I avidly read a book every day, but I love great characters and classic literature. I've got a huge fondness for writers such as Ernest Hemingway and Oscar Wilde and can drop quotations from Dylan Thomas into everyday conversation, often to the surprise of the person I am talking to, as most people don't expect that from a working-class ex-boxer! Oscar Wilde is a particular hero of mine. A few years ago I actually paid his cigar debt off. He owed something like £113 to Fox's in London and I went in and paid it off for him. They gave me a certificate to confirm I'd cleared the debt then, a couple of weeks later, they called me up to tell me I wasn't allowed to do that. I pointed out that they had accepted my money and I had the certificate to prove it. They told me that the amount I paid would not have been enough as interest meant that the actual current debt would have been a far higher figure after over a hundred years. I simply said, 'I don't care. I've paid Oscar Wilde's debt off – it was in the paper!'

My literary tastes surprise many people and it's the same with music. Yes, I like Rihanna and other contemporary singers and I occasionally watch MTV but, when I'm in the house alone or I'm out in the car, I almost always listen to classical music. It's never Radio One. My dad loved Caruso and Mario Lanza, whose films I watched as a kid. My favourite, though, is Katherine Jenkins. She's a fabulous singer and great to look at too! I went, by myself, to see her at Newcastle City Hall when she last toured and I thoroughly enjoyed the experience. It may seem weird but then I'm all about opposites. My good friend John Gibson said to me recently, 'You're an enigma Glenn. You're the roughest kid I know and yet you listen to classical music and you've just quoted Dante – I've never known anyone like you.' Like I said, perhaps many people wouldn't associate opera, poetry and literature with an ex-boxer. Like I've also said – never try to pigeonhole me.

# 3

'One of the great untold stories of boxing unfolds through the life
of one of the most loved of all British fighters. Glenn McCrory,
World Champion, is but a small part of a great man. The noblest
achievement of my friend – everybody's friend – Glenn, was the
selfless championing of his brother's right to as full and rich a life as
humanly possible. Glenn is even more of a hero outside the ring.'
Jeff Powell, Chief Sports Writer, *Daily Mail*

Perhaps the most significant event in the life of our family,
and certainly in my own life, took place in 1972. None of
us realised at the time the huge impact about to hit us. It
was when we first met David.

What a new chapter this was going to be – one of
love and heartache, caring and suffering. One of bonding
against seemingly insurmountable odds and yet somehow
overcoming them. One of doing what people told us we
could never do. Of achieving the impossible.

It came about partly because my mother had seen something in the local paper which tugged her heart-strings and partly because Father Phelan thought it would be doing Mam and Dad a favour financially. David would be going to a loving home and there were benefits for fostering a child. There were six kids already so what harm could one more do?

Little did Father Phelan realise that David had a degenerative disease which would lead to years of unending toil and struggle for my mother. He had no idea what he was about to unleash.

David was born on 2 March 1966. He was six years old when we first went to see him and was living at Nazareth House, an orphanage in the Sandyford district of Newcastle upon Tyne. I believe he had been placed with a couple of different potential foster families but it hadn't worked out and he had ended up back at Nazareth House.

I remember the eight of us (Mam, Dad and kids) arriving for our first visit. There were a lot of young ones there in the care of the nuns who ran the home. The one responsible for David was Sister Lydia, who was lovely but couldn't have been more than a teenager. Such devotion.

I was seven years old and I didn't take to David at first. It wasn't love at first sight. That took time. My first impression was that he looked 'a bit funny', a typically forthright thing that kids often think and say. David wore National Health glasses and walked in a slightly awkward, clumsy way.

Nevertheless before long we started to play with all the kids in the home. Coming from a big family we were good mixers, but then all of a sudden David, who was sitting closest to me, put his arms around a toy and moved it away from me as if to say 'that's mine'. We all shared everything at home, we had to, and it seemed so strange to me that I have never forgotten it. It was different for David of course. He had very little in his life and he didn't want to give up anything he could lay claim to.

When we left after that first visit, I think my mum's feeling was that she wasn't sure he would fit in. As the days went by, however, she was unable to get him out of her mind. I don't know whether something in her conscience couldn't let her overlook him because she knew he'd been out to a couple of families already but, despite her misgivings, she made up her mind that she wanted to give him a chance.

We went to visit him on several occasions and he would also come to stay with us for short periods until everyone got used to each other. At first it wasn't just him who was coming. We had jumped straight into playing with everybody so all the other kids loved us too. When David started coming to visit us they would bring him in a minibus full of other children. When it came time for them to go back, half of them would go missing because they all wanted to stay. Ours was that sort of house. There was so much love and fun and although we didn't have much money we'd always have the best biscuits! My mother was always one for buying the top brands. Our cupboards contained Kellogg's Cornflakes, Lurpak butter and Heinz ketchup. We were always well fed. We never had luxury food, but we had good old basic food from the most reputable brands.

The following year David came to live with us permanently. The final papers were signed by the Hexham and Newcastle Diocesan Rescue Society in March 1974. I get the feeling that they were desperate to try and provide David with a chance of happiness and once my mum had decided she wanted him to join us then the job was done quite speedily.

I'm not sure that today the authorities would allow a family on such a low income with six young kids already to foster another but, at that time, with the family being good Catholics, highly regarded by the local church and with us all being so fit, healthy and happy, it just seemed to sail through.

From the start it was known that David had a few problems. It was obvious even to me at seven that he walked a bit clumsily. What nobody knew was just how serious David's problems actually were. Even the doctor didn't think his condition would get significantly worse.

Initially I had reservations, not helped by losing my bottom bunk and being forced to share a bed with Gary and Shaun, which went down well as you can imagine! But things were to change on one particular morning on the way to school.

David started to attend St Patrick's with me. It was a long walk along various streets and up and down hills just to get to the bus stop, where we would catch the bus to Dipton before walking the final hill to reach the school itself. David's slow walking speed was forever holding us up so, one morning, I became exasperated, told him he was always dragging behind and made him get on my back so I could carry him there quicker.

And that was it. That was the connection made.

From then on I would look to carry my brother and David was always eager to climb on for a ride. My mum would tell me to put him down and let him walk because she was scared that I would damage my back and that David wouldn't get the exercise he needed, but for some reason that was my connection with David and we loved it. Maybe it is another example of my desire to look after people and to help them. Maybe I just wanted not to be late because I would get the cane and David wouldn't! Whatever the reason, it became my thing to put David on my back and carry him to school every morning. I'd simply say, 'Come on, let's get to school,' put him up there and away we would go. From that moment on we bonded and never looked back.

I always had a protective streak about all my family, but it was heightened with regards to David. I recall one kid at school calling David a 'spacker' and I punched the living daylights out of him in the schoolyard. It was a real frenzied attack and it needed several teachers to pull me off him. No one was going to pick on my family, David in particular, and after that incident it didn't happen again.

David went through a period when his walking became noticeably worse and his feet seemed to be turning inwards. Expert opinion seemed to be that it was something that could be fixed rather than a degenerative, wasting disease and so he underwent a series of operations in the hope that his legs would return to normal. He hardly ever walked again. My dad tried to encourage him by telling him to march like a soldier and other such motivational ideas but, after a brief improvement, he began to deteriorate.

David's decline was very gradual. Every now and again I would realise that things were getting worse. I'd notice that he was struggling to walk more than he used to, or that he had stopped doing certain things that he used to be able to cope with. His speech was getting worse and he had to start using a spoon instead of a knife and fork at mealtimes. It was a gradual deterioration, but very distressing for all of us. On more than one occasion he nearly choked, which frightened everyone and must have been horrendous for David to go through. Incredibly though, David was always smiling. He never seemed to complain about the way his life was turning out. He used to attend a club for handicapped children which ran discos and all sorts of other entertainment, which he loved. His bravery in the face of what must have been miserable circumstances continues to inspire me to this day.

My recollection of events is that when David was around fourteen my mum took him to hospital for a check up. I believe it was around the time that I was on the way to winning the National Junior Amateur Boxing Association Championships (the Junior ABAs as they are known), so positive things were starting to happen for me. I was getting occasional reports in the *Stanley News* and things were looking up. I have this memory of my mum taking David to the hospital in Newcastle and coming back in tears. The doctor had told my mother the extent of David's problems. He was suffering from Friedreich's Ataxia, it had become far worse than expected and, as it was now affecting his throat, he did not believe he would last much longer.

To that point, David had always called my mum and dad 'Auntie Gloria' and 'Uncle Brian'. After that hospital visit things changed. My mum told him that from that moment on he was to call her 'Mum'. My parents loved him, he had become part of the family, and now they thought they could lose him at any time. However, my parents decided not to tell any of us, including David, what the doctor had said at this stage. They wanted us to remain a happy family for as long as possible.

That was a really bad time because not only did I have to come to terms with David's increasing problems, but also I felt that, once again, I was being forgotten. I had finally accomplished something worthwhile by winning the Junior ABAs and all of a sudden it was almost as though it had been taken away from me again. Somebody and something else was suddenly more important than my achievements. I again felt that sense of wanting to yell, 'What about me? I'm here! Can't you see me?' Finally people were starting to notice me and then all of a sudden it was a case of, 'No Glenn, David's more important right now.' As I progressed through my adolescence I was constantly wrestling with my concern and love for my brother and my need to be recognised for my own achievements. It was a difficult time.

Despite the gloomy prognosis the doctor had given my parents when David was fourteen, he continued to fight through his difficulties and to enjoy life. At one point the doctor expressed astonishment when my mother arrived with David for a check up as he admitted that he had not expected to see him again.

As David's condition worsened he moved to a special school called Cedars in Gateshead. He was provided with a wheelchair and the house was fitted with a stair lift. As you can imagine with a houseful of youngsters, pretty soon nobody was walking upstairs anymore. Everybody, including family friends, enjoyed the novelty of taking a ride to the top. The twins and I would also play wheelies in his wheelchair as everybody continued to make the most of the way things had turned out. He briefly had a motorised wheelchair but, quite frankly, he was a menace to society in it! He started to attend a day centre after his schooldays were over and the older people were terrified of him as they had to keep jumping out of his way. Our dog was equally petrified, so David's motoring days were soon over.

The literal carrying had long since ended, but the metaphorical meaning went on. I had my connection with him. All the others had their own relationships with David – I wasn't unique in that – it was just that we had this personal little bond between us and it seemed obvious to me that he felt the same way. In a way, he enjoyed much of his life by living it through me and my activities. He got excited when fight nights were approaching. He wanted to know what was happening. He'd want to be there at the fights when they took place and so on.

After a while it became a question of just who was carrying who? Who needed who more? I found that I needed David every bit as much as he needed me. His zest for life in horrible circumstances, circumstances that would have caused lesser human beings to give up, was a constant source of inspiration to me. He was there to provide me with the boost I needed and, in a way, to give me someone and something to fight for. I think he needed me to achieve great things to help keep him going, because he fought on for fifteen years longer than the doctors had expected. He certainly lived for something and I hope that in some way I played as big a part in maintaining his desire for life as he did for me.

# 4

'If brains were a disease Glenn would be in perfect health.'
Jim Watt, former World Lightweight Champion

My rebellious streak was seen to its greatest (or should that be worst) effect at school. I went to St Patrick's Infant and Junior Schools until I was eleven and I can honestly say that I hated it. I can still remember my first day like it was yesterday. I just recall crying my eyes out because my mum had left me. The teacher put me in the nursery school sand pit and I can still remember sitting there, sobbing my heart out the whole day. It never got much better and I hated every single day I went to school. St Patrick's was a Catholic school run by nuns and they were vicious. Sister Mary Edward and Sister Joseph are two I remember for being strict and, quite frankly, terrifying. I recall standing in assembly singing one day when Sister Mary Edward came up, dragged me out of the line, sat me down and said sharply, 'You can't sing. Sit down.' I've never been able to sing since! I don't even do it in the bath thanks to Sister Mary Edward.

At the age of eleven I moved to St Bede's School in Lanchester, just after it changed to a secondary modern. Gary had attended it as a grammar school pupil and my parents had saved up to ensure he had a briefcase, tie and blazer for his first morning. When I started my parents couldn't really afford new items for me and I wasn't about to insist that they tried, so I went in a second-hand Wrangler jacket and a black jumper, despite the uniform demanding a red one. I found myself pinned up against the wall by the Deputy Headmaster on my first day. He told me to make sure I was in uniform the following morning. Well that was it – a red rag to a bull, or perhaps that should be a red jumper? Anyway, from that day on, I made sure that I never wore the correct uniform for any single day I went to that school.

Right from the start, my stance was that if they are saying that my parents had to somehow afford the proper uniform then I was going to reply, 'No they don't.' It felt to me like people were picking on my parents and I've always tried to look after them, as I have done with my brothers and sisters. That, crossed with my rebellious nature, led to an uncomfortable time at St Bede's – for both parties.

To be honest I was hardly ever there. And when I did turn up I was such a difficult pupil that, to my knowledge, they never once went to my parents to ask why I wasn't at school when I was absent without leave. I think they were just glad to have me out of their hair.

I would be a pain in the arse to the point of real disruption to the class and I really didn't care. In lessons with Miss Green I would often just get up and walk out of the classroom and then come back a few minutes later. Then I might start talking so she'd tell me to stand at the back of the room whereupon I'd get up and walk back out again. Eventually I'd get sent to see the Headmaster and he would tell me off and send me to Mr Fagan to be given the strap. It was just a silly, ridiculous, pantomime performance.

Mr Fagan, despite this, was actually my favourite teacher. To be perfectly truthful, I was virtually a delinquent at school and none of the other teachers wanted me in their classroom. Mr Fagan used to stand up to me, which I respected. He would literally start some lessons by coming in and saying, 'Right McCrory. I know you're going to do something so let's get it over with.' And I would come to the front, hold out my hand, he'd take out his leather strap, give me a whack and everybody would laugh; including me. He'd probably go to prison for doing that now and yet he was probably the only teacher I liked! I liked him because he wouldn't be pushed around. I could manipulate the others but he wouldn't let me get away with any of that.

Corporal punishment was something that went right through my whole schooling. It was a joke. I ranked the teachers by who could use the strap the best, and alongside Mr Fagan I would place Mr Cuthbertson who could be pretty nasty with the strap. He looked a bit like Catweazle and was always smoking. If he gave you the strap it would hurt. There was also Mr McCormick who was just a little guy but had a fiery temper. The rest of them wouldn't hurt, but those three were painful.

I think my parents are the most wonderful people but, although I'm sure they wanted the best for all of us, I can never remember them sitting down and doing homework with me. They had seven kids and were struggling to survive: to feed us, to clothe us, to bring us all up, to take us to church, to do all that sort of stuff. With everything that was going on I guess there was no time for either of them to sit down and ask how my History lessons were going or anything like that.

I do remember getting many bad reports and on one occasion my mother coming upstairs, ripping one up in my face and shouting 'this is diabolical!' at me, so I know they cared. I don't know if they'd perhaps given up on me a little bit, or maybe they didn't expect me to do well; I'm not sure what their thoughts of me as a schoolboy actually were. They knew I really didn't like school though. I can't say how strongly that came across, how much they knew that I genuinely hated going, or how aware they were of how often I played truant, but perhaps that had an effect on how they approached my schooldays.

Also, I'm fairly sure my parents will have assumed that the boys would all get jobs with the Consett Iron Company, or down the pit, and the girls would marry somebody who worked in one or the other, and that would be that. The same as their lifetimes and their parents' lifetimes had been. I knew from early on that that was not for me.

At school there was a group of us who went from St Patrick's to St Bede's as mates. There was Ian Callaghan, Sean

Ward, Hylton Marrs and Micky McKee who, God bless him, is no longer with us. We got up to our share of mischief, but when I got to St Bede's I met up with a whole new bunch of kids every bit as delinquent as I was. It was great! Sadly, several of them have died far too young through drink, drugs and motorcycle accidents. I guess I was lucky that I managed to get myself away in time.

I remember going to Ozzy's tattoo parlour in Byker at around twelve years of age, telling him I was sixteen and coming home tattooed. I had the world 'Mother' on my right shoulder and, shortly afterwards, got both forearms done with a rose and a dragon respectively. School were not pleased. I also wore earrings and carried a knife. I was a complete lunatic quite likely heading for jail. The movies I loved were such things as *The Warriors* and *The Wanderers* and all those gang films of the time. Me and my mates would sometimes cut off our sleeves to emulate what we had just seen on screen and that's also why I went for the earrings and tattoos. We all wanted to be in little gangs and would chase each other over the coal heaps and were forever nicking stuff. At that point in my life I felt as though I had no hope, which contributed to my becoming the rebel that I remain.

My worst days were up until the age of fourteen. I started going to the boxing club at twelve, but I was a big lad and, as a result, I was difficult to match. I therefore didn't start boxing properly until I was fifteen. After that I started to calm down, but beforehand I was running wild. I used to be out stealing and shoplifting on a regular basis. I even used to take David with me to the Disco, which was the name given to the local supermarket in Annfield

Plain, as my accomplice. That was a great ruse because I'd take him round in his wheelchair and everybody would be thinking, 'Aww how sweet. It's Glenn looking after his little brother,' yet all the time we'd be sticking all sorts of sweets and what-have-you down the sides of his wheelchair. We had it off to a tee.

Most ridiculously of all I broke into St Bede's School and nicked the school video. Video recorders had pretty much just been invented and our school had saved up to buy this machine. My thinking was that I could tape boxing on TV and watch it whenever I wanted. That shows how daft I was back then. Where did you get video cassettes from in those days? Nobody had them. How was I going to explain buying them even if I could find some? And how was I expecting my parents wouldn't discover it? Especially if I was hoping to link it up to the television! Anyway, rather foolishly, I didn't realise it would be that big a deal; but obviously it was. The police were called and CID became involved. I realised that there was no way I could keep it so, two or three days later, I put it on the cross-country course and they found it. I hate to think what would have happened if I had been caught.

Unlike many of my contemporaries, I wasn't into drinking or anything like that as a kid though. I always wanted to be the fittest and the fastest. I loved my sports and drinking didn't fit in with that. Plus, if we got up to anything we shouldn't, I wanted to make sure that I was the one that got away!

They pulled down the old Annfield Plain Co-op brick by brick, then rebuilt it as part of Beamish Museum. It must have taken them a damn sight longer to rebuild it than they were expecting, however, because we nicked all the lead! We would never break into houses or anything like that, but we didn't have any money and so we saw ourselves as foragers. I never had pocket money in my life, so I felt as though I was fending for myself. We were just out finding scrap metal and, if somebody's pulling an old building down and there were bits of lead there, then we were just going to take it, weren't we?

Sport was always big in the family in a way that it seemed education never was. My dad was working class and at home never really talked of books or anything like that, so sport was very much the thing.

I was lucky enough to be good at most sports, especially football and athletics. As far as my early interests in boxing are concerned, I remember my dad would come in from the Demi – the Democratic Club – after a couple of pints and I would enjoy spending some quality time with him in front of the TV. Sometimes there might be a fight on that we'd sit and watch and after a drink or two his cogs would be a little bit oiled for chatting, which would get him talking about his father and my Uncle Jim and telling tales. Like when my granddad would take him to St James' Hall in Newcastle, and how he would meet famous boxing characters. Tales of meeting Randolph Turpin and Don Cockell and stories of North East boxing legends like 'Seaman' Tommy Watson and 'Cast-Iron' Casey. All these names would suddenly float back into his memory from days gone by. That romantic nostalgia simply added some colour to the dull and grey existence that was life in a small North East mining village for a young boy.

As well as talking about football and boxing, my dad would occasionally get Gary and me to put the gloves on. There were always a tatty couple of pairs in the house, old and knackered with no padding, and we'd put them on, use the old punch bag that my dad had brought into the house, and occasionally spar a little. Gary was four years older than me and would often be a little bit spiteful. He seemed to feel that he would have to try and hurt me. It would always end in tears – and they would invariably be mine. Sometimes he'd take the gloves off and we'd roll around wrestling. He would get me in the scissors position, where his legs would be wrapped around me and his being four years older than me made quite a difference when I was eight or nine. Those experiences perhaps helped to build the fight in me, which may have come in handy later in my career. So my first experiences of boxing were always a little bit painful, but I think from listening to my dad talking of the characters from years gone by, and then seeing my first images of Muhammad Ali on TV, there was an awakening of something inside. As with so many boys of my age, Ali was the key to selling me the sport of boxing. Just seeing this character, the magic that he brought, sowed the seeds within me.

Looking back, my first experience of Ali must have been the famous Rumble in the Jungle with George Foreman, just after my tenth birthday. The fight received so much publicity and has now gained legendary status, yet the fact was that Ali was not supposed to win. Nobody gave him a chance but, not only did he tell everybody he was going to win, he pulled it off in such fantastic and spectacular fashion that the whole fight and everything surrounding it has magic memories for me. It was something special and I started to wrap myself up in the whole Ali mystique from then on.

There was a little cut-price store in Annfield Plain and I can remember, in 1975, seeing a book about Muhammad Ali in the window. I just had to have it. It was *Muhammad Ali: The Holy Warrior* by Don Atyeo and Felix Dennis. I still have a copy today, although not the one I bought originally because I cut that one up so I could stick pictures of Ali everywhere. Back in the mid-seventies all the kids used to have things stitched to the back of their jackets. Names of bands like Led Zeppelin or whoever else was around at the time. This book contained a picture of Ali and the phrase 'Bear Hunting' from the days when he used to follow and taunt Sonny Liston, whom he described as 'the Big Ugly Bear' in the run-up to their first fight. I made my mother stitch 'Bear Hunting' onto the back of my jacket! It was Ali for me, not some rock group.

The guy who brought me my first pair of decent boxing gloves was a friend of my father's called Brian Railton. The Railtons were a really tough family, with prison time among them. Brian was one of many hard mates of my dad who always seemed to protect us somehow.

Brian was an amateur boxer who fought under the name of 'Rocky' Railton and is still a dear friend of mine. He was as tough as old boots, but a lovely guy. I remember one New Year's Eve my dad invited him back to our house and he brought two pairs of old sixteen-ounce horsehair boxing gloves for me and Gary. Our tatty ones with no padding could be cast aside as we now had a set of proper sparring gloves. Looking back they themselves were just old, brown, horsehair, leather gloves, but they were a huge improvement and it was another step along the way to making me want to become a boxer.

Rocky never turned pro himself but he loved to fight and was always tough and entertaining. I think my dad brought him round with gloves for me because I was starting to show a little bit of a knack for it, but it was more for Gary's benefit as he was about sixteen. One night my dad came in and told Gary that the following evening Rocky and he were going to take him to the local boxing club in Consett. As soon as I heard this I piped up, 'Take me! Take me!' I was only about twelve and my dad told me I was too young so I started to cry. This perhaps just proved his point, but I pleaded and pleaded with him until eventually he gave in and agreed to take me along just to shut me up as much as anything.

I remember entering Consett Sports Centre for the first time and walking past the indoor bowling green, through the doors at the end and discovering a weight training room. Gary was excited by this and wanted to have a go as soon as possible. Meanwhile I looked through another door and saw a scene that I can only describe as looking, to my twelve-year-old eyes, utterly magical. Twenty-five kids skipping, hitting bags and sparring stirred up such emotions within me it is hard to describe.

In actual fact it was just a standard room in a normal sports centre. It had a shiny, wooden floor and the ring itself was just made up of posts that fixed into the floor with no canvas. There were no pictures on the wall or anything that would give you a feeling of a boxing gym in the traditional sense. It was very much a sports centre gym but I loved it. The shorts, boots and vests struck me straight away. Other kids were in fleece jackets and they were all either skipping or hitting the bags and it was just mesmerising.

As I got older, the lustre faded and I didn't particularly care for it for the very reasons that there weren't any pictures on the wall and there wasn't any canvas or a proper ring. Every time you came to train you had to drag all the equipment in from outside and someone had to climb up and pull the bags down. We had to fix the runners from which the bags were hung and then put the ring posts up to create this makeshift boxing gym and it was a very sterile sort of environment. It had none of the romance of the gyms I'd seen on TV. All the great old gyms with posters falling off the walls and discarded tape and Vaseline bottles lying around; the air dense with memories of countless bouts fought in bygone eras, ready to be breathed in by the latest in a long line of hopefuls who were using the gym to hone their skills under the gaze of battle-hardened boxing sages who had seen ten thousand rounds and could tell you about them all. That was what I wanted and Consett Sports Centre was never like that. But, as a twelve year old, I was sold 100%. This was what I was going to do from that moment on. I went straight to reception and told them I wanted to join and asked for a form there and then. Gary didn't fancy it and so he didn't bother, but I couldn't wait.

Gary did in fact take the sport up a few years later, after I had started to make a bit of a name for myself. He had a reasonable career and eventually had a handful of professional fights at heavyweight. Later we would be joined by our brother Shaun, who also boxed professionally as a super-middleweight. Back in the beginning, though, it was only me who wanted to join on the spot. My dad told me that he'd have to see as the cost of membership was a lot of money to us back then, but once I've set my mind on something I won't take no for an answer. I'm terrible that way. I was just so excited about the whole idea of being part of this boxing club that I decided that I simply had to get hold of the money somehow. In addition to the 'foraging' in which I used to participate, I would also sometimes use my free dinner vouchers at school to earn a few quid. I was entitled to free dinners due to the level of my parents' income. However, because I knew my parents didn't have the money and I always ate a good breakfast every morning and a decent meal on an evening, I figured that I didn't always need to eat at lunchtime. I decided to sell my free dinner tickets in order to fund my joining fee.

Before I was allowed to join properly I had to undertake what seemed to be nothing more than a money-grabbing six-week course which taught boxing basics. I went through all this rigmarole and was ready to be a full member for the season which would have started around my thirteenth birthday. The club itself was on two nights a week: Mondays and Wednesdays. That wasn't enough for me so the rest of the week was spent training at home. I would push the chairs back in the sitting room and that was where I did my workouts. My dad, or even my mum occasionally, would put on the pads from time to time. We still had an old punchbag which I would use and I trained literally every day. You can't become a champion on just two days a week and from the start I was determined to emulate Ali and become Champion of the World.

My new-found interest in boxing served one particularly important purpose around that time, which was to finally give me a connection to my grandfather. Granddad Joe, as described earlier, was a gruff, hard-drinking, tough guy who communicated by way of grunting and who scared me silly. Around the time I started visiting the boxing club he was suffering with the later stages of terminal cancer.

He knew he was dying and one day I got summoned to see him in his bedroom. I was terrified and didn't really want to go upstairs, but my parents insisted so I went with my dad. He was quite ill by then and was thin and haggard. He smoked a lot so his fingers were yellow, as was his lip, and his head was bald, so it was all a little frightening for a young boy.

Suddenly my granddad, this man with whom I had never really had a proper conversation, said to me, 'They tell me you're into boxing.' I told him that I was and he turned to me and asked, 'Who do you think would win – Muhammad Ali or Joe Louis?' I loved Ali and told him that was my answer. Quick as a flash he replied, 'No way. Joe Louis' jab was the best in boxing history. He was heavyweight champion for eleven years. Ali just moves about a lot. He can't even throw a hook properly.' All of a sudden I had connected with my granddad. I had something I could share with him at last. He loved boxing and he knew his stuff. And so there was finally a bond between us which made our future meetings great until, after what seemed like no time at all, I was carrying his coffin.

His was the first dead body I ever saw. My dad brought me in to say goodbye to my granddad as he lay in his coffin, as happened in Catholic families. It was too much for me at the time. I was only thirteen years old and I wasn't ready for anything like that. It was horrible. I was a big kid for my age and so I was expected to help carry the coffin, which I dutifully did, but it was all a very harrowing experience. Death has been a spectre which has come back to haunt me far too often during my life.

Back at the club I became friendly with the club secretary, who was a lovely guy called Tommy Gardiner. Tommy was a bald, robust guy who always seemed to have a bit of a tan from working on the roads. I think he saw something in me from very early on and he took me under his wing. I would accompany him on trips to see fights all over the place. He also took me to his house where he showed me the best collection of boxing books I have ever seen in my life. I would go round regularly after that to borrow those books.

One of the first books I borrowed was *Give Him to the Angels* by James R Fair. The book told the story of Harry Greb, Middleweight Champion of the World during the 1920s and an extraordinary character. It was written in a somewhat disjointed fashion and dated back to just after the Second World War. Nevertheless, I thought it was great. It was the story of a guy who loved to fight and loved women in equal measure and from an early age I've felt the same way. To be honest, I think most fighters do. I would say that the make-up of 99% of the fighters I know is that they love to fight, or at least they love the sport of fighting; they're usually gentlemen and lovely guys outside the ring; they tend to love a drink, love fun and love life, because often it has been hard or painful and could well be relatively short, so they like to make the most of it. And, ninety-nine times out of a hundred, they *love* women! I don't know whether it's because we have so much testosterone, or there seems to be a constant need to show our machismo, but you find that in almost all fighters' stories there's a large number of women. So it was with Harry Greb and it fitted the bill for everything I liked and everything that fascinated me. I read about his hundreds of fights, his travelling all over the country in his old, busted car, heading from one adventure to the next, one woman to the next, one crazy fight town to the next.

I think that book embedded in me my love of these wonderful stories. I couldn't wait to borrow other books and I swiftly became something of a scholar as regards boxing history, great fighters and the people in and around the fight game. Boxing lends itself to writing in a way that perhaps no other sport can match. Great drama, poverty, bravery, overcoming adversity, gladiatorial combat, people making good after starting from nothing. Some of the greatest writers of the last hundred-plus years have written about the sport; Hemingway for one. As a kid I got caught up in all that and these fighters became my heroes. I loved to read about their dreams, their achievements and the world of Hollywood glamour, high society, women, mobsters and gangsters they inhabited. I remember thinking 'wow!' when I discovered that Wyatt Earp had refereed for Bob Fitzsimmons and James J Corbett. Heavyweight boxers mixing with a cowboy legend, a cowboy that I'd seen portrayed in the movies. All of that had a big effect on me and I think that's where my subsequent love of literature comes from. Like I said, in some way or another, pretty much all my education has come from boxing.

Unfortunately, reading about boxing was about all I had to enjoy during my first two seasons, as I didn't manage to have one single fight in that whole period! I would go to where the matches were taking place, often with Tommy. I'd take my gear here, there and everywhere. Often the opposing club would have some kid that was lined up to fight me, but when I got there he would turn out to be something like eight pounds lighter and they'd refuse to put him in with me. Or perhaps there would be someone who did weigh the same but who had already had around a dozen fights and our guys wouldn't let me fight someone with such an edge in experience. It was just a case of disappointment after disappointment, week after week. I began to wonder whether my career would ever get started.

Despite my frustration with not getting the chance to actually test myself in the ring, I continued to immerse myself in the sport utterly and completely. Soon after joining the club I started getting *The Ring* magazine every month. I also used to get the British-based *Boxing News*. I used to do anything I could to get money in order to spend it on boxing. I would sell scrap, chop wood, anything. This was also the height of my 'foraging' period. I didn't really consider it as a real crime if I took something that had just been left lying around. Even if it happened to have been lying in somebody's garden or on a building site at the time! Somehow it still didn't seem like it belonged to anyone in particular. I felt that if it had just been left there then it had been abandoned and was fair game.

At one point I even sent off to *The Ring* to buy a cine projector. We had a basic black and white television set at the time and there was hardly any boxing on for me to watch. I saw an advert in *The Ring* offering this projector and three reels of fight films for something like $29.95, which would have been around £12 or £13 back then. Quite a substantial amount in those days for a kid who didn't get pocket money. I guess I must have 'found' quite a lot of stuff at that particular time! I saved up and sent away for this projector, which duly arrived, and it was incredible. I set it up in my bedroom and David and I would sit with a blanket over our heads watching these films in hushed awe as they flickered against the dodgy bedroom wallpaper.

One of the reels featured some of Muhammad Ali's 1960s contests including those with Sonny Liston and Cleveland Williams. Another featured Joe Louis against the likes of Max and Buddy Baer and his famous knock-out of Max Schmeling. There were also fights featuring Ezzard Charles and Jersey Joe Walcott, who I saw for the first time and immediately loved. Jersey Joe Walcott had great footwork and was doing the Ali shuffle before Ali was born. As I watched I found myself taken back to a time when these boxers were the most respected and adored men on the planet. Their acts of skill and bravery in the ring further instilled in me a desire to test myself against my peers in gloved combat. I, too, wanted to hear the roar of the crowd and receive their acclaim as I was lifted shoulder high after a hard-fought victory against the very best. All the time my ambitions were being fed.

I continued to buy *The Ring* throughout my teenage years. Over time, my bedroom wall became covered in posters, because every issue featured a pull-out picture of a great fighter. Later on I would go to gyms and see some of the same pictures that adorned the chimney breast above my bed as a teenager. All the legends of the seventies and early eighties: Aaron 'The Hawk' Pryor, Tommy Hearns, Sugar Ray Leonard, Alexis Arguello, Roberto Duran and my namesake, Milton McCrory, they were all there.

What I realise now is that the guy who's been on Sky Sports for the last twenty-odd years was formed back then. It was then that I picked up my knowledge of the sport which stands me, hopefully, in good stead today. At fifteen or sixteen I could name every World Heavyweight Champion there had ever been, as well as every current World or British Champ in whatever weight category you wished. It was all part of the development of my love of the sport; but reading, watching and learning about it was not enough. I needed to start fighting.

# 5

'When Glenn was a boy I'd take him down the gym and I'd never get out. As a man he'd take me to a bar and I'd still never get out!'
Rocky Railton, family friend

Many of my early fights blur into one at this stage of my life. I can remember names and occasions, but specific details often escape me. However, one thing that is true in life is that you never forget your first time! My boxing debut took place at Witton Gilbert Working Men's Club on 6 October 1979, a fortnight after my fifteenth birthday, against Michael Harvey of Horden Boxing Club.

Despite the disappointments of the previous occasions there was a confident expectation that this time the fight would actually take place. For a start I knew he was a little bit heavier than me. I also knew he had competed in three or four fights already. I was therefore giving away both weight and experience. With those two things against me I felt sure the fight would be allowed to take place as Michael Harvey also happened to be Ron Harvey's son. Ron was the secretary of the Tyne and Wear Amateur Boxing Association. When you seem to have the odds against you, and you're fighting the ABA Secretary's son, you feel pretty sure that it's going to be allowed to happen.

Although it took place in Witton Gilbert, it was our home show. Prior to my joining, the club had previously been based at Langley Park. The venue used in the days of Langley Park Amateur Boxing Club had been the Witton Gilbert WMC and that had never been changed. So it was that Witton Gilbert WMC was to be the first step on my way to Las Vegas.

I remember waiting for my turn to fight and seeing a little kid with big ears and ginger hair sitting near me crying. I asked him where he was from and if he had fought already, to which he tearfully replied that he was from Sunderland and had just lost his third fight out of three. Before we could talk any further it was my turn to fight. After all the waiting, my time had finally arrived. Most of my family were there to support me and I had seen how upset this little kid from Sunderland was having lost his first three fights. I was determined that wasn't going to happen to me.

I remember I had a black terry-towelling dressing gown onto the back of which my mum had ironed letters which spelt out the name 'McCrory' especially for the occasion! There I was, a fifteen-year-old kid with no fights whatsoever to this point, and already I had a personalised dressing gown and proper blue boots, which I had funded by whatever means had been necessary. Later, as a pro, I had a black satin dressing gown with a hood. This one had no hood and being terry towelling the name 'McCrory' didn't look all that impressive if I'm honest, as it's not the ideal material to iron transfers upon.

I stepped into the ring a beginner and left it a winner following a victory on points after three rounds. It was brilliant. I was given a trophy, which my mother still has to this day I believe, and the whole evening was just an amazing experience. After all that time spent waiting I was on my way at last.

And what of the skinny, ginger kid who cried after having lost his first three fights? Well he could have been excused for giving up the game but, thankfully, he didn't. His name was Billy Hardy and he became my longest standing friend in boxing, a friendship that continues to this day. We were born only a few days apart and we were to go through our whole careers together. We won Junior ABA titles at the same time and we travelled on the train together to represent Young England. We then turned pro in London together, albeit with different promoters. As pros we both won British and Commonwealth titles. Billy also added the European Featherweight crown having come within a hair's breadth of winning the World Bantamweight title, losing on a split decision, just months after I had taken the IBF Cruiserweight belt.

All that lay in the future. For now the important thing was that I was up and running as a boxer and from then on the fights started to come quite regularly. By the end of 1979 I had won five out of five and in February 1980 I won the North East District Junior ABA title. That set me up to go to Leeds to fight for the North Eastern Counties

ABA Championship against Gary Crawford. The winner would head to the finals in London.

Gary Crawford was one of the best young amateurs around. He was highly rated and would later go on to prove just how good he was after turning pro under the name of Crawford Ashley, when he became British, Commonwealth and European Light-Heavyweight Champion. To be fighting people of that calibre already, in only my eighth bout, was a mark of how far I had come in only six months.

The fight took place in April 1980, shortly after I had started dating Amanda Walsh, a girl I knew from school. Mandy's brother, Rob, had boxed in the Navy and had started to come to our club. To me he always seemed to regard himself as the greatest thing since sliced bread and I don't think he was too fond of me either, because all of a sudden I had started both going out with his sister and doing quite well in the ring myself. It may not sound like much, but I was starting to get my picture in the *Stanley News*. For a kid who always wanted to be noticed that's a start. Anyway I think there was a little bit of animosity or jealousy with Rob, because he and I never really got on.

On the night of the Crawford fight in Leeds, my coach couldn't make the trip. With Rob helping the club out at the time, and with me dating his sister, it somehow came to pass that he was to be in my corner for the most important fight of my fledgling career to date. I remember clearly being in the dressing room beforehand with him being ever so cocky. He was bouncing around, throwing jabs and I was sitting there thinking that it was me that was about to fight so surely I should be the one shadow boxing. Anyway, I leant forward to say something to him and – bang – I took a left jab right in my eye. He couldn't have been more apologetic, but there was I, about to take on a top junior for the North Eastern Counties title, with a fat eye given to me by my own cornerman! Apologetic or not, I couldn't help but think he was a prat.

The fight itself was a total anti-climax. I was wary of him and his reputation and I think he must have heard good things about me too. When the bell rang, he went one way and I went the other. We were both fearful of each other it seemed and it turned out to be a really dull fight. There was nothing in it, but I suffered my first loss, going down to a narrow points decision. Gary went on to win the national title that season and returned the following year to win the national final in the 77kg division. He was a good fighter, as his subsequent pro career proved, and it was certainly no disgrace to have suffered my first defeat to someone of that standard.

The loss to Crawford was my only defeat in my first season. I won five more fights over the next eight weeks to finish the boxing year with a record of twelve wins and only the one defeat, all thirteen fights having gone the full three rounds.

My second season began badly when I started off by losing three out of five fights including suffering my only knockdown as an amateur en route to a points defeat at the hands of an excellent Scottish fighter called Steve Williams. He was something of a nemesis for me. We fought three times and Steve won twice. I believe he now runs a training camp in Spain. In that first fight he put me down on my knees. He was a good kid.

For the rest of the season I never looked back. I clinched the North Eastern Counties title that I had narrowly failed to win the previous year and moved on to reach the National Junior ABA 74kg Championship final where I was scheduled to face Lou Gent.

The Consett Amateur Boxing Club's head coach at this time was a guy called Johnny Cuthbert from Langley Park. He'd been a good amateur boxer and was an excellent technical coach who had worked with the English national team. He was also the Assistant Manager of Consett Sports Centre and I always got the impression that coaching us was more his job than his passion. In addition to Johnny there was an assistant coach called Alan Walker who had boxed at regional level and was a really great guy. Alan was always around to offer help and support and I've always been someone who likes to be loyal to those who have been there for me. That is how Alan ended up working in my corner the night I won the world title, but that is getting ahead of myself a little!

As far as I was concerned, Johnny had never really shown any interest in me during the early stages of my career but, as I progressed towards the national finals, he started to appear in my corner. Johnny, being a former national coach and current assistant manager of the leisure centre, wasn't going to be travelling here and there for just any fifteen-year-old kid. Although I can understand that to a certain extent, to be truthful I resented Johnny a little at the time. Alan had helped me all the way and then, when I started winning stuff, everybody else was out and Johnny was in. He just seemed like a bit of a fair-weather friend to me.

I also saw him as being something of an old fart. He would go over and over how you stood, how you moved, how you pivoted, how you blocked a shot, how you slipped a shot until you were sick to death of it. I have touched upon the six-week course he ran prior to new members joining the club already. At the time I found it boring and saw it as nothing more than a way of making money for the leisure centre. It was constant repetition of defensive moves: inside parry, outside parry, block the jab, inside elbow, outside elbow, block-guard, block-guard, etc, etc. After that there were the balancing exercises – learning to move your feet in the right way so you were always balanced. All of it seemed tremendously dull to a twelve-year-old kid who just wanted to climb into the ring and fight. Later on I realised what a valuable experience all that had been. Yes I was bored to tears, but it helped me so much throughout my career. So, although I may have thought him an old fart at the time, Johnny taught very good basics.

Anyhow, Johnny was in my corner for the fight with Lou Gent, a decent fighter who went on to box at a good standard as a pro. He fought Nigel Benn for the World Super-Middleweight crown, having previously lost two attempts at winning the British Cruiserweight title, one of which was against future world champion Johnny Nelson and the other against some guy named McCrory. On the night of 29 May 1981 though, we fought for three rounds, after which I was awarded the decision and, less than twenty months after my first ever contest, I was the National Junior ABA 74kg Champion. Nobody from north-west Durham had won a Junior ABA title before, so I thought that could end up being the pinnacle of my career. I'd done great. I was in the *Stanley News*. I was legendary!

By the time of my triumph over Lou Gent, my life had already started to change in a number of ways. Once it became apparent that I had a real talent for boxing I became increasingly dedicated to the sport. Training was everything and my previous bad behaviour stopped. Okay, so I didn't bother going to school very often, but everything else was now history because my dreams revolved completely around being a boxer. I never really had amateur ambitions at this stage; I didn't really know what the Olympic Games were. I went into boxing to be a pro and when I first went to Consett at twelve and saw they had vests on I was puzzled. Not only did I not know you had to have an amateur career first, I didn't even know what an amateur was. I wasn't bothered about the money but I wanted to do what Ali did. I wanted to do what Joe Louis did. I wanted to be Champion of the World.

As well as my delinquency coming to an end, so did my participation in other sports. From a young age I was very athletic. I was a county athlete and a pretty decent footballer. I played football from day one at school. At St Patrick's I was the leading goalscorer, banging goals in for fun. There's a picture somewhere of me being presented with a certificate for my goalscoring achievements by a member of the Sunderland 1973 FA Cup winning team. I believe it was Dennis Tueart, but I can't remember for certain because, cards on the table, I am very much black and white and not red and white when it comes to football!

After moving to St Bede's I was converted into a centre-half, as are most big kids I suspect. I did pretty well in that position and went on to represent Stanley District along-side Barry Venison who became one of that rare group of players to be popular with the fans of both Sunderland and Newcastle United.

Barry and I were both scouted by Sunderland and offered trials. Barry went along and did quite well I believe! For me that offer pretty much ended my football career. I thought that if it was going to be as bad as playing for Sunderland then it was time to quit!

I didn't go for the trial as I had started to lose interest in football. Boxing had well and truly taken over by this stage. I remember Charlie Errington, a Sunderland scout who ran a local shop, telling me that if I had cared about football as much as I cared for boxing then I could have made it but, to be honest, by that time I no longer did care.

Once again the teachers at St Bede's had played their part in my lack of enthusiasm. I was starting to come up against a negative feeling at school about my boxing. They offered no support, no encouragement and never gave me any pats on the back. If they had said something to me along the lines of, 'It's brilliant what you're doing with your boxing. If you can do the same with your football you could go a long way,' and encouraged me, then maybe I would have been more inclined to keep at it. Instead they were wholly negative. They threatened not to pick me or to refuse put me forward for the district team if I didn't start taking football as seriously as my boxing. Well, me being me, my attitude was simply to think, 'Well fuck off then!'

The final straw between me and St Bede's occurred after I won the Junior ABA title. I still remember to this day being in assembly at the age of sixteen, having just won a national title. That is a really big deal for a kid, but they never announced it. They read out details of a second or third place achieved by someone in the East Stanley District Cross-country Championship, but not one word about my becoming champion of the whole country. I remember standing there almost in tears, just so dejected. I still hold a sense of bitterness about that occasion even after more than thirty years have gone by. Apparently they've got a picture of me in the school somewhere as one of the old boys, but I've never been back to see it.

The Junior ABA final against Gent turned out to be my last fight in the junior ranks. Despite the next season starting around the time of my seventeenth birthday, I would only be fighting grown men.

Things could scarcely have gone better in the ring for me. I was on a high after becoming national champion and, despite giving away age and experience to all my opponents, I racked up a sequence of eleven straight victories in the first four months of the boxing year, including my first ever wins inside the distance. In my own mind I was becoming a superstar. People were starting to take notice of me. I may have just turned seventeen, but I was called up to the England Under 19 squad and was training with the likes of Errol Christie and Chris Pyatt. My ambitions were growing and I had half an eye on the Olympics coming up in Los Angeles in 1984.

While life could not have been going any better inside the ring, outside things were taking several turns for the worse. At home David's physical condition was starting to deteriorate noticeably, causing a great deal of concern and distress to all of us. In addition to the trauma of my brother's increasing problems there were other awful events which happened around that time and which had a significant effect on me.

I had a good friend from Annfield Plain called Shaun Curry who was a year younger than me and who started boxing around the same time as I did. He would get a lift to training with me and my dad every Monday and Wednesday. At sixteen, Shaun became a boy soldier, went away with the army and boxed while he was there. A matter of weeks later he had a fight which he won. His hand was raised in the ring, then he suddenly collapsed and died shortly afterwards. It was a devastating loss. He was such a lovely boy and a real friend with so much life in front of him. I helped to carry his coffin.

Around the same time I also lost the wonderful Tommy Gardiner, the man who had taken me under his wing and introduced me to the world of boxing literature. He wanted me to accompany him to a Junior ABA event, but I chose to stay at home and spend some time with Mandy. He went on his own and just a few hours later I received a phone call from my mum to tell me he was dead. He had suffered a massive heart attack and died on the spot.

I still think about Tommy and I wish he could have been there to see me win the world title. It would have made him so proud I'm sure. I still see Shaun's family from time to time and I miss him too. In life you never know what's around the corner, which just adds to my determination to make the most of it while I can.

My run of victories led to my being included in a North East select team which travelled to Norway for a match in February 1982. That was a trip in which I feared for my own life and developed a fear of flying that lasted throughout my ring career and beyond.

Having been selected for the trip, I had to get myself my first passport. I'd visited my Uncle Tony in London once or twice and boxed in the ABA Finals and trained with the Young England squad down there, but the furthest I'd been other than that was to Blackpool on a family caravanning holiday. Norway was to be my first experience of foreign travel and very nearly my last.

The Tyne and Wear ABA Secretary (and father of my first ring opponent) Ron Harvey was there, as was Billy Hardy's trainer, Gordon Ibinson, although Billy himself was not part of the team. They were the officials, and there may have been one other trainer, together with about half a dozen boxers. I was only seventeen, but it was a senior team and I was going to be boxing a senior international. I'd never flown before and when we saw the plane it turned out to be a propeller job. I didn't know anything about planes, but it was a lovely day and we all boarded quite happily and off we went. We had a tailwind as we crossed the North Sea and flew over the fjords and I remember feeling exhilarated with the view and the whole flying experience.

We spent a couple of days in Oslo and had a great time which included a trip to check out one of the Olympic ski jumps. We stood in the area in which the jumpers land and looked up at the ninety-metre ramp. And people say boxing is dangerous! When you stand in the landing area for a ninety-metre ski jump and look back at where the competitors would actually be taking off it makes you realise that they must all be completely insane!

Anyhow, we had a lovely time in Oslo. The fights went okay – I hurt my thumb during my contest and lost a close points decision, but all in all it was a really positive experience. And then we had to fly home.

For the return journey we were flying in the dark and almost as soon as we were up I realised I didn't like flying in the dark all that much. Shortly into the flight the weather took a turn for the worse. No longer did we have a nice tailwind as on the journey over; instead we were flying directly into it and we were getting hit pretty hard. Despite this the other guys seemed calm enough and settled down to play cards. As things progressed the weather got worse and worse and we started to drop regularly. Sweat was soon pouring out of me and the others had stopped playing cards pretty swiftly. I remember Gordon Ibinson scoffing at the rest of us, saying, 'Lads, I had fifteen years in the RAF. This is nothing.' This reassurance was not enough to stop one of the guys throwing up. When someone is sick in a plane it doesn't half stink! That just added to the general sense of unease in the air.

I then remembered the pilot. On the way over I had noticed that he wore gloves to fly the plane. He stayed at the hotel with us, where I found out the gloves were because he only had three fingers on one hand and four on the other. He also had a noticeable scar on his neck. At this point I was starting to think, 'I reckon this guy's crashed before!'

After more buffeting in the wind and significant drops in height we became aware that the pilot kept turning on the lights for one wing only. To me something had to be wrong for him to keep doing that and my suspicions proved correct. He informed us that one of the wings was icing up a little too much. He told us we couldn't turn back as we'd gone too far by that stage, so we would have to carry on to England. By this time I was thinking that this is how it was all going to end. My first trip abroad was destined to end with me being plunged into the freezing cold North Sea in pitch blackness.

Because of the dark we had no idea how high up we actually were. We could just feel ourselves dropping and dropping. Soon enough everybody was petrified. I resorted to prayer and even wrote a farewell note to my mother to tell her I loved her and to say goodbye, which I then put in my wallet. How she would ever have found it to read if we actually crashed into the North Sea I have no idea, but that is where my mind was at that moment.

The next problem occurred when the pilot contacted the airport to request permission to land and was told that they were closed because of the conditions. We would need to divert.

We were told to try Edinburgh, but flying into such a strong headwind had used up our fuel so we wouldn't be able to get there. Newcastle Airport cleared us to make an emergency landing. We arrived to the emergency services clearing the runway and waiting for us. We landed with Gordon Ibinson puking up. Fifteen years in the RAF was it Gordon? I genuinely fell to my knees to kiss the ground once I was off the plane. I don't think I have ever been so relieved in my life.

That one journey began a horrendous fear of flying which lasted around fifteen years. I would dread every time I had to get on a plane, which happened more often as my career progressed and even more so once I had started working for Sky. In my mind the Oslo experience could happen every flight. That's what happened when you flew; they were life or death experiences. I was pretty convinced that we were just up there by luck. As time went on I tried drinking to get past the fear, but I'd never manage to get sufficiently drunk because I was just too scared. I tried sleeping pills; the works. Nothing seemed to be able to relax me sufficiently to enjoy the flight.

Eventually I managed to overcome my fear in quite an unusual way. It would have been during the late nineties. I was having a bad time at that point and would often be in the depths of a private despair. I remember sitting on a flight coming back from a job with Sky and I was in the midst of a really black moment. I felt as though I didn't know where my life was going and was utterly lost and hopeless. I found myself sitting there during a violent storm, with the plane shaking about, thinking to myself, 'Come on then, let's crash. I'm ready so let's get it over with. Just crash right now.' And we landed safely. The next time I flew I did the same thing. I dared the plane to crash. I had had enough, but would never have dreamed of taking my own life. This seemed an easy way out. But again, we landed safely. I don't know how I managed to get to feel so low but that's where I was at the time. After this happened a couple of times I remember thinking, 'You know what? They just don't crash do they?' It dawned on me that I had been on countless flights and had never had any problems at all after that one experience on the way home from Norway. Since then I have really enjoyed flying. On long haul flights you get to relax in pure peace. I would go so far as to say I actually love flying these days.

In fact, I've even flown an aircraft myself. I won an auction for a flying lesson at Newcastle Airport. I turned up and the instructor told me to get in the front and he sat behind me. No dual controls or anything. I thought, 'This guy's an idiot! It's my first lesson – what does he think he's doing?'

The next thing I know he's telling me to put my foot down and we're hurtling along the runway when he stated, 'I'm going to count to three and when I reach "three" pull that steering wheel back six inches and we'll take off.' And we did!

Once we were airborne I was holding the controls tightly when he instructed me to let go. Well I couldn't, I'm not relinquishing control to just nobody. So he changed the instruction to just letting go with one hand. I did and nothing happened. He then told me to just keep two fingers on the wheel. I didn't really want to, but I managed to ease my grip and again, nothing happened. Suddenly I realised that I wasn't really doing anything, the plane was doing it all by itself. He smiled at me and said, 'It flies itself mate. They're built for it.' Obviously a human being needs to control them from time to time, but once you've got them sitting there safe and stable that's what they do. You merely need to point them in the right direction and let them get on with it.

I flew over Stanley, Burnhope and St James' Park and loved the experience until his next comment, 'Okay, time for you take us down.' I believe my initial response was, 'Noooooo!' Again he was insistent that all would be well. He pointed out some lights on the wheel, there were five or six in total and if you're too high or too low they all go red. If you're leaning too far to the left or right some will go red to tell you which side you need to raise. What you need to do is to make all of them turn green and if you manage that then you're bang on target for landing. As we approached the ground the instructor advised that when he counted to three again all I needed to do was carefully push the wheel forwards again, in other words the exact opposite of the process for take-off. I followed his instructions and we landed safe and sound. It was so simple. I appreciate that I've probably just set aviation back a hundred years with that statement and pilots everywhere may be thinking 'there's a bit more to it than that mate!' but all I can say is that if I have taken off, flown and landed a plane safely then it isn't as difficult as I used to think it was!

Although my first experience of flying had not been a good one, I was certainly flying metaphorically in the ring. I felt a close fight with a Norwegian in Norway was always unlikely to go in my favour so I wasn't too perturbed by my defeat. However, I did lose my first match back at home when I was outpointed by John McKenzie, a tough, tattooed, hard kid from Ashington. It was a time when I was really struggling with southpaws. The first time I came across one I asked my dad, 'What's he doing? Why is he using the wrong hand?' It took me a while to get the hang of them.

After the McKenzie loss I was swiftly back on the winning trail. I was only seventeen, but I was already training in London with the England Under 19 squad. I was just a young kid but back in the North East people were beginning to talk about me and I was winning awards so I felt as though I was a star in the making. Then I went down to join the England Under 19 squad as the youngest member and I was a nobody again. People were pointing at me and asking each other, 'Who's he? What's his name?' There were the likes of Errol Christie, Chris Pyatt and Duke McKenzie down there who had really strong reputations already. Errol was only a year older than me but was already being talked about as one of the best amateur boxers we had ever produced.

Training with those guys was a great experience and I'm sure it helped me to cope with boxing at the senior ABAs and to beat the likes of Paul Lister and Les Purvis while still a teenager. I actually beat both John Fairbairn and Les Purvis on the same night in the Senior ABA Championships, boxing first and then seventh on the bill. Les was a big knockout artist who shook me up and gave me my first standing eight count although I held on for the decision.

My continued improvement and work with the Young England squad led me to have half an eye on the 1984 Olympics. I beat a German called Christian Honhold in my debut performance for the England Under 19 team and was presented with my trophy by Alan Minter. As my bout finished Michael Caine's brother introduced himself to my father and told him, 'Your boy's gonna be a star. Here, take that for him.' He then leant forward and slipped something into my dad's breast pocket. My dad thanked him, but never thought anything further of it until we were back in the house. He then remembered the exchange and went to fetch his jacket to find a £50 note in the pocket. We'd never seen a £50 note before and didn't even know there was such an item in existence! £50 notes over thirty years ago were quite a thing – we thought we were rich.

Things were looking up, but my Olympic hopes suffered a setback when, in my next fight, I lost to David Cross in the ABA Championship North East Counties Finals. I won't mince my words. That result was an absolute disgrace.

David Cross was a respected England international from Bridlington who worked as a policeman. We were pretty much the last bout of the night and by that stage the North Eastern representatives were beating their Yorkshire counterparts about eight-nil. I went at him and he backed up against the ropes. As I moved in he suddenly threw himself backwards over the top rope and let out a yell. I was wondering what he was doing – I hadn't even hit him. The referee immediately deducted a point from me! He thought that I'd pushed him over the ropes, but I swear I never touched him. I was utterly perplexed. The fight continued and I was hitting him with some good shots. Eventually I backed him into a corner and as soon as we got to the ropes he did it again and the referee deducted another point! I got two public warnings. He didn't disqualify me, but I lost unanimously on points. I know fighters often say 'I was robbed!' but that result was a downright scandal. That a grown man, a supposedly respectable police officer, should resort to such tactics against an eighteen-year-old kid was appalling. And I'm not convinced it would have happened if the North East were not eight-nil up already. I was out of the Senior ABAs, beaten unfairly by a copper, which was ironic because I was as sick as a pig.

Soon after that I gained revenge on John McKenzie, the Ashington southpaw, and racked up a few more wins before getting a wonderful opportunity to visit America as part of a GB Select team. It was fantastic. I roomed with Manny Burgo, who was a pal of mine from North Shields, and we had a great time. It was at a time when New York was the craziest city in the world. It was as though everybody I walked past was a lunatic. Just a bunch of crazy people. It was fabulous though and I fell totally in love with the place. We visited the Empire State Building and were driven round the Bronx in a blacked-out bus. We also rode in the service elevator, the fastest elevator in the World Trade Center. I've loved New York ever since that trip, everything about it was amazing. Even the danger was right up my street.

I had two bouts while I was over there. The first was a points win in Atlantic City, New Jersey. For our second contests we were fighting a very strong US Navy team and, for some reason, most of us seemed to be fighting somebody from the weight division above our normal one. Manny, who was a heavyweight, boxed a superheavyweight and I boxed a heavyweight who had just returned from representing the USA in the Soviet Union. I wasn't too bothered by my subsequent majority points defeat as it was all part of such a great experience.

After the contests were over we went out for an evening on the tiles. We all wore our GB jackets and ventured from the navy base where the fights had taken place to some bars across the road. Our English accents meant we were getting loads of attention from the local girls and we were all having a great night.

Later we were coming back in a car which, luckily it turned out, was being driven by the son of one of the NYPD officers who had been chaperoning us on our trip. There were three of the team in the car, one of whom I forget, but the other was a decent young fighter called Mark McCreath who was a nice kid but a bit mouthy at times. We were laughing and chatting away when we heard a noise and turned to see the car behind us swerving about and driving erratically. Then they started beeping the horn as if they wanted to get past, so we slowed down and the next minute there was a crashing sound as they smashed a bottle against our car causing the window to disintegrate. We pulled in and Mark ran over to the other car to remonstrate with the group of guys inside when one of them leapt out and smashed a pool cue in his face, slashing it open. At that we all dived in and jumped on them. They obviously knew we were the boxing team and probably shouldn't have picked a fight with us, but the next minute there's a siren and we found ourselves handcuffed with guns at our heads!

Mark didn't seem to have learnt from his experience, as he was still mouthing off while we were bent over the bonnet. At one point he exclaimed, 'Jesus man, this is just like the movies!' to which the copper holding a gun to his head replied, 'This won't seem like the movies when I blow your brains out!' Meanwhile I was pleading, 'Mark man, just shut the fuck up!'

So it was goodbye Olympics. Even though we were entirely exonerated, the whole incident meant that I was unlikely to be considered, although to be truthful it was never likely to happen anyway. It was very much the time of the old-school British selectors who tended to go with experienced guys in their mid- to late-twenties rather than teenagers. Later on they discovered that taking a chance with young fighters like Amir Khan can pay dividends, but back in the early 1980s it didn't seem that that was the way they thought.

Of course, had I been selected for the 1984 Games I would have run into a young man called Evander Holyfield, so thank you NYPD!

# 6

'The only time I nearly lost it live on air was when Glenn told me
during an interval that whilst on a holiday he had woken and didn't
recognise the apartment he was in. Some bird had taken him there
the night before and done a runner, nicking his wallet and phone.
He had to wander the streets for hours just to find out
which town he was in!'
Richie Woodhall, former World Super-Middleweight Champion

After returning from the States I decided that the time was
right to turn professional. My final amateur fight, during that American trip, was just days after my nineteenth
birthday. My instincts told me to forget the amateur game
and give professional boxing a go. To be honest, ever since
day one, all I had ever wanted to be was a pro. All I'd seen
was professional boxing and all my heroes were pros. As
a kid I was hugely disappointed when I discovered that I
had to do this thing called amateur boxing, wearing a vest
and only boxing for three rounds per fight, before I could

get into the pro game. I was never really into the whole amateur thing so I used the first excuse I could to turn my back on it and join the professional ranks. I finished with an amateur record of fifty-six wins and ten defeats.

Looking back this was the first of many occasions where the lack of any experience around me, and the absence of sensible guidance, had a significant negative effect on my career. If I'd had somebody with me that knew anything about business and who could find a sponsor to recognise my potential then they would have sat me down and said, 'Right, we're going for the Olympics in 1988. You'll still only be twenty-three and we can all make some serious money if you make a success of that.'

Less than a year after the 1988 Olympics I was good enough to win the World Cruiserweight Championship. Therefore, I have little doubt that I would have been able to bring back a gold medal from the Seoul Olympics and that would have enabled me to turn pro around the time of my twenty-fourth birthday with any amount of offers from promoters, sponsors and TV networks on the table. My career would have been easier as I wouldn't have had to take on ridiculous fights against much bigger men while I was still practically a kid myself, plus I would have been picking up significantly more money along the way. Bear in mind that I was still on the dole when I fought for the world title. That's how hopeless my career planning turned out to be.

But all that lay in the future. As it was it was late 1983, I had just turned nineteen and I was on the lookout for a professional contract. Being in the North East I'd looked at the Deans brothers, Frankie and Brian, plus Tommy

Conroy who was doing bits and pieces in Sunderland even back then. But generally it seemed as though there was very little going on in the area. There were the Feeney brothers from Hartlepool, George and John, who both became British Champions in the eighties, but the scene was largely quiet. I had never actually been to see a live professional bout as they were not all that prevalent in the region.

I didn't have many conversations with potential managers. I think Tommy Conroy had asked Tommy Gardiner about me around the time of my winning the Junior ABAs, but I pretty soon decided that the lack of action in the North East meant that I was never likely to stay up there. I was aiming for bigger things.

I remember someone my dad and I spoke to was Eddie Thomas from Cardiff. He had managed Howard Winstone and Ken Buchanan to world title success and had a near miss with Colin Jones. He also handled the wonderful Eddie Avoth, former British and Commonwealth Light-Heavyweight Champion and a close of friend of mine today. In his favour, Eddie Thomas was from a mining area like us, I liked the fighters that he'd handled and his record spoke for itself. We chatted on the phone and he invited me down so he could have a look at me. Both my dad and I thought he seemed a lovely man and maybe it could have been a good move for me to make, but the stumbling block was simply the location. Cardiff was even further away than London and much harder to get to. Just the logistics of travelling there and back unfortunately made it a non-starter.

Even though I was very much from the sticks, the working-class North East, I always had a fascination for the bright lights of London. Everything seemed to happen down there. It was the base for all the top British fighters of the era in which I grew up: Alan Minter, the Finnegan brothers, John H Stracey and Charlie Magri. They all topped the bill at the Albert Hall and promoters Jarvis Astaire, Mike Barrett and Mickey Duff would hold regular big fight nights that I would watch at home on TV, waiting for the day when it would be my turn. Everything seemed centred around London. I always had a bit of a fancy for the place and that played a part in my eventual decision.

Another key player was my amateur trainer, Johnny Cuthbert. He had been to an Alan Minter-led training course in Jersey with an England Schoolboys team or something of that nature. While there he met not only Alan but also his manager, Doug Bidwell. He'd had a pretty good time with them by all accounts, with a few good laughs and a few too many beers thrown in. Anyway, Johnny seemingly forged a bit of a relationship with Doug and told him he had a kid who Doug should look out for. He told him about my record and Doug expressed an interest. My recollection of events is sketchy, but I believe this conversation took place before I represented England Under 19s against West Germany after which I was presented with my trophy by Doug's most famous fighter, Alan Minter. I think there was a little chat with Johnny that evening and from then on I felt as though Johnny was gently pushing me in that direction. To be honest, I would probably have been happy to go that way anyway simply because Minter had become undisputed Middleweight Champion of the World under Doug's management and he was based in London, right in the heart of things.

My dad and I travelled to London to meet Doug properly. From the start I took to him as a person. He was quite the smoothie. I mean, anybody who looks like Del Boy and had the rings and patter to match was instantly likeable, and that was Doug. He introduced us to his family; his wife, son and daughter, and they were all really nice. He took us out to Alan's pub and then on for a meal at a posh restaurant. Well, it seemed posh to us anyway. I remember my dad asking what all the different knives and forks were for! I was trying, with not much more experience of such places than my father, to prevent the pair of us looking like total idiots. Meanwhile Doug was giving us the patter about how he had taken Alan to a world title and promising similar things for me. I was a little bit in awe because Alan's achievement in becoming undisputed champion by winning in America was massive at the time.

I was very young and impressionable. The whole lifestyle that I was shown seemed exactly like everything I had read about. It was as if I had entered into another world – and I liked it. I felt as though I was moving from a world of black and white, of darkness and grey, to a new world of colour. All of a sudden I was in swanky restaurants and bars and was discovering another way of life that had never been accessible to me before.

I signed a contract to be managed by Doug Bidwell at the headquarters of DAF Trucks on Teesside. There was some sort of sponsorship deal which meant I would fight with the company name on my shorts, although I didn't receive any money for it. Nor did I receive anything for signing up. That perhaps should have served as a warning of what was in store.

I moved to London and stayed in a pokey bed and breakfast in Beckenham that Doug had arranged for me. The old guy who ran the place with his wife was suffering with cancer and would sit there coughing, yet still smoking all the time. I had a small single bed which wasn't long enough for me and for breakfast I would get one egg and one slice of bacon.

What I didn't realise at this stage, because one thing for sure is that Doug never mentioned it, was that Doug Bidwell had never trained a boxer before in his life! I didn't realise that Alan Minter had a brilliant trainer called Bobby Neill with him during his career. Doug sold me a great story but I had no idea I was to be his guinea pig. What followed was almost the perfect example of how to mismanage a boxing career. In fact, if you were trying to list of all the possible mistakes that could be made in a pro fighter's career, I don't think you'd come up with as many as Doug managed to make with mine.

My initial experiences were not of the kind of glamour that I had been expecting. I was still on the dole, surviving off a few quid a week. I'd seen a bit of the glamorous side in the initial press conference at the signing, but this was the reality and it was hard.

I started to train at the Thomas a Becket gym on the Old Kent Road. The Thomas a Becket was *the* gym in London. Ali had trained there before fighting in the capital, as had Sugar Ray Robinson. Anybody who was anybody had worked out in that gym and it was almost a museum of boxing, just crammed with memorabilia. Precisely the sort of gym I had craved during my days at Consett Sports Centre. It was also where I met Ivor Thomas. Ivor was a London bookmaker who loved boxing and could often be found in the gym with me, Gary Mason, and many other top British boxing names. He's kept in touch and been a friend ever since but back then he was crazy! He must have been in his forties and never had a professional fight, but he loved a good scrap and would happily jump into the ring and spar with me, Mason and the rest. He used to reckon that it would cheer us all up, at the end of a hard day sparring with each other, to see him climb in so we could have fun beating him up!

The gym was in a room above the pub of the same name and had Danny Holland, Henry Cooper's old cut-man, on the door. He took me under his wing a little, did old Danny. I'd have to pay him my subs, which was always a struggle, and before long I had people paying them for me. This included Joey Pyle, a well-known London character who had been associated with both the Kray twins and Charlie Richardson. He was one of several guys who used to hang around that would feel sorry for me and pay my subs as it became apparent to everyone that I was struggling financially.

Once inside the gym it was just me and Doug. From the start he had decided that I was to put on weight as he seemed to entertain the idea that I was to be that Holy Grail of boxers – a great, white, British heavyweight. For my last fight as an amateur I had been around the 12 stone 7 pound light-heavyweight limit, but Doug was telling me, 'You're growing; you're going to be a heavyweight and we're going to build you up into one sooner rather than later.' Right from the start he had me drinking full-fat gold top milk and eating bacon and sausages by the pound. The truth is I was little more than a big light-heavyweight and should have been matched as such, but at only nineteen who was I to argue with a man who had guided Alan Minter to a world title?

My debut fight in the pro ranks was strange in that it was almost the making and the breaking of my early career rolled into one. The making because it gave me some instant positive press coverage and the breaking because it confirmed, in Doug's eyes, that I was a heavyweight champion in waiting. Initially I was scheduled to fight a tough cruiserweight from Newcastle called Steve Abadom. His family were well known in Newcastle as a hard lot and Steve was a tough character. However that fight fell through and, all of a sudden, I was fighting a heavyweight called Barry Ellis who'd won three out of three. Now I didn't know much at that age, but I knew it was unusual to match a nineteen-year-old light-heavyweight debutant with an undefeated heavyweight who outweighed him by nearly a stone and a half. Before I went on I was already having doubts. I hadn't won a senior ABA title and I suddenly felt like a boy in a man's world.

When the time came to fight I made my way to the ring and spotted Alan Minter and Howard Winstone at ringside, among others. Doug was nothing if not a salesman and he had persuaded Colin Hart from *The Sun*, top journalist Walter Bartleman and a reporter from the *Daily Mail* to be there to witness the debut of his hot new prospect. I wasn't top of the bill, but I was the one they'd come to see and I can honestly say I was terrified. I had never even seen a live pro fight in my life, let alone taken part in one. The first professional contest I ever encountered and I was in it! I looked across the ring and saw this big guy staring back at me. All I could think was, 'Well, the pro dream was good while it lasted. What a short career this has been!' I feared that I was about to become a sacrificial lamb in front of all these luminaries who were sitting within touching distance.

The opening bell went and we danced around each other for a little while and then, through fear, I started throwing punches. Not through any strategy or planning, just sheer terror. I can't describe what happened exactly as it was all just a blur. The next thing I remember the referee was dragging me off, Barry Ellis was lying crumpled by the corner post and the fight was over after just ninety seconds.

Naturally enough, after the bout I was on an enormous high. It was unbelievable, mainly because I couldn't remember it. Several of us went out to the Rheingold, a dodgy old club full of mostly slightly worse for wear women. I was with Doug, some of his friends, and a group of guys still in their dinner jackets and everybody was all over me. Everyone wanted to buy me a drink and were busy telling the girls that I had just won my professional debut with a first-round knockout, how I was destined to be a champion and all of that bluster.

I remember talking to one particular lady who disappeared only to return five minutes later to tell me she had a present for me after my win. She put her leg up on my seat to display a suspender belt and announced, 'That's for you. Take it.' She also happened not to be wearing any underwear! That night was the start of my career both in and out of the ring!

It was laid on a plate for me if I wanted it, but I was just a very naïve kid at the time so nothing further happened on that occasion. But it was certainly a real eye-opener which I had never imagined happening to me. To be in a glitzy club, with blokes in dinner jackets and girls offering themselves to me – this was the world I had read about and now I was experiencing it for real.

The next day's copy of *The Sun* featured a picture of me throwing my left hook and the caption 'The White Bruno'. The report included the phrase 'the sweetest left hook since Henry Cooper'. Colin Hart, who remains a good friend to this day, still maintains he discovered me.

In the midst of the excitement of my professional debut I was missing home, in particular David, whose condition was getting worse. As the disease continued to ravage him he was struggling more and more with simple things like swallowing food. Those lonely nights alone in my London digs were tough, but each time I thought of how tough my brother had it I was humbled. What I was going through was manageable and I had a dream of what I was going to achieve as a result of my efforts. David's dream was just to wake up the next morning. He was desperate for me to be a success so he could share my joy. I was carrying David with me as I sought to achieve the dreams of boxing glory that drove us both on.

My return to the ring was another early example of the rather unorthodox matchmaking and management that was to haunt me throughout my career. Denroy Bryan, like Barry Ellis before him, was another unbeaten heavyweight, with two wins from his first two professional bouts. The fight was to take place a mere fortnight after my initial contest. I was thinking that it was a funny old piece of matchmaking and there was a further surprise in store when I learned it was scheduled as an eight-round contest. What madness! Who does eight rounds at the Albert Hall in only their second pro fight at the age of nineteen?

Something I still remember from that night is the DAF Trucks shorts fiasco. Alan Minter had been sponsored by DAF Trucks, but I didn't know any details of the deal he had with them. I didn't know what deal Doug had done with DAF Trucks either. I did know that I hadn't done any deal with DAF Trucks whatsoever and I wasn't getting a penny from them, nor a car, nor a DAF truck for that matter. I did, however, get a pair of shorts with 'DAF Trucks' written on them. I was scheduled to box around third on the bill and was in my dressing room all gloved up and ready to go when an official came down and told me I couldn't go on next after all. We asked why. Apparently, because there was a TV crew present, I was not allowed to appear with advertising on my shorts. Instead I had to hang around until after the main event had been completed and the cameras had stopped filming before I was allowed to go on.

Denroy Bryan was a pretty tough fight for a kid. I managed to win a points victory after having lasted the eight-round distance, despite having never gone beyond three in my life before that night. Denroy became something of a journeyman after that, but he could handle himself.

Next up came the match with Steve Abadom which had originally been planned for my debut. He was a tough southpaw against whom I suffered my first cut eye. I got cut almost every time I fought a southpaw – never from a punch, always from a clash of heads. It was just one of those things that seemed to happen to me. I would miss with a jab, they would slip inside, and with me usually being the taller fighter their head would connect. Bang! I'd be cut again.

Despite the injury I won a six-round decision and went on to face Frank Robinson at the Grosvenor House in Mayfair. It was a night that I will remember for the rest of my life because it was the night I got to meet Muhammad Ali.

I think the evening was in honour of Henry Cooper's fiftieth birthday. I wasn't too sure because I was just some undefeated three-fight prospect who went along because his manager had fixed up a fight for him. I had no idea Ali was going to be there, then I happened to catch sight of the top table and who should I see but my all-time boxing hero? I worshipped Ali. I grew up loving this guy – the guy who took me into the world of boxing, the guy whose flickering footage on my bedroom wall had inspired me and whose pictures used to gaze down upon me from above my bed. This amazing spirit that made me desire to be a world champion above everything else. The man who made me believe, despite coming from an area where there had never been any world champions, where there were no top gyms, where there were no internationally renowned trainers, where there was nothing to suggest a champion could possibly come from that area; that I could still fulfil my dreams one day. And now there he was sitting just ten yards away from me. I couldn't get over the fact that *he* had come to see *me* fight! That night I didn't care about anything else. I didn't care about the fight or Frank Robinson. All I cared about at that moment was how to let Ali know that I loved him and that I thought he was the greatest in the world; to acknowledge the inspiration that he had been and the pleasure he had given me from the age of ten until that moment at nineteen. I just needed to connect with him somehow.

So what did I do? I did an Ali shuffle.

Looking back now I can't believe I had the audacity to do an Ali shuffle in front of Ali. Then I raised my hand above my head. All I was trying to do – though I didn't know if he'd get it or whether he'd think I was taking the piss – was just let him know I loved him. To let him know that this is what he meant to a poor white kid from Nowheresville. The fight itself was a disappointing performance as, quite frankly, I was too busy doing Ali shuffles and worrying about how he would react to it to concentrate on the job in hand. I won a points decision over six rounds and then went on to stop the same opponent in the fourth round of a rematch a mere nine days later, which I think goes to prove that I should have been so much more impressive on that night at the Grosvenor House, but I was too wrapped up in Muhammad Ali.

After the fight was over I went upstairs to get changed and to see my dad and Uncle Tony who had come to stand at the back and watch me as best they could, as they couldn't afford tickets for the tables near the ring. It dawned on me that I had just embarrassed myself in front of my two heroes: my dad and Muhammad Ali. You know how you often do something when you're full of excitement and adrenalin and then afterwards you sit down and think: what a numpty?! Well I was thinking that right at that moment. All that was going through my head was: what an idiot! What have I done? I was sitting in the changing room with all those negative thoughts for company when Jarvis Astaire and Mickey Duff came bursting through the door. Jarvis barked, 'McCrory. Fasten those boots up again – Muhammad Ali wants to meet you.' I couldn't believe my ears. Muhammad Ali wanted to meet me! I had been quite early on the bill too, so the bigger fights were now taking place and Ali had left them to come and see me!

I rushed out of the dressing room but then, on my way downstairs, a new fear swept over me. I suddenly found myself thinking, 'Oh shit. What's he going to say?' Yes he wanted to meet me, but why? What if he was to say, 'What did you think you were doing you idiot? You showed me up. Don't ever do that again!' My knees were shaking as I approached the great man. As it was Ali just looked at me and declared, 'Man, you're gonna be champion one day. You'll be Champion of the World – mark my words. But... cut that nonsense out!' He then pulled the famous Ali face. The one he used to give Joe Frazier and George Foreman. The one in which he bites his bottom lip and mock-glowers.

As luck would have it Derek Rowe, a lovely man and a top photographer, was there and he captured the moment for posterity. The picture of Ali gurning at me still hangs on my living room wall to this day. And, as my career entered some dark days, I would think back to that night and say to myself, 'Ali said you were going to be Champion of the World and Ali was never wrong!' His achievements and personality never ceased to inspire me throughout my career.

Following the stoppage of Robinson in the return bout, I travelled to Port Talbot to outpoint Andrew Gerrard over six rounds in my sixth fight in four months. When does a teenage heavyweight fight six times in four months? I was beginning to have my doubts as to the way Doug was handling my career, even at this early stage. And from the start I'd be told I'd be getting a purse of, for example, £1,000 and then, after Doug's deductions, I'd actually be handed something like £250. That's why I was still on the dole. I'd receive an amount, they'd stop my giro for a couple of weeks until that was gone and then I'd be straight back on the dole again.

At least my career was progressing in terms of victories in the ring. I moved out of the digs in Beckenham, which I was delighted to do as they were awful and I wasn't putting on any weight with their miserly breakfast portions. Doug obviously realised that I was now regarded as an undefeated heavyweight prospect, so any idea of my fighting in any other weight category was out of the window. It was now a case of 'how much can you eat?' That was my training plan.

My thoughts are that I should have begun my professional career at light-heavyweight. Like I said, I was pretty much that weight when I left the amateur ranks and I'm sure with a healthy regime and a decent trainer I could have continued to make the weight for a good couple of years. I was still able to make the 13 stone 8 pounds cruiserweight limit when I was almost twenty-nine, so I'm sure I could have continued to make 12 stone 7 pounds for a year or two after I turned pro at nineteen. Doug wouldn't have needed to keep me at that weight for long, he could have kept me there till I was around twenty-one or twenty-two and seen how far I could make it in that division before moving me up to cruiserweight. Sadly, however, Doug had decided the heavyweight route was the only option from day one, which was to have an almost catastrophic effect on my career.

Doug began by training me himself, but I think he soon realised that he was not up to the job and brought in a trainer called Lenny Lake, who was also a taxi driver and a nice guy. Doug must have known he needed the help but, typical Doug, once he had hired Lenny he never really let him actually help at all. I think he was scared that if he let someone else in then they would get my ear and tell me a few home truths about Doug's methods and ideas. Doug wouldn't let anyone get close: trainers, promoters, other managers, none of them. So poor Lenny had a hard time while he was trying to train me. Doug would butt in and pull Lenny away for one reason or another so he could never really help me significantly and I pretty much had to do without a proper trainer my whole career.

All Doug really did, apart from to feed and weigh me, was to get me some top-class sparring partners. I sparred with James 'Bonecrusher' Smith before his fight with Frank Bruno and with Trevor Berbick when he came over here to fight on a Bruno bill at the Empire Pool. I was a young up-and-coming fighter and I was being asked to spar with men who went on to be world heavyweight champions. Later on I sparred with a previous champion in Gerrie Coetzee, as he also prepared for a meeting with Bruno. It was all hard and painful work. These guys were genuine, world-class heavyweights. I remember leaving the gym with tears in my eyes after one Bonecrusher session. Things were getting really tough.

Despite a promising start of six wins from six contests, things were not going well in any other aspect of my life. I had recently moved to The Jolly Gardeners pub in Wandsworth, which was anything but jolly let me tell you. It was rough in there. There were stabbings in and around the area and the whole thing was all becoming pretty unpleasant. I was still on the dole but, because I was winning fights, everybody back home seemed to think I was some kind of big shot – the Fancy Dan from London.

I was coming out of every fight with next to nothing in cash and had an even bigger problem with the training. It literally seemed to consist of Doug asking me how heavy I was. Honestly, it was a case of turning up and being told to get on the scales. He had me drinking gold top milk, which is just pure fat. He had me eating bacon, black puddings and sausages – basically just fry ups all day. This is what I was training on. Anybody reading between the lines could have foreseen a disaster was coming inside the ring. What I had to deal with first was a total disaster outside of it.

# 7

'I covered Glenn's professional debut at a Mayfair sporting club
and although the fight lasted less than three minutes the Geordie
lad made a major impression and it was no surprise to me when
he became the North East's first world champion. Outside the ring
Glenn is happy-go-lucky, laid-back and wonderful company and
I'm proud he regards me as a friend – even though there were times
when I upset him with some of my criticism.
That's the mark of a big man.'
Colin Hart, Boxing Columnist, *The Sun*

My first proper girlfriend at school was Claire Gilbert. She
was the first one that I really thought a lot of. I used to run
from Annfield Plain to her house in Byermoor, a distance
of around five miles. I ran there and back just to see her
because I didn't have money for the bus fare. Every four
weeks or so she would behave a bit differently and seem to
be in a huff. She'd be a bit off with me and I couldn't get
over the change of emotion which seemed to take place
roughly once every month. Well duh! I've clocked on a

bit since then but, at the time, instead of either staying away or treating her differently, I didn't understand and couldn't really accept her changing behaviour. I had no idea what was going on, which goes to show how young we were. As a result of this nothing really developed between us although Claire remained part of my life, or at least around it, from then on. She was always there until we had both married and she went off to Australia. Tragically she took her own life a few years ago. She once told me that I was her great love but that she never showed it. It could all have perhaps been so different.

My first serious girlfriend was Amanda Walsh. We were fifteen years old and in the same year at school. It was just kids' stuff at first. I'd go and see her at her mother's house for a cuddle and a bit of tea, or take her to the pictures. But from kids' stuff it changed so quickly and drastically that within a few years we were facing all sorts of horrible things. Looking back that whole period was just terrible and it was probably the same for her. It was definitely a time when we needed somebody to say: You know what? You two need to sort yourselves out. You're not getting on, you're not suited to each other. Just make a clean break and get on with your lives. It was a relationship in which one minute we were all over each other and intensely passionate and the next we were shouting and yelling and she was demanding that I gave up boxing and all sorts of other stuff. It was definitely a situation in which I should have just walked away instead of getting too involved.

After we finished school she left England to work with her sister in a hotel in Germany. I didn't want her to leave but she told me she was young and wanted to experience life and she was right. We were only seventeen; it was going to be exciting and fun for her. Meeting lots of American soldiers and that kind of thing is precisely what she should have been doing at that time of her life. I certainly wouldn't have wanted her trying to stop me from doing what I wanted to do with my life at that age, so I had no alternative but to let her go. It was a perfect opportunity for me to make a fresh start, but instead I decided to wait for her and wrote every few days.

She came back after the best part of a year and there was a massive row when I discovered a picture of her with an American soldier. It was another one of many times we finished only to come back together soon afterwards, which was the pattern of the whole tempestuous relationship.

I remember being at her house one evening, during one of our regular periods of being together but not particularly happy, when there was a knock at the door. It turned out to be a lad called Chris, who was her ex-boyfriend, or so I had thought. They had been together before we had started dating at fifteen and then, all of a sudden, he had called round to see her. I wasn't buying it. At the time, I thought that was pretty much it.

By the end of my amateur days we were over, as far as I was aware. But once I turned professional and went down to London, she was immediately back in touch to ask what it meant for us. I remember being totally confused by what was going on. If I mentioned Chris she would just refuse to discuss it as though it never happened.

It seemed to be on and off more times than it was possible to keep track of. All the same, we were not an item in

September 1984 when I headed up to Newcastle to have my first fight in my home region since I turned professional.

The reason for heading north to fight was that, because I was doing everything down in London, I was making a bit of a name for myself everywhere except back home. Doug began to reason that if he was to take me to Newcastle and build up a following in my local area then we could get home support to develop and really start to make some money. The decision was taken that I would fight a number of bouts up north over the following few months.

I outpointed Andrew Gerrard again over eight rounds in Gateshead. I hadn't invited Mandy and she wasn't there on the night. We had fallen out of touch and we were no longer together, although nothing had been said officially.

Later, while at my parents' house, I received a phone call from her mother who was almost hysterical. It turned out that Mandy was in a critical condition in hospital. I rushed down with Father Phelan who gave her the last rites. It was a horrendous situation for someone still only nineteen years of age to experience.

The whole of the previous few years was flashing before me. I was living in London and trying to survive on dole money. I was on and off with a girl and I didn't know from one week to the next whether we were supposed to be an item or not. She didn't want me to continue with boxing – then she did, then we were split up – then we weren't, now we're on – now we're off. It had just been totally crazy and was having a serious effect on my own state of mind. Finally it seemed to me as though we were definitely over and I could move on and concentrate on my career and – boom! – there I am by her bedside as she fights for her life.

Luckily she pulled through but once she recovered I found myself in an impossible position. I felt I couldn't possibly break up with her while she was recovering from something so serious. How could I tell her it was over and just walk away? Whether she knew it or not she had a hold over me. I was so scared of everything I did and said. I remained in the North East for two more fights over the next two months and by the end of that period we were back on. Just months later and she was pregnant. What do I do now? I was a good Catholic boy and I was thinking that I would have to do the right thing and marry the girl.

Looking back I wish my parents had told me to do what I could for my child, but that marriage would never work between us; but they didn't. They remained non-committal and sent me to see Father Phelan. To my astonishment he said, 'You don't have to do it my boy.' That was the last thing in the world I expected him to say, but I'm sure, deep down, he knew what would be in store if I did the honourable thing.

By this time I was totally confused, but my Catholic upbringing kicked in and I decided that I would do right by Mandy and the baby and so we got married on 1 June 1985.

It had been a period of my life which had been sheer hell and things were not about to get any better. The one thing that had been going well throughout that time was my boxing career. After my wedding day even that was to see the wheels fall off in spectacular fashion.

# 8

'Glenn is boxing through and through – a Geordie icon.'
Frank Warren, boxing promoter and manager

If life is a rollercoaster, I was about to hit an almighty bump. No one relishes losing. To do it at home before your own folk is totally demoralising. The world suddenly seems a very empty place.

Looking back, my boxing career was heading for disaster at breakneck speed. I had just got married and bought a little house in Mitchell Street from my sister Karen. One problem was going to be the mortgage. Another was that Mandy didn't like Doug Bidwell. She hated his rings and greased back hair. She thought he was slimy and on top of that she felt I wasn't getting paid properly, which was true of course. Mandy would repeatedly press me to give up boxing and 'get a proper job'. No pressure there then!

I was on the dole, struggling in my personal life and being fattened up into an overblown heavyweight which meant I lost my speed. I was a car accident waiting to happen and, sure enough, I crashed headlong into a Geordie showdown with big John Westgarth at Gateshead Leisure Centre three weeks before my twenty-first birthday. The key of the door? More like the dungeon!

The ironic thing is that a lot of folk up here thought I was a flash git, some Big Time Charlie back from the smoke. They expected a huge car and a fat bank balance. They couldn't see the real me.

I had been ticking over defeating the likes of Joe Frazier's nephew Mike Perkins; Nate Robinson; a gruelling fight with Alex Williamson, a tough undefeated Canadian trained by the legendary Angelo Dundee; and Gypsy George Carmen.

Bidwell can come up with his usual flights of fancy which resulted in us going to the States to meet Don King, the notorious promoter of all fights gigantic who looked as though he had been plugged into an electric socket with his hair standing bolt upright.

I spent some time in Larry Holmes' camp as he prepared for his title defence against David Bey. I was still a bairn, only twenty, but I was thrown in with some top heavyweight names. I sparred with Randall 'Tex' Cobb and Mike Dokes, who were preparing to fight one another on the Holmes undercard. Boy, was my sparring card collecting a host of impressive faces.

Bidwell got us seats from Don King. The announcer started introducing celeb guests who would take a bow and built up to a couple of 'special guests.' In walked the two Sugar Rays – Leonard and Robinson – who proceeded to make their way to the seats directly in front of me, arm in arm. Was I impressed!

Doug had been touting me as the big, young, undefeated British heavyweight and sure enough I got to shake hands with two legends of the ring. Brother, I was so proud my heart almost jumped out of my mouth! I've always considered Sugar Ray Robinson to be the greatest pound for pound fighter in boxing history and to shake the hand that had shaken so many fighting men was a phenomenal experience for me, a kid from Annfield Plain.

The truth, though, was that Bidwell was just playing a game. We had sat in Don King's office to allegedly discuss a possible deal but we had come out with nothing but a couple of ringside tickets. That was the last King ever saw of us.

The bottom line was that Bidwell was making enemies for me just to get Vegas tickets and put me on *World of Sport*. Everything was short-term gain with no thought for my long-term future.

It was the same when I fought Gypsy George Carmen. He was living in the Norwich area and as my fight in Gateshead was three days before the Milk Cup final between Sunderland and Norwich City, Bidwell had the brilliant idea of making me a Sunderland fan to cash in on the rivalry. Oh yeah? The Mackem punters weren't buying it. Now Newcastle folk who didn't know me wouldn't cross the Tyne Bridge to support me. I always kept the bitter football rivalry 'twixt Tyne and Wear away from my boxing career and here was *my* manager putting me right slap bang in the middle of it.

If Doug did me no favours there, he did me even less when I fought John Westgarth. Here was my moment of truth. Everything that was going wrong behind the scenes came together to deal me a blow. You can only hold back the tide for so long. Ask King Canute!

On fight night the Gateshead Leisure Centre was jammed. There was a searing, tense, expectant atmosphere. I had weighed in at 208 pounds, my heaviest ever, and as soon as the fight started I felt slow and cumbersome. Despite this, I absolutely boxed his head off in the early stages. It was like taking candy off a baby. I realised he was big, strong and wild, but I knew if I could keep away from him and use my jab I would handle him with no real difficulty, so I jabbed and jabbed and gave him a boxing lesson.

After a couple of rounds of this I came back to my corner to find Bidwell screaming, 'Take him out! Take him out! You can knock him out. He's gone!' He was nowhere near gone. He was still as strong as an ox and throwing me about in the clinches. I went out again, jabbing, jabbing, jabbing and again, after the third round, had to listen to Doug telling me to make a name for myself by knocking him out. I began the fourth round and jabbed him some more. Doug was yelling at me and I found myself thinking, 'Should I? Perhaps I should? Maybe I shouldn't...'

Boom! The minute you start to doubt yourself and stop to think about things in the ring is when trouble turns up. I was caught with a big shot and went down. I wasn't badly hurt but it had been enough to put me on the canvas. I remember looking around while I was down and everybody in that room was up and cheering. I could have sworn that even my friends were on their feet! Honestly, it was the loneliest time of my life, the loneliest place I had ever been. The whole of my beloved North East wanted this. They wanted me to lose. They thought I'd sold them out for fame and wealth yet the truth was the complete opposite, I was having the worst time anybody could imagine. I climbed to my feet but he jumped on me again and the referee stopped the fight. My unbeaten record was over.

I've been around the game long enough to know that fighters always blame their trainers, their managers, everybody but themselves. I know I was the one in the ring, I was the one doing the fighting, but I wasn't the one giving the bad advice. I wasn't the one forcing me to remain on the dole by paying me peanuts with the knock-on mental effects of worrying how I was going to pay my bills. And I certainly wasn't the one that was virtually force-feeding me pounds and pounds of bacon and sausages every day and kicking off every session by asking, 'How heavy are you today?' before demanding that I put yet more weight on. I went into the Westgarth fight at least twenty pounds heavier than I should have weighed at that time. You don't feed fighters shit, you don't feed fighters bottles of gold top, you don't tell them to go out and fill themselves full of cream and all that sort of stuff to put weight on. That's not how you build muscle – it's just pure fat. Doug was simply in a hurry to have a heavyweight prospect that he could tout around for big money. Perhaps if he'd put me on a proper bodybuilding programme and had me eating supplements and doing all the right stuff then that would have been fair enough, but he didn't have me doing anything like that because he wouldn't let anybody near me who may have been able to come up with a sensible programme.

All I was doing was just eating and sparring. Around a year or so before the Westgarth defeat I remember training at the Thomas a Becket and the Park Tavern in Mitcham Lane with the other guys in the Bidwell stable such as Jimmy Cable, Trevor Cattouse and Doug Jones. My sparring partners at that time included Gary Mason, Derek Williams and Funso Banjo – two future British Heavyweight Champions and another who fought for that title. Derek Williams has since told me that they would often have a conversation with each other beforehand to discuss ways they could handle me and try to beat me up. These guys were top heavyweights, so I must have had a fair bit of potential because they had to gang up in order to beat me despite all being naturally bigger and stronger than I was.

I sparred with Trevor 'Hughroy' Currie about six months before the Westgarth fight and handled him no problem, I was all over him. That was back when I used to be fast. The one thing that I had going for me against these big, strong guys was speed. I could handle myself, but only due to my speed and movement. Once I started putting the weight on it got harder and harder. A few years later I sparred ninety-six rounds with Mike Tyson in his heyday. You don't go ninety-six rounds with Mike Tyson without being able to handle yourself. I managed to cope because I had the speed. If they'd put the Glenn McCrory that fought Westgarth in with Tyson I'd have been killed. I was just a big, fat plum.

\*

My first fight after the Westgarth debacle saw me earn a straightforward victory over light-heavyweight Roy Skeldon. By the time of the Skeldon fight I had become a father following the birth of my daughter, Victoria, in November 1985 – about the only happy event in my life during that entire period. Because I now had a wife and daughter I decided I wanted to live and train at home in the North East. I could no longer afford to train in London, either financially or emotionally. Mandy was constantly pushing me to get a normal job so I went for interviews at the job centre and in the meantime I trained on my own. Visions of belts, titles and glory had begun to disappear in the cold, hard reality of the life in which I seemed to be trapped.

Following the Westgarth defeat I think it had begun to dawn on Doug that I was not going to be his great heavyweight world champion and from then on he started trying to maximise the money he was able to make out of me while he still could, making whatever match would earn him a few quid. Quite simply, I went from being an exciting, undefeated prospect to a journeyman in the space of a year. And I was only twenty-one.

Due to my being up north Doug would arrange a match then call me to tell me where I needed to be and when. That is how I got to face unbeaten young Welsh heavyweight Rudi Pika at the Albert Hall and was then expected to take on former European Heavyweight Champion, Anders Eklund, in Denmark just nine days later! I mean how crazy is that?

Rudi Pika was a highly promising young Welsh south-paw from the Mickey Duff stable of boxers. He had won twelve out of twelve prior to our meeting. It was a close fight which could perhaps have gone either way, but he got the decision and I slipped to my second defeat. He never fought again after that. Little over a year later he took his own life in a tragic waste of talent and promise.

Anders Eklund had been European Heavyweight Champion until he lost his crown to Frank Bruno six months prior to our meeting. I was to be the first fight on his comeback. This shows how quickly I had been switched from up-and-coming fighter to stepping-stone opponent. To be expected to take on a fighter of that calibre, a giant of a man at 6 feet 7 inches tall, only nine days after a tough eight rounds against a promising unbeaten heavyweight, was madness.

To begin with the crowd were all chanting: 'Lillen! Lillen!' which was Swedish for 'Little Guy' and was Eklund's ironic nickname. By the end they were chanting for me. I put up a really good show despite everything that was against me, but I was never going to get a decision over there. The fight was actually on the undercard of the contest for the European Heavyweight title, which Bruno had just vacated. In the main event John Westgarth only narrowly failed to win the European crown as he lost a split decision. The same John Westgarth that I felt I had been handling comfortably until my moment of hesitation just a few months earlier. It was victory over me that propelled him into the limelight and brought home just how narrow the margins between success and failure can be in this sport.

Although my second and third defeats had been close decisions against good quality fighters in difficult circumstances, things were to get still worse before they would get better, both in and out of the ring.

Mandy and I were really up and down at this time. I was still a little resentful of how I felt I had ended up married at the time and in the way I did. Constant arguments and fights at home and the pressures of bringing up a baby were never designed to help a boxer whose career had hit a rough patch.

My next fight was against Dave Garside in Blackpool and that night was an absolute disgrace. I felt I was outboxing him when, in the seventh round, he nutted me. It wasn't a clash of heads, he just pure and simple nutted me. It was blatant. The referee gave him a warning and asked if I was alright. I had been cut but otherwise I felt fine so the fight continued. As soon as we got in close he did the same again – a clear headbutt. The referee took him to one side to give him a final warning. He then came across, looked at my eye, and promptly stopped the fight to award him the victory due to my cut! It was scandalous.

It was such an outrageous injustice that one person in the audience, someone I never met and who had never seen me fight before, was moved to send me a telegram which read simply, 'You may have lost a fight but you will win the war. I am a fan.' It was signed by Les Dawson. I have kept that message to this day. Les Dawson didn't need to take time out to send telegrams to me, but he had been so appalled by what had gone on that he went to the trouble of sending something to boost my spirits and it worked. I wish I had had the chance to thank him for it. Clearly Les had no idea how low I was at that point, but there I was just about to hit rock bottom in the ring and he gave me just enough encouragement to persevere. I may have lost a fight, but I sure was going to win the war.

There was one more defeat to follow the Garside debacle, which came when Doug plunged me into a fight with heavyweight contender Hughroy Currie with no time to train beforehand. I went into the ring at a career high of 15 stone 8 pounds. Mandy had to put the pads on for me in the couple of days before the bout. That is all the training I had. I entered the ring knowing I had no chance at all and it was no surprise when the big and powerful Currie knocked me out in the second round. I had only agreed to take the fight in order to pay more bills that were coming in. Mandy, the baby and I were still managing to keep the house at that point. That wasn't to last much longer.

The Currie defeat was the low point for me inside the ring. Mandy's attempts to get me to give up the game were becoming more appealing. I had just celebrated my twenty-second birthday and had lost five of my last six fights. I had turned from young star to no-hoper in less than a year, in the eyes of both the boxing world and my own manager. All I had done in almost three years since turning professional was spar and eat.

This was a time when anybody normal would have just walked away. As well as Mandy, my dad was also showing signs of concern for me. Like any decent father he didn't want to see me fail and potentially be emotionally or physically hurt in the process. The thing is though, he had a different attitude towards life than me. Both he and my mum stayed safely in their little cocoon and never seemed to have great and grandiose dreams. That's never been my way. I've always felt you've got to have dreams and then get out there and have a go at making them come true. So, deep down, no matter how bad things were getting, I knew I couldn't give up yet. The more people tried to protect me by telling me I wasn't going to make it and was only going to get hurt, then the more determined I became in my desire to prove otherwise. My inbuilt rebellious nature came to the fore. The worst thing somebody can do to me is to tell me not to do something. That's just lighting the touchpaper. Plus, the more I saw David defy the odds to fight on, the more I knew I couldn't let him down.

Clearly something had to change however and, out of the blue, an event happened which transformed everything for me. I remember sitting at home one night watching TV, drinking milky coffee and eating Maltesers. This had become my routine and I was only doing it out of sheer habit. Suddenly I started to feel really ill. I don't know what was wrong with me, but I started sweating and feeling dizzy and nauseous. I went upstairs and before I managed to reach the bathroom I puked. I didn't stop puking for hours. I went through that horrible period when you have seemingly brought up everything that was in your stomach and all you can do is retch. I felt more ill than I can ever remember. Then, after hours of sweating and being sick on the bathroom floor, something else came up. I thought there was nothing left inside me but up came this dark gunge which I thought at first was congealed blood. I thought I was dying. It turned out to be largely chocolate. Chocolate mixed with whatever else was lining the pit of my stomach.

I was in bed for about three days unable to eat. A few days later I walked into my parents' house and everybody was stunned. I was so white and had lost so much weight that my dad asked me if I was okay. I told him I felt fantastic. He couldn't believe what I was saying and exclaimed, 'but you've lost so much weight!' I looked at him and replied, 'I know I've lost so much weight. Why do you think that is? It's because it was all just shit inside me. I was fat!'

It was as if a light had suddenly been switched on in my head. I told him clearly, 'You know what's wrong with me, Dad? You know why I'm getting beat? It's not because I can't fight; it's because I'm two stones heavier than I should be! I've become slow. I feel good now – I don't feel fat anymore.'

I felt like a weight had been lifted from me both literally and metaphorically. I was newly energised because I had realised what had been wrong with me and I knew how to put it right. I found myself believing again. My career was not over after all.

# 9

'Glenn is an honest gentleman whose straight-talking, no-nonsense
attitude to boxing is justified by his extensive knowledge and
personal experience of the pro-boxing game.'
Carl Froch, three-time World Super-Middleweight Champion

Having decided that my career was far from finished,
what happened next was right out of a *Rocky* movie. I
decided I didn't really have any faith in Doug being able
to do it for me. If I was going to achieve anything I would
have to do it myself.

I needed to find somewhere to train and I managed to
locate premises in Catchgate, near Annfield Plain. It was
nothing more than a derelict room above a fruit shop with
plaster falling off the walls, but I asked the shop owner if I
could rent it and we agreed a deal which pretty much took
up my entire dole money. I got a mate of my dad's, Alan
Cruddas, to come and help me work on it but it really was
a tatty old shithole of a place.

I thought I could put a bag up if I found a large metal bar to fit across the room so I met up with my brother Neil and off we went to Gallagher's Haulage Yard and nicked a long bit of metal, which we then brazenly carried on our shoulders through the streets until we got to Catchgate – only to find it wouldn't fit! So, instead, we had it cut into four sections which we used to fashion corner posts for a makeshift ring.

We obtained another metal scaffold bar and put a single bag up. There it was – a dilapidated room with one bag, no shower and no toilet. If you were caught short you had to use a bucket in the corner and empty it out later. The ring was nothing but a roped off area – there was no canvas and you couldn't even lean on the ropes because if you did you would hit the wall and a big chunk of plaster would land on your head. We used some wood to box off a little area as a changing room and that was that. From that small room (you can barely call it a gym) I won the British, Commonwealth and World titles. Honestly, Rocky has nothing on me!

I paid a visit to my old amateur club and spoke to Johnny Cuthbert about the possibility of him training me. Johnny was committed to the leisure centre though and, to be honest, he had never really been that close to me during my amateur days, so that never came to pass. Instead I asked Alan Walker, Johnny's assistant, if he would like to get involved with the pro game and he jumped at the chance.

Alan was a lovely guy, but he had no pro experience whatsoever. He never did learn how to hold pads properly and never did that for me during my entire career. What he did do was simply be there with me every single day. We would go up to the moors at Consett and run together. That was just what I needed. I already knew how to fight. I'd sparred with Bonecrusher Smith, Trevor Berbick and all those other top heavyweights. What I needed was somebody with me, to push me, to motivate me – I needed someone like Alan. Perhaps I could have been so much better with a Freddie Roach, a Terry Lawless or an Emmanuel Steward, but it didn't matter. My aim was to win a world title. Alan bought in 100% and was with me every step of the way on that road – on every run and at every training session. He gave me something that fighters often don't have. You can have great trainers and do great technical work, but Alan was like my best friend, my mentor and was there when I needed him most.

My brother Neil also came on board, along with my Uncle Anthony, despite neither having any boxing experience, and they too worked in my corner. It really was the most motley crew you've ever seen in your life. No experience at all, working out of a ramshackle, one-bag gym, and yet together we took on the world and won.

A new approach was to be matched with new influences on my career but things were not to follow a smooth, clear path. That's just not the Glenn McCrory way!

During the early part of my professional career I had been asked to spar with Dennis Andries on a few occasions in the Thomas a Becket gym. At that time he was working with an American from Lafayette, Louisiana called Beau Williford. Dennis was British Light-Heavyweight Champion from 1984 and won the world title in 1986, but I was more than holding my own with him despite being just a raw young kid. Because I was fighting as a heavyweight at the time I didn't think much of it, in fact I expected to be better than him in a way, even though he was a world contender. Beau Williford, however, was impressed and had a couple of chats with me, enquiring who was looking after me and who my trainer was and so on. Just putting a few feelers out I guess.

A couple of years later and with my career having seemingly gone off the rails in the meantime, Beau got back in touch. He wanted to know what was going on with this promising young fighter he had seen in London. I told him that I felt I had been too heavy and had since started losing weight. He confirmed what I already knew, which is that I should never have been a heavyweight and should not have been fighting the likes of Currie, Eklund and Pika. My future was in the cruiserweight division.

At the end of the chat he told me to pay him a visit in America to see if we could look at doing something together. By this time my relationship with Doug had become very strained. I felt that I had been a lamb to the slaughter in recent fights. Doug was treating me as a journeyman and sending me in to fight bigger, heavier, stronger guys with only days' notice and no proper training whatsoever. My family were all telling me that he wasn't looking after me, he was merely cashing in, so, despite the fact that Mandy and I were struggling so badly, I borrowed money and flew out to the States to see what Beau could offer.

Doug hadn't really complained when I told him what I intended to do. He was still my manager but, quite frankly, he didn't seem to care what I did because in his view

I was now a nobody going nowhere. He let his defences down for the first time and so it was I found myself in Louisiana. Beau paid for me to fly out and I stayed in a store room in one of his properties there. It was full of junk and I slept on the settee for a couple of weeks while I prepared for my first pro fight in the States.

I was staying with Beau in a real ghetto area, living in a storage room and training in a basement with some pretty useful heavyweights, all of whom seemed to be trying to kill me! It struck me that nobody else in Britain was doing things the way I was.

The fight Beau had lined up was in Louisville, Kentucky, birthplace of Muhammad Ali. Of course I made a point of walking down Muhammad Ali Boulevard and visiting the places in which he had grown up and trained. I think every fighter would have done the same in my position. The actual fight itself wasn't particularly memorable. I weighed in at around 200 pounds and had a pretty easy points win after six rounds with a big pudding of a heavyweight.

One other result of my linking up with Beau was that I acquired a boxing nickname. I had never had one throughout my career, but Americans seem to go mad for nicknames and so Beau decided I needed one. Because to Beau I seemed polite, well-mannered and neatly turned out he decided that he would borrow the name used by one of the legends of boxing in its early days – nineteenth-century Heavyweight Champion of the World, James J Corbett. Corbett had been known as 'Gentleman Jim' and from then on I would enter the ring with 'Gentleman Glenn McCrory' emblazoned across the back of my dressing gown. I like to think that it was quite appropriate, although more than one person has since told me that it was the biggest misnomer they had ever heard!

While in the States I sadly missed my daughter Victoria's first birthday, which had been the day before my fight in Louisville. I returned home for a few weeks over Christmas and signed straight back on the dole in order to try to get hold of some money. I can understand how Mandy would have been peeved trying to make ends meet with a young daughter and a husband with an erratic source of income who was hardly ever there. To make matters worse, our house in Mitchell Street had been repossessed and she was back living with her mother. It was all pretty dire and real hand-to-mouth living, but for me it seemed like I had the chance of a new start and a bit of brightness on the horizon after a very testing year. I felt I could not turn down the opportunity being presented to me and so, immediately after New Year, I flew back out to meet up with Beau who had lined up another fight for me.

When I think back to my time with Mandy it is clear that I actually wanted to be away as much as I could because I wasn't happy at home for almost the whole time we were together. I don't think she really wanted to be with me either and I seemed to infuriate her by just being there. I can't speak for Mandy but, looking back, I sense that we both felt that we had made a mistake and were now trapped with the consequences.

Despite our problems we still managed to maintain a physical attraction for each other and so, every now and then, after we had made up we would have a really passionate time. But things could change so quickly and she would suddenly turn into the last gunslinger in town. She would often just hit out. There were times when she would get so frustrated that she would whack me and slap me and I hated it.

We'd had our time when I thought the world of her. When we were together as teenagers I felt that I loved her, but by the time we were nineteen or twenty our lives had started taking shape and we were heading in different directions in terms of what we wanted. From then on it was never the same. When I was back at home it was horrible, the whole thing was just a mess. We were in a relationship neither one of us wanted to be in, but we didn't seem to know how to get out. She wanted a normal, reliable guy with an ordinary job and I wanted to be special, unique and conquer the world. It was obvious that she hated the insecurity. I can say now that she's a nice lady. I'm sure she's great in her current relationship and she's been a good mother, but I'm positive she would agree that we were totally wrong for each other.

When we were together we just rubbed each other up the wrong way. Anything that could take me away from the pain and the misery was something I seized upon. Basing myself in London, flying to America to spar with the guys in the Larry Holmes camp and later working with Mike Tyson all helped me escape. And, for now, it was Beau Williford and the promise of a career resurrection.

My next contest was to be in Houston, Texas. A whole new world was opening up for me. I ate in Tex-Mex restaurants and thoroughly enjoyed the attention I was suddenly getting from women thanks to a combination of my physique, my English accent and, I like to think, my devilishly handsome looks! Life was exciting while I was away, all of which helped put thoughts of my depressing home life out of my mind.

I fought in the Marriott Hotel against a huge guy known as Calvin 'The Killer Monster' Sherman. When I first got into the ring I remember wondering what was going on and whether history was going to start repeating itself – I was being put up against a much bigger heavyweight opponent once more. The difference was that now I was lighter and I was so much better. I weighed in at fourteen stones, the lightest I had been since my professional debut, and it was all coming back. I was fitter and quicker. My reflexes and timing had returned so it didn't matter whether they were big or not. Sherman was nothing special, he was basically just cannon fodder, but I hit him with a left hook in the first round and knocked him out. The other thing that was coming back was my confidence.

I flew back to the UK and within weeks had a really tough fight back in Newcastle against Danny Lawford and, less than a fortnight later, there was a rematch with Barry Ellis, the opponent against whom my pro career had begun three years previously. It was another of those situations where I was wondering how I had ended up fighting another heavyweight and there was little motivation in fighting Ellis a second time. However, my backing in the North East was growing again now that I had returned to winning ways and of course I had a large family and a great many long-term friends up there. Doug Bidwell lined up the fight with Ellis in the West End of London and I remember bringing two or three busloads of people down from the North East to give me support that night.

Yes, Doug Bidwell had jumped back into the picture. I was winning again and there seemed mileage in the idea of me as a cruiserweight so Doug wanted to be back on the scene. Beau didn't really like Doug but they made an attempt at working together because I was still under contract with Doug. Beau had recognised something in me and he followed me to the UK. I was still on the dole and had recently lost my house but found myself having to pay his expenses.

Throughout my career it had been almost impossible to pin Doug Bidwell down to tell me what I was actually going to get paid for any given fight. With Doug it was always, 'Well I don't know exactly. I'll get as much as I can for you.' If I pressed him he would maybe say that it would be around a certain figure but he couldn't be sure. Over time I cottoned on to the fact that whatever he said was meaningless as I would always end up with less than half the number he had mentioned. I would tell Mandy that we were going to get some money and Doug had promised a thousand pounds and I would come home with less than four hundred. Or we'd expect six hundred and get two hundred and fifty. Naturally Mandy used to go mad. She'd ask me where the money had gone, as you would expect from someone who needed to feed and clothe a small child as well as herself. I was getting so much hassle from her and I just felt that Doug was ripping me off hand over fist. I was paying for his meals and everything. The second Barry Ellis fight, however, topped the lot.

I won the fight on points and in the dressing room afterwards asked Doug for my money. He looked at me and said, 'Listen Glenn. You weren't supposed to be on this bill tonight. We had to fit you in at the last moment and had to pay for your opponent from your share of the money. Your purse and ticket money was X, we had to pay him Y, so now you owe me £150.' I swear to God that he stood there, looked me straight in the eye and, bold as brass, told me I owed him £150. Now imagine going home to your wife and telling her you've just had a fight in London, which you won; that you took two to three coach loads of supporters down to boost the ticket revenue and that at the end of the night you owed your manager £150 for the privilege! By this point I was just absolutely sick of the whole thing. I decided that I could not be bothered to put up with Doug Bidwell any longer. I thought it was terrible what he was doing to me, it was absolutely criminal.

I spoke to Howard Gold, a local solicitor and a lovely man, and enquired about getting out of my contract. I told him the situation, but explained that I couldn't afford any legal help as I had no money. Doug was so complacent he was even writing down on my payslips details of just how far he was ripping me off. Deductions, expenses, meals, hotels – they were all listed. Howard took a look at the contract and the paperwork and told me that he thought it was so terrible that he would do it for nothing. That's how bad it was – a solicitor actually agreed to work for nothing! I thought that would be it and left it with Howard to set in motion. Little did I realise just how difficult breaking from Doug Bidwell would prove to be.

# 10

'Aside from him being a world champion I remember watching the
big fights as a kid and Glenn being the voice and commentating
with such knowledge and enthusiasm. I've since got to know him
personally and he's an even better character in the flesh.'
Darren Barker, former IBF World Middleweight Champion

I often wish that Frank Warren had been my manager. I
admire and respect Frank tremendously and I regard him
as a friend. Unfortunately he always seemed to be in the
opposite corner during my career. It was through Frank
opposing me, however, that I got my first major nudge up
the ladder towards some serious professional success.

Frank was acting for Andy Straughn at the time and
Andy had recently lost his British Cruiserweight title.
Frank was trying to get him in a position to win the belt
back as quickly as possible and so, only a month after his
title defeat, he had arranged for Andy to fight an official
eliminator in order to secure an immediate opportunity

for him to regain his crown. Frank needed somebody competent who would provide a 'name' on Andy Straughn's record but wouldn't be expected to beat him. It was my name Frank came up with.

It was understandable enough. I had been developing a name as a heavyweight before the wheels came off. Since moving down to cruiserweight I had won a couple of fights but I hadn't faced anybody special and so I wasn't thought to be too dangerous. On top of this they only gave me about ten days' notice, so I am sure they were pretty confident that I would put up a reasonable show but would be very unlikely to derail Andy's march back to the British title.

Andy was a very good fighter and he did go on to regain the British title a year or so later, but that night was my night. I had been given an opportunity to revitalise my career and I wasn't going to let it pass. I won the fight on a tenth round stoppage and all of a sudden Doug was back with a vengeance. I had gone from zero to hero and so Doug linked up with Billy Aird and lined me up for a shot at the Commonwealth title against Chisanda Mutti at Gateshead Leisure Centre.

Chisanda Mutti was a tough Zambian who had recently failed in two world title attempts – that was the level he had been fighting at when he came to Gateshead to defend his Commonwealth crown against me.

Also on the bill that night was a decent heavyweight from Liverpool called Noel Quarless and we'd been down to the Grainger Park Gym a couple of times to spar with each other in preparation. My style had really developed by that stage and I basically had a good left jab, a very damaging left hook to the body and a solid left hook to the head. My right hand wasn't worth shit but my left was pretty useful. One of the things I was working on while sparring with Noel was throwing left hooks to the body. I remember stepping in and throwing a left hook to his midsection but connecting with his elbow instead. There was a sudden flash of pain and I was in so much agony it was unbelievable. Doug tried to take my glove off but it wouldn't budge and the pain was just horrendous. They had to remove all the laces before the glove would come off, and they discovered that my thumb was bent back at almost 180 degrees! It was completely dislocated. I nearly fainted on the spot.

We dashed straight to Newcastle General Hospital and into A&E. They gave me an injection to numb the pain and tried to put the thumb back but it wouldn't go. I was still in phenomenal pain, despite the injections. To be honest I've always needed about treble anybody else's injections when dealing with teeth and local anaesthetics, normal doses don't seem to have an effect on me. A couple of hours went by, because they were unable to try again straight away, but even after a long wait they still couldn't fix it. By this time it was late at night and they told me they were almost certainly going to have to operate.

This news was devastating. I thought I'd lost my chance. The Mutti fight was only four weeks away. My big opportunity had finally arrived and I'd blown it. I had no idea how the rest of my career would pan out. Fighting for the Commonwealth title in the North East could well have been the greatest thing I would ever get the chance to do in boxing and a twist of fate may well have robbed me of that moment. But then, at nearly midnight, they gave it one more go and finally managed to get it back into place. I was put in a plaster cast and told to return to have it removed on 15 September. The fight with Mutti was scheduled for the fourth!

Such was my need for money there was no way I was going to cancel this fight. I figured that once it was bandaged up on the night the adrenalin would get me through. Doug Bidwell went along with this, which is crazy really, but then I suppose it meant money. The remaining four weeks of preparation were spent shadow boxing with a cast on and throwing right hands only on the bag. The day before the fight I cut the cast off and the first time I used my left hand in a month was against Mutti in the ring. It was insane.

The fight got to about the fourth or fifth round when I started to hear the same old thing from Doug: 'Take it to him. Go and fight him. Knock him out, knock him out!' Memories of the Westgarth disaster came flooding back but this time I was older and wiser. I became so sick of hearing the shit being spouted in my ear by somebody who didn't have a clue what he was talking about that I decided to take control of my own destiny. In an act of defiance I simply got up between rounds, walked to a neutral corner and stood there on my own rather than listen to him anymore. I would never have done that in the past. It was a defining moment. It was the first time I had ever stood up against authority in the boxing ring in the same way that I had done in other aspects of my life. That moment was another step closer to the end of mine and Doug's relationship.

The fight itself was extremely tough and close. He was very good was Chisanda Mutti – an excellent fighter – but I won a points decision. I was Commonwealth Champion!

Around three days after winning my first professional title, I took a call from Beau Williford. Beau hadn't been with me for the Mutti fight as he was working with James 'Quick' Tillis in Atlantic City. Beau congratulated me and offered me an incredible opportunity – did I want to fly out and spar with Mike Tyson? Of course I did! Mike Tyson was the biggest name in boxing having taken the heavyweight division by storm. I thought it might earn me a few quid but Beau quickly corrected me on that score. He told me he may be able to get me a couple of hundred bucks a week but they were unlikely to offer more as Tyson was knocking heavyweights out every day and I was just a cruiserweight. Still, they would be paying my fare, so I agreed to go. I was given £20 by my dad, took a holdall for hand luggage and a case with the rest of my gear and headed off to face Mike Tyson. I'd just won the Commonwealth title so I didn't give a damn about my bad thumb any longer! Looking back it says much about the state of my marriage that I would rather fly to America with a bad thumb to be thumped by Mike Tyson for next to no money than stay at home with my wife, but that's the way things were.

I flew in to Philadelphia and Tyson's people were waiting for me. Everyone from the flight collected their luggage from the carousel and drifted away bit by bit until there was only me left and nothing coming round. I had twenty quid in my pocket and my hand luggage, which luckily contained my headguard, gloves and gumshield; the rest was nowhere to be seen. I was left stranded. I had no clothes, no gear and I'd been flown over at Mike Tyson's expense in order to spar with him tomorrow. How could I turn up in the gym without my gear? I was devastated.

I got a call to go and meet Beau who told me that Mike Tyson wanted to see me. I met Mike and he was as nice as could be. As soon as I said hello he was unbelievably friendly. 'Great to meet you Glenn. Thank you very much for coming. I'm really looking forward to sparring tomorrow.' He couldn't have been lovelier and all the time I was thinking, 'Shit. I've got no gear!'

I didn't get one wink of sleep that night. The next morning I managed to find an Army Surplus store and used the money from my dad to buy some emergency kit. And so it was that I found myself climbing into the ring with the meanest boxer on the planet wearing a pair of cheap white shorts, a white vest and a pair of plimsolls. I'd spent the previous day travelling across the Atlantic in economy class. I had lost my luggage and had no sleep whatsoever. Everybody wonders how I managed to survive in there but, to be honest, I don't think he could stop laughing at me!

To be fair, the one thing Mike Tyson did not do very often in the ring was laugh. He was utterly focused. When I first arrived it was all, 'Hi Glenn, great of you to spar with me. It's so lovely to see you; thank you so much.' Just such a polite, nice kid. Then we climbed into the ring and he snarled, 'I'm gonna kill you, you white motherfucker. I'm gonna rip your fucking head off that skinny neck.'

I'd never known such a complete change in a personality so quickly. That he could be my best friend one moment and threatening to kill me the next was incredible. I found myself thinking, 'What's up with this idiot? He's clearly never met a Stanley lad! Bring it on!' And believe me – he did.

Despite how I looked, I did really well. He couldn't catch me. I was whacking him with jabs and he couldn't nail me down. I did great, completed four rounds with him and that was it – I was part of the camp, the only white kid in the place. Anybody who was anybody was there: James Broad, Oliver McCall, James Tillis. Many of the top heavyweights in the world were there to spar with Mike and then there's me – this kid from Stanley. It was amazing. I got so much respect from Mike and it was all because I felt I had nothing to lose. He thought life was tough but he was making millions. I was on the dole and didn't have a pot to piss in. I had nothing. I thought I had nothing to lose against Tyson so I fought my heart out and it won me so much respect. After training we'd go and play on Space Invaders together or hang out on the boardwalk and it was great.

After he knocked Tyrell Biggs out to retain his title he came up to me, obviously full of emotion, gave me a kiss and said 'you did that' because I had a similar style to Biggs and had given him some problems in the gym which he then had to work on. I still have a photo of the two of us together in his dressing room after the fight on my wall at home.

Beau had only brought me across for himself initially, so that he had a reason to remain involved in the camp, but it was also great for me to get away from Doug again and to work with Beau because, having had the major problem with my thumb, I needed my hands to be protected. The one thing Beau knew about more than anything else was how to bandage hands. The minute I started working with him for the Tyson sparring sessions I had the most fantastic hand wraps on. My hands were taped perfectly, which I'd never known before. It was almost like having plaster casts. I never had one iota of hand trouble from that moment on. The extra confidence you have when your hands have been wrapped properly is unbelievable.

I returned to the UK over Christmas and in the process signed a contract to fight Tee Jay for the British Cruiserweight title on 21 January. On Boxing Day I flew back out to the States to rejoin the Tyson camp in preparation for his fight with Larry Holmes on 22 January. It may seem strange to be jetting off so close to a British title fight, but my thinking was clear. I had no money to enable me to prepare at home – I simply couldn't afford sparring partners or anything like that – so when I got the call from Beau to tell me that the previous trip had gone so well that they wanted me to be Mike's chief sparring partner this time around, it was a no-brainer. They felt I could mimic Holmes' style and move around and keep Mike on the end of my jab, as Holmes would probably try to do. All of this meant my money was to be increased to $1,500 per week and I wasn't even getting that for fights at that time. On top of that, what could be better preparation for a British title fight than sparring with Mike Tyson? I was challenging Tee Jay for the title and he was a bit like Tyson, he was stocky and powerful, but clearly he was no

Mike Tyson. After a week or two of staring at Tyson across the ring, what possible fears could I have about Tee Jay?

The only downside of the whole experience in that second Mike Tyson camp was that he was fighting Larry Holmes. I loved Larry Holmes. He had been so good to me when I went out there early in my career. I really looked up to him and thought he was great so, in all honesty, I was probably more a Larry Holmes fan than I was a Tyson fan. In a way I was glad that I would have to return home to fight Tee Jay and therefore wouldn't be around for the Tyson-Holmes fight itself.

Of course, January in Atlantic City was freezing cold. I ran every morning with Matt Baranski, one of Tyson's corner men. Matt had taken me under his wing to an extent because he thought my people were crackers for letting me anywhere near Tyson. His exact words on the subject when we first met were, 'Tyson loves to knock sparring partners out and he especially likes to fuck white boys up.' He thought I was a lamb to the slaughter.

Anyway, I was running with Matt in the freezing Atlantic City mornings and then Beau started getting involved and had me diving into the Atlantic Ocean in January. That toughens you up, let me tell you!

The camp was another great experience but it was hard work. It was like casualty central at times. I managed to get through my second Tyson training camp without any injuries myself and I even blackened his eye at one point. Mike Marley of the *New York Post*, who has always referred to me in regards to my roots rather than my country of birth, wrote an article about this Irish cruiserweight who was bashing Tyson about. That led to Mike duly seeking his revenge over six rounds one Saturday. He never knocked me down but that wasn't the nicest six rounds I've ever spent in the ring, as he punished me for Mike Marley's story.

I flew back to the UK just a day or two before the Tee Jay fight. I got off the plane about the nineteenth ready to fight on the twenty-first. Doug Bidwell had told me that jet lag won't hit you if you leave it till the last minute. If I had returned five days beforehand it would have affected me. Doug insisted there were only two ways to avoid the problem: either give myself plenty of time (ideally don't go out there in the first place) or come back right at the death.

Tee Jay had become British Champion by knocking out Andy Straughn's conqueror, Roy Smith, in around ninety seconds. He hadn't had many bouts but that victory had frightened a few people so in that sense working with Tyson was ideal preparation.

The fight itself was tough and Tee Jay was a good opponent, but I won it pretty comprehensively with my superior boxing. At the end of the day I had just been sparring with the meanest man on the planet, so fighting for the British title was no big deal.

Unfortunately I suffered a cut eye against Tee Jay which meant I had to cancel plans to fly to Tokyo to spar with Mike again in advance of his meeting with Tony Tubbs in March. Instead Beau took my brother Gary who was just about to turn pro and who struck me at the time as being almost half into it and half not, but clearly he was nowhere near that level. I knew what was in store and I tried to warn him, but Gary and I have had a bit of a funny relationship our whole lives and he wanted to prove he could do whatever his younger brother could do. I believe he did a couple of rounds with Mike but then got his nose smashed up by Oliver McCall and had to fly back. I had tried to tell him but unless you have experienced it for yourself you can really have no idea what life was like at that time around the most feared man in boxing.

Looking back at that period in boxing history, my view is that the Mike Tyson of 1987-88 was on his way to becoming perhaps the greatest fighting machine that's ever been built. I don't think they will ever again find someone who was totally programmed to destroy like Mike Tyson was. After he burst onto the scene they briefly had him in a place where he was the closest I have ever seen to the ultimate destructive force in the ring and where, in my opinion, he could well have beaten any heavyweight who ever lived.

Purely by chance, I just happened to be with him in his absolute prime. They wanted me to go back as a sparring partner in preparation for the Michael Spinks fight but I didn't go for a couple of reasons. Firstly, I was now British and Commonwealth Champion and wasn't sure I should just be seen as Mike Tyson's sparring partner. And secondly, there was a problem with Doug Bidwell. He wanted to come out with me – he saw an opportunity to make a few contacts. Tyson's camp weren't prepared to pay for Doug to accompany me and that's ultimately why I didn't go, because I certainly couldn't afford to pay him, his flight out and his hotel room.

Tyson's people felt I would have been perfect preparation for Spinks as, again, he was a lighter guy who used to box well, but they were not hugely bothered when I couldn't go because they had absolutely no doubt whatsoever that Tyson would win. Spinks was an amazing boxer, a truly great fighter. I don't think he genuinely beat Larry Holmes, but he was a great fighter nonetheless. It should have been a really tough fight for Mike, but Kevin Rooney told me it was going to be easy. I thought it was potentially a tough fight for Mike because of the success I'd had with Tyson. He couldn't quite get the hang of my style. Obviously he would have probably caught up with me and pulverised me over the course of a proper fight, but over two- and four-round bursts he struggled to deal with me. The movement and quick hands gave him trouble, so I thought Spinks had the right style to cause problems.

The one thing I didn't take into consideration, but the Tyson camp believed completely, was that Spinks was terrified. They felt he was going to be frozen with fear. The reason why I did well against Tyson, and why Holyfield and Douglas did well, is that we all had no fear. None of us felt we had anything to lose and so we just went for it and wouldn't let him bully us, but if Spinks really was shitting himself there was only going to be one outcome. That was something the Tyson camp had worked on from the start. In reality the Mike Tyson image was largely manufactured. Everyone who had ever been around him had all played their part: Cus D'Amato, Jim Jacobs, Steve Lott, Matt Baranski, Kevin Rooney – the whole camp was such a great team. They took a kid from the ghetto, a wild, crazy thug who was perhaps a little short but who was fast and powerful, and they harnessed him to become a complete wrecking machine. They got the whole image right. He wore black shorts, no socks and had no dressing gown. He would walk into the ring with a towel over his shoulders, which he would throw off aggressively and prowl around oozing menace. In the dressing room beforehand he would punch the walls knowing that the opponent was next door. I remember banging on the wall myself before the Tyrell Biggs fight in the hope of intimidating Biggs. A few of us were thumping the wall and banging the lockers as if it was Mike. It was great to be a part of this whole intimidation scheme.

At the time the camp was also like a family who treated me really well. Matt Baranski and I used to sit after training and sign Mike's autographs for him. It really was a close unit and sparring partners were all part of it.

But things were changing. Robin Givens came into the camp for the Holmes fight and I thought she was horrible. As Mike's success and fame grew, others got involved and deflected his attention away from fighting and perhaps the family aspect in camp was lost. I'm glad I got out when I did because my memories are of how it was at its best and it was great to have been a part of that family even for just a short while.

In total I sparred ninety-six rounds with Mike. I know that because when I had to leave early they gave me a jokey certificate saying something along the lines of 'Glenn Mc-Crory survived ninety-six rounds with Mike Tyson'. They were geeing me up for my British title fight and Oliver McCall, James Broad and the others were all involved in handing me this certificate. As an aside, can you imagine how tough sparring could get when on my day off from sparring Tyson I would be facing these guys instead. Some day off!

It was due to my sparring sessions with Mike that I had my only feature in the *News of the World*. It was a complete stitch up. They came out to do a piece on the white English boxer who was sparring with Iron Mike. Who is this madman from Stanley who's getting into the ring with the scariest man on earth? That sort of thing.

They turned up with about three photographers and I wondered what on earth was going on. I was talking to them about the sessions but I could see it was all going over their heads. There seemed no interest in anything from a boxing angle at all. Then they asked me what sort of seat I had been given for the Biggs fight. I explained that the sparring partners didn't actually have seats but we did have all-access passes, meaning I could go anywhere I wanted and watch the fight from somewhere in the arena. They seemed fixated by the fact that I hadn't been given a specific seat ticket and although I kept trying to explain that I could get into the guy's dressing room with a pass they just ran with the story 'Tyson treated me like rubbish'. The whole thing was written around the idea that a British boxer had flown to America to help out Mike Tyson and didn't even get a seat for the fight in return. They just twisted my words and stitched me up completely. When I went back after Christmas, to join the camp in preparation for the Holmes fight, I had to explain what had happened and assure them that I felt I had been treated extremely well by Mike and everybody on the team. I was not impressed by the standards of British tabloid journalism in that story.

From having been a part of his camp for two fights and wanted for the next two, it would be a couple of years before I saw Mike again. By that time the wheels had come off and the whole Tyson story had begun to implode. He had lost his title and was attempting a comeback and I was making an early appearance as a pundit, so the first time he saw me in a couple of years was when I was sitting in a nice suit holding a Sky Sports microphone. I don't think he could quite get his head around that. He saw me as some crazy kid with no money and who didn't give a fuck about anything and then there I was in a suit holding a microphone. He could not seem to comprehend this and for pretty much the next ten years he treated me casually and almost with contempt because I was the media. It was as if I had sold out.

Our paths crossed several times during the nineties as the Tyson story spiralled out of control. Everything went horribly wrong for him. He spent four years in prison and after he came out he was so bitter and surrounded himself with such terrible people that being near him was just a horrible experience. Sky would always send me to get the story because of our previous connection, but I hated it.

Mike seemed to feel that it was the press who had been responsible for all the bad things that had happened to him and he looked down on me because I was now sitting with the journalists. He had known me as a devil-may-care guy that couldn't afford a decent pair of pants, who seemed more into shagging than fighting, and yet would stand up and have a good battle with him in the ring. Then he saw me in a blazer and a tie and I'm sure he thought I had sold my soul. The truth is that he had his million-dollar investments whereas I was just trying to make a living, to pay for my house and feed my kids, all while going through whatever troubles I had at home. The fact that he seemed to be looking down on me and treating me with contempt just pissed me off.

And it was the same routine every time we went to interview him, whoever was with me and whichever gym he was in. We'd turn up and someone would let us in. We would hang around for a short while with nobody speaking to us. Then he'd throw us out. We would be told that while Mike was training we had to leave the building. He wouldn't have spoken to us directly or even given us any acknowledgement at all by this stage. We would be made to wait outside for an hour or two, often in temperatures of over one hundred degrees before, eventually, we would be invited back in. Then he would catch my eye and say, 'Glenn.' I would reply, 'Hi. You alright Mike?' and slowly he would start saying a little bit more and a little bit more and before long we would be able to carry out an interview. By the end of the session he would pose for pictures and give me a hug and all the rest of it. I hated it. Always the same rigmarole time after time. To be honest, all I wanted to do was smash him in the mouth and tell him he was being stupid, but it was my job and I had to do what I had to do. Plus he would have probably killed me!

I thought that he had let me down badly as we used to get on pretty well and I had really liked him when we were younger. Throughout the years in which his unpleasant, dismissive behaviour towards me continued I always remembered the time when we did have some friendship. And I knew he thought the same, because otherwise he wouldn't have let us in in the first place, let alone ended up being quite friendly. I just couldn't get my head around what the whole tirade of shit was all about each time. I didn't understand it. At the end of the day I am a street kid from Stanley. I can't be doing with mind games. If he didn't like me I felt he should have just told me what he thought and got on with it.

A few years later, after he'd been beaten by Lennox Lewis, he came over to England to be a guest at a dinner in Liverpool. Former heavyweight champions Tim Witherspoon and Tony Tucker were also there. Tim was a pal of mine and Tony I also knew. They were fighters I had sparred or shared camps with back in the eighties when we had all played second fiddle to Tyson. When I first arrived at the venue, Mike invited me into his dressing room to meet his missus. He gave me a hug and seemed back to the 1987 Mike. During the course of the evening my name was mentioned and I ended up on stage with him. He told everybody how he thought I was nuts and how great and how fearless I was and how much he thought of me, respected me and how much I had done for him. He was lovely all evening and I thought, 'Mike – we've got you back!' Since then we have been friendly again. We had never been close. Our lives crossed when we were young and we got on quite well for a while without being bosom buddies, but it was nice that the decade of awkwardness was behind us. I don't suppose either of us knew exactly what the other was going through in those days, but I hope that whatever demons were troubling him back then have gone forever and we can remain on friendly terms.

In April 1988 I defended both my Commonwealth and British titles against an old foe, the opponent I had beaten eight years previously to win my Junior ABA title, Lou Gent. I beat him again, this time via an eighth-round stoppage, and then focused on trying to score an equally decisive victory over Doug Bidwell.

Before I could focus on that there came another heart-breaking moment in my life when, in May 1988, Father Phelan died. He was only in his early fifties and it was a sad loss for all our family. Father Phelan loved his golf – he was a total golf nut – and was very good at it. He died of a heart attack as he made his way home from a round. To this day they still compete for the Father Phelan Memorial Trophy at South Moor Golf Club in Stanley, where I am a member.

Father Phelan had been a real character. He was something of a John Wayne type to me – a big man who loved a drop of whisky and a smoke – and he seemed to take our family under his wing and would always be popping round to visit. And of course we shall always be grateful to Father Phelan for bringing David into our lives.

Due to how close he had been to the family, and how well he had looked after us over a great many years, it ended up that my dad, Gary and I all carried his coffin. I remember while carrying Father Phelan that I prayed from the moment I put his coffin on my shoulder until we reached the church, some 200 yards away, that I wouldn't drop him. He was a huge guy; well over six feet tall, and he must have weighed around twenty-two stones at the time of his death. His coffin was so heavy and carrying it on my shoulder was agony. I literally prayed that I wouldn't collapse.

He took me aback when I went to see him about what to do having got Mandy pregnant and he told me I didn't have to get married. It totally confused me at the time, but he obviously knew that it wasn't the right thing to do. That showed me something about the Church; that it wasn't all hell and damnation and based on fear. I was, and still am, a religious person and, as I've grown older, I have realised that God is a forgiving God.

I never missed Sunday Mass until I was around twenty-six and work with Sky would take me all around Europe and across the world. That really took me out of my normal routine. Prior to that I missed it occasionally when I was living in London at the start of my professional boxing career but, as a youngster, I was part of a big Catholic family and we used to attend Mass every week at St Teresa's Church in Annfield Plain. There was no big fuss made about it, it was just a simple routine – Sunday was Church. Before Father Phelan there had been a slightly grumpy old priest who reminded me a little of my granddad, a bald headed Irishman called Father Finnegan.

I have my faith and I believe that everything that happens is all part of God's plan, but I don't tend to go to confession like I probably should. Whenever I do go it always seems like there's a fair bit to say! I don't feel as though I am that bad a person, but it does seem that I've always got quite a bit to confess. I prefer to confess my sins to God directly at home by myself. To be honest that is how I felt when I was young too, just in case the priest went and told somebody or, more likely, that Father Phelan would have throttled me!

So I wouldn't say I'm the best practising Catholic in the world. I'm a sinner, but I truly believe that God is my Father and that life is His test. I would accept that I've probably done a million things wrong and I've got a lot of work to do, but I have faith that, hopefully, I will pass the test one day and be with Him and, ultimately, that's all I want at the end of it all. I want to be with my God.

Having said my goodbyes to Father Phelan I linked up with Howard Gold, the solicitor who had agreed to take on my case against Doug Bidwell, who had been working away in the meantime. Howard asked if I wanted to take Doug to court, but my dad persuaded me not to, as the idea of such places made him nervous, added to the fact that I had no money to begin legal proceedings in the first place. Instead we took the matter to the British Boxing Board of Control – my thoughts being that boxing people, who were my people after all, would look after me. We met them at the Station Hotel in Newcastle with Howard and a barrister who Howard had also managed to rope in for free. It really was extraordinary for two legal representatives to agree to work for nothing, but that was how much they were on my side.

The hearing went on until about one in the morning, which was unheard of. Eventually the Board announced their decision which was that I was out of the contract and free to sign up with somebody else, but that I still had to pay Doug Bidwell his percentage up until the end of the contract term! This meant that I would still be paying Doug a percentage of my subsequent world title fight income.

I felt that the outcome was utterly disgraceful. I have since heard a rumour that the Board may well have decided to do that to me because they thought I was flash for bringing both a solicitor and a barrister along. Clearly they had no idea that they were doing it for nothing because I didn't have a penny to call my own. I was shocked and hurt to discover that this was how my own looked after me.

# 11

'He's a fucking doughnut.'
Chris Payne, friend

With Doug now out of my corner, if not yet out of my wallet, I flew back to America to link up with Beau for a couple more fights and to raise my profile over there a little further. I had been lined up to fight a fairly decent cruiserweight in Oklahoma and we turned up on the day expecting a tough battle against a good opponent. We arrived to be told that the police had picked him up the night before and he was currently in an Oklahoma jail cell! His trainer, a guy called Ron Lee Warrior, told us that the fight was off. Beau told him I'd flown in from the UK especially so somebody had better fight me and so it ended up that Warrior himself stepped in the ring as my opponent! Ron had been a half decent boxer in his day, but he had fought at either light-middleweight or middleweight and was now coming in two stones heavier than he had been a couple of years previously to fight someone who had been competing as a heavyweight until only recently. Still, he performed pretty well before I stopped him in the fifth round despite being scared to hit him properly.

Next up I was off to New Orleans where I took on Lorenzo Boyd. Boyd was the perfect example of a journeyman. I knocked him out in two rounds but I knew he was nothing special. What was special about that night was that I got to meet two legends of the sport, Joe 'Old Bones' Brown and Willie Pastrano, after the fight. Pastrano had been World Light-Heavyweight Champion from 1963 to 1965 and Brown held the World Lightweight title from 1956 to 1962. They came to my dressing room after the contest and we had a great evening together. The occasion is marked by yet another photo of me with a boxing legend or two on my living room wall.

Those latest two fights in the States had done nothing to improve my stature as a cruiserweight contender, but what had been important in that regard was my period as a sparring partner for Mike Tyson. Although my stint in the Tyson camp hadn't lasted long it was of huge significance to my career because I caught the eye of Cedric Kushner. Kushner was one of the USA's major promoters and much of the boxing game is about who you know. When Doug was working with Frank Warren I moved forwards. When he associated briefly with Don King my profile rose. Whenever Doug allied himself with people who had influence things started to look up for me, but he would never actually sign me up for any kind of official deal with anyone because he wanted me all to himself. I was his plaything, his project to work on to his benefit.

However, when I was in America and away from Doug's prying eyes, Beau was able to introduce me to some important people in the fight game over there and once Cedric Kushner came on board things took on a whole new perspective. I have a great deal of time for Cedric. He was a person who would sit me down and effectively say, 'Glenn, I'm about to rob you now.' Well to be fair he would actually say, 'I'm going to do the best deal I can for myself,' but I could read between the lines! If I'm honest I really respected him for that. He told me straight, up front, that he was going to do the best deal he could do for himself. Beau, Doug and so many others were guys that would tell you how they were your best friend and how much they loved your family while taking a huge chunk of your purse at the same time. Cedric was just a straightforward businessman and I could deal with that. He'd tell me how much I was going to get paid, in my hand, at the end of the day, and he would mean it.

I've always been very forgiving of people because I never like to fall out with anyone. I could still be friends with Beau. I'm sure I could be friendly with Doug if he was still alive, God bless him. I understand that people are just trying to get by and make some money for themselves and their families and that's the way the world works. Sometimes they make mistakes or go too far, but I don't harbour any ill will for anybody for any length of time. I had fun and friendship with those guys and I've never really hated anybody in my life, but I can honestly say that I have always liked Cedric. I thought he was a good guy and he was certainly influential. He said he'd get me a world title fight and he got me a world title fight, so I have nothing but respect for him.

Before Cedric, I had feared that my lack of connections would mean that the door would never open. Then, in 1988, Evander Holyfield vacated the undisputed title in order to move up to heavyweight. I wasn't scared of Holyfield and would have been happy to take him on had he remained in the cruiserweight division. I'd been sparring with Tyson so Holyfield held no fears for me. I admit he was a great fighter and would probably have kicked my arse, but I certainly wasn't scared of him – I wasn't scared of anybody. The difficulty would have been manipulating myself into a position where I would even get a chance to fight him. There were so many decent cruiserweights all vying for a crack at the title that a kid from the unfashionable North East of England would never have been given a shot. Now, all of a sudden, there were three belts up for grabs, which meant six fighters would get an opportunity to fight for a title. With Beau having got Cedric on board, he was the key. We left it with him and waited to learn our fate.

In the meantime I signed up to fight Steve Mormino at the Marton Country Club in Middlesbrough. John Spensley promoted the fight and I found him to be a good guy. Mormino himself was nothing special, but I was on the verge of a crack at a world title and that scared me. Everything I had worked for in the ring since the age of twelve was close to being realised. My whole life depended on this possible world title fight. When you're so close to your dream, a fight against the likes of Steve Mormino, someone who I should have just brushed aside without thinking twice, suddenly becomes a terrifying prospect. What if I blow everything now? I couldn't get the thought out of my head. I didn't set the world alight that night, but I felt relieved to get a comfortable points victory out of the way. I was now free to concentrate on a potential title shot. Cedric had promised me something, what would he have in store?

Of all the boxers at the top of the cruiserweight rankings, there was only one person that nobody wanted to fight: a Swedish-based Kenyan called Patrick Lumumba. Nobody wanted to fight him for two reasons. Firstly, he was very, very good. Secondly, he was a lunatic! He was the scourge of the division because he was so good coupled with being a complete madman. I remember Colin Hart came back with some fellow journalists from watching Tyson in training with stories of how Tyson had been given a hard time by 'that African nut from Sweden'. As far as I was concerned I was happy fighting any of the ranked cruiserweights other than this guy. Plus, being a nutcase born in Kenya and living in Sweden, he had no fans, so you could factor in that he wouldn't generate much interest around the world to boost the purse. He was definitely the man to avoid.

His amateur record was extraordinary. He had been World Amateur Champion and had lost only six amateur contests out of over three hundred! That is phenomenal. I saw him fight once as a professional, when he took on my fellow Tyson sparring partner James Broad, the former North American Boxing Federation Heavyweight Champion. Lumumba lost a close and controversial decision to

Broad, but in the first round he knocked Broad almost co-matose and he was giving away over five stones in weight! In his fight before that he had beaten Spanish heavyweight Alfredo Evangelista who, in his very next contest, went on to reclaim the European Heavyweight title. After Broad, Lumumba beat former World Cruiserweight Champion Alfonzo Ratliff and then future champion Jeff Lampkin. He could only get fights against heavyweights and top cruiserweights because nobody else would touch him.

I was hoping I might get matched with former champion Carlos De Leon because I reckoned I would have punched holes in him. He was overweight and didn't seem to have his heart fully in it any more. There was a French-Tunisian guy called Belbouli I would have happily taken on too. He was nobody to worry about. The division was wide open except for this one bad bastard that, of course, Don King would have. And then I got the call. 'Glenn, you can have a world title fight and you can have it in the North East.'

Music to my ears!

'It's for the IBF title and it's against Patrick Lumumba.'

Bloody typical.

On the day of the fight itself I looked at the paper. Perhaps it was a mistake, perhaps it was what I needed as a final spur to drive me to victory. Either way I saw an article written by a friend of mine, the man who 'discovered' me on my professional debut, Colin Hart. I didn't need to read the article itself to know his opinion, all I had to do was glance at the headline. 'Glenn's a Goner.' And this was by my friend!

I had been staying at the Royal Derwent Hotel in Consett to prepare myself for the fight at the expense of owner Mac Murray who had sponsored me, put me up and made me feel like a champion for the only time in my life. He had given me a training camp of sorts in the shape of a couple of Portakabins in a field in Derwentside.

I went for a walk on the morning of the fight with Colin Hart's words still fresh in my mind. I knew Lumumba was good. I usually had a quick look at an opponent on video as part of my preparation and I remember watching Lumumba and thinking 'oh shit!' So seeing Harty's headline in the paper could have destroyed my confidence completely. But that fails to take into account the kind of person I am. I am quite a stubborn and determined individual. The one thing you must never do is count me out.

I looked to one person above all others for inspiration. David. They had written David off years ago. They were writing me off now. Don't ever write us off. We may have been different in so many ways but we were bound together by our spirit. Spirit is something immeasurable but I know both David and I were blessed with more than our fair share. David wasn't expected to live much beyond fifteen. He was now twenty-three.

Throughout my life I had to live with the fact that every day there would be someone shaming me. Someone who would always be achieving more than me, despite my belts and titles. That someone was David. Every time I thought I was doing something special he'd do something more special, such as climbing the stairs, eating his food or any number of things which to most people would be entirely normal, but which to him was a colossal triumph of will. If you had handcuffed me, blindfolded me, tied my feet together and then put me in with Patrick Lumumba I'd have had no chance whatsoever, but in those circumstances David would still have had a go. His spirit was ferocious. He fought with every fibre of his being, every second of the day, just in order to live life.

I fought tough men, David fought death. Every day of my life he was there; at times inspiring, at others almost shaming. He would be outdoing me day after day. Occasionally I even found myself in bed crying because, whatever I did, he made all of my achievements seem so small by comparison. He would fight to eat his breakfast or to get down the stairs. He would push your hand away if you tried to help him. He would not let this horrible disease defeat him without giving everything he had to fight against it, every single day. This had a huge effect on my own emotions and behaviour on a daily basis. His example drove me to achieve far more than I could ever hope to have achieved without him and not a day goes by when I don't think of him and use his inspiration to pull me through and drive me onwards. I always wear a crucifix and rosary beads to this day, because he gave me his and wanted me to wear them for him.

I cannot overstress how unlikely this night had seemed for most of my career. Yes, I had some talent. Yes, I had drive. Yes, I had David to inspire me. But I also had the mismanagement, the personal problems, the absence of proper training, the wasted time in the heavyweight division, the do-it-yourself approach and the total lack of money. I can't know for certain, but I'm pretty sure I must be the only fighter in history who signed on at the dole office just two days before fighting for the world title! How

I ever got to be there that night was miraculous. How David got to still be around to see it years after he was expected to have lost his fight for life equally so. Once again our spirit and sheer bloody-minded stubbornness had led to our both managing to achieve the seemingly impossible and the moment of destiny had finally arrived.

As the fight drew closer I was dropped off in Stanley to see Mandy and kiss my little princess Victoria, and walked to the venue with my bag over my shoulder just like usual. I saw a number of people milling around and a couple of swanky cars going by. I was wondering what on earth was happening in Stanley for there to be people in dinner jackets in limousines in the town. It was only when I approached the Louisa Centre itself and several of these immaculately dressed people saw me and began to clap that I realised they were there for me!

To this day, Ian Darke, who was providing commentary for BBC Radio, will tell you how that occasion in Stanley provided one of the most unbelievable atmospheres he has encountered in his boxing career. There hadn't been a world champion or even a world title contender from the North East of England in the history of boxing. On this night it seemed as though the whole region played their part in helping me to put that right.

As for the fight itself? Well, to put it bluntly, I smashed him! I nearly knocked him out in the first round when I hit him with a left hook that sent him reeling. I also had him in all sorts of trouble in the fifth, but the bell rang before I could finish the job. The fight was tough, but I was on top throughout. A unanimous decision by the judges and I was Champion of the World. In a life of drama and theatre, that night in Stanley was the end of Act One.

Right: Looking more of a heavyweight rather than a cruiserweight as a toddler!

Below: My first belt! Karen, Kelly, Neil, me, Shaun and Gary at my confirmation in 1971.

Left: David in 1979. We were already aware that there was something wrong with him.

Above and left: Becoming Champion of the World by beating Patrick Lumumba in Stanley.

Below: Another celebration after retaining the title against Siza Makathini.

Above and right: Being World Champion was fun, but the hard work didn't stop.

Below: Facing Lennox Lewis in the ring. I took a beating but earned a few bob.

Meeting legends – with Muhammad Ali and chatting to Robert De Niro on the set of *Grudge Match*...

...and with Teofilo Stevenson (note the bulge on his hip) and Mike Tyson.

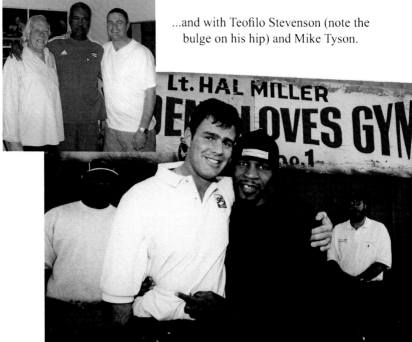

Left: The early days of Sky. If only I looked so young now!

Below: Working with Sky takes me to some of the finest places in the world. Here I am ringside in Wigan!

Lt. HAL MILLER
LOVES G

Right: With my friend and long-time Sky colleague Ian Darke.

Left: Meeting the Queen in my role as Deputy Lord Lieutenant of Northumberland.

Below: With fellow actor and buddy Len Trusty in Rio.

Above: Top journo and my best mate, John Gibson.

Right: Cooking is a passion of mine – I love to spend time in the kitchen.

# Act Two

# The Sky's The Limit

# 12

'Hope is the thing with feathers
That perches in the soul,
And sings the tune without the words,
And never stops at all.'
Emily Dickinson

Champion of the World! Four small words, but ones with a monumental meaning. I said them slowly, bathing in every syllable. It was sweet. I had conquered my Everest from such unlikely beginnings. I was standing on top of the mountain and it felt bloody wonderful. Who said I couldn't do it?

The atmosphere, the excitement, the spine tingling feeling. Everything that happened on that championship-winning night would never quite be repeated. How could it? I've had so many letters, so many people coming up to me and saying 'that was the greatest night of my life'. It would be an amazing compliment if only one soul ventured such an opinion but honestly I've had scores and scores. It's so heartwarming.

I know what prompted such emotion. The underdog had triumphed against all odds – me – but another underdog had ridden the ride with me. The North East is often portrayed in this way, so the region could rejoice as well as myself. I was their first ever world champion. We did it together. It was the ultimate Rocky story because it was real, not a figment of Sly Stallone's vivid imagination. It was the story of the kid who had nothing conquering the world. The dole boy who became king. When I was handed the mike in the ring by the MC to say a few words in victory I announced, 'I have a message for Stanley Dole Office. Thank you, but I'm not coming back.'

I hadn't made a fortune. Far from it. But I was the richest man on earth at that particular moment. You cannot buy what I had. I would never feel it again, because you cannot a second time, but right at that moment I wouldn't have swapped places with anyone on earth.

The post-fight press conference gave me an opportunity to resolve matters with Colin Hart. I had been so absolutely horrified that he'd written me off that morning that I had used it as inspiration for my winning the world title. It was probably the final deciding factor, the last piece of the jigsaw. Even now I still feel passionate when I think back to how I felt when I read it. I sat in the press conference and announced, 'I've only got one thing to say, and that's to you Colin. "Glenn's a Goner." How could you?'

He confessed, 'Hands up. I thought you'd lose.' At the time I was gutted. I took it as a total insult. After a quarter of a century as a boxing pundit I have long since realised that you have to say it how you see it and I haven't managed to last as long as I have in the job without picking my mates to get beaten from time to time. I respect Colin for that today and I love him to bits. He's a close personal friend of mine who was a guest at my second wedding, but on that one particular morning I could have killed him!

I drove back to the Royal Derwent in my newly acquired car from Vauxhall. It was a tiny little Nova that they'd given me in a sponsorship deal now that I was world champion. I could barely fit inside it! I returned to join the celebration party which was in full swing. I remember sitting there, looking around the room and thinking, 'Who are all these people?' I hardly recognised anybody. The room was full of strangers including singer PJ Proby, well-known disc jockeys and former challenger for Muhammad Ali's title, Richard Dunn. It was as if, for one night only, the little mining town of Stanley had become the centre of the world. It was crazy. It was a Saturday night and the fight had been live on ITV with Jim Watt and Reg Gutteridge providing the commentary. There had never been a world champion from the North East so the world came to Stanley to see history being made. It was a big deal, a massive occasion. The actor Tim Healy had also been at ringside. Tim was a friend of mine who I had known for years and would later appear alongside on stage. During the fight I looked at him and winked. I just felt that there was a mate of mine sitting at ringside who had come to see me doing what I do best and where

I feel most comfortable, so I gave him a friendly wink. I was having fun.

Looking back to that night the scale of what we achieved never ceases to amaze me. Not only had there not been a North East world champion before that moment, the fact is that we have hardly been churning out British champions with any regularity since then, let alone world beaters. I was honoured and delighted when I was invited to walk to the ring with Darlington bantamweight Stuart Hall in December 2013, on the night that he emulated me and became a world champion from the region, but that was almost twenty-five years on from that night in Stanley. When you take into account the circumstances in which I was operating it becomes even more remarkable. To become world champion with only a makeshift gym above a fruit shop, without a professional trainer and having my brother Neil in my corner, with no boxing background whatsoever, sounds like a fantasy. That is precisely what it was. We were probably the oddest group of people to ever take on a world title challenge together. We should have had no chance at all. There was no way we could possibly have succeeded in those circumstances – and yet we did. The truth is that I couldn't have had a better team. Beau was there too, and Johnny Brown, who was a great cutman. I couldn't have asked for a better bunch of misfits who were going to work together to achieve something extraordinary.

There is something about me as a person that makes me believe I can do anything. I have had that belief bashed and bruised over the years, but I still feel that if you believe strongly enough, or perhaps if you're just stupid and bloody minded enough, then you actually can. Every single individual who's ever done anything in this world was just a normal person. You might have more money or something but that doesn't give you any advantage. All my life I've felt we're not the real heroes; sportsmen, film stars, musicians and celebrities. We're just ordinary people who believed they could do something and went out and did it. The real heroes are people like David. People for whom every day is a struggle against the odds and their very survival an achievement. The many people who have to deal with severe handicaps on a daily basis but who just grit their teeth and get on with it – they are the real heroes and anything the rest of us do with our lives pales by comparison.

I deliberately live in a dramatic way and always with a sense of theatre. It has been a recurring theme throughout my life and it will be there until the day I die. At many stages I have blurred dreams with reality, which leads me on occasions to almost forget the real world and try to live the dream instead. Sometimes things get so mixed up that I think to myself, 'You know what Glenn, you can do it.' And when I believe I can do something then that belief is pretty hard to shift. This can have its drawbacks, and has got me into trouble on many occasions, but it also made me champion of the world.

Mandy hadn't been at ringside, but she was in the crowd somewhere. It felt to me as though she didn't really want to be there. Later, when I saw her, I felt almost detached in some way. Looking back, I find that sad that because she was my wife and, despite all we had been through, I still loved her, but things were clearly not right, even on the happiest night of my professional life. In fact, if any-thing, winning the title probably made the dynamics of the relationship even worse because all of a sudden I was famous Glenn. Famous Glenn was in the limelight and it could be crazy at times. I remember going to Middles-brough as a guest for some occasion that I have long since forgotten but at which I was asked by more than one girl to sign their breasts! It was all so unbelievable to me. I'm sure pop stars have that kind of experience all the time, but if you're a fighter suddenly faced with all this madness it can be hard to take in. But, despite the obvious perks that kind of thing could bring, it never made me feel any better. In fact it only made me sadder when I thought of how I had a wife at home with whom I could never seem to get things to work.

Other than the ongoing state of my marriage, you would have thought I would have been on cloud nine. I was the IBF World Cruiserweight Champion. Mike Ty-son was the IBF World Heavyweight Champion. I was right up there in that company. On my wall as a kid in Mitchell Street there had been all those posters of fighters from *The Ring* magazine. Now I was travelling to New York to have my photo taken so I could be in the centre pages myself. It all seemed a little unreal.

The truth is that I had gone to bed on the night I won the title feeling better than I've ever felt in my life. I wore my belt to bed and it was the happiest I have ever been. I woke up the following morning feeling utterly de-pressed. I realised that my goal had been to win the world title. I had done it. I had never been aiming to defend the belt, merely to win it. Now I had achieved that it was as though my candle had gone out. I didn't care about fighting anymore. I had won the title despite everything being stacked against me and all the handicaps and obstacles I had to overcome. I had proved it could be done. I can remember my feeling that first morning as champion as though it were yesterday. I wanted out. I really didn't want to fight anymore. The trouble was that I still didn't have any money. That meant quitting was not an option, but something inside me had died. I woke up the morning after the night before realising that it was a case of 'same shit – different day.' David was still dying. I still had no money. And to top it off, I didn't want to fight anymore. Sadly, I knew I had no choice.

Before making my first defence, I received a phone call that was to change my life. Becoming world champion hadn't altered my situation dramatically at all. I only received $15,000 for the Lumumba fight, which enabled me to sign off the dole at last, but I had very little in my pocket to show for it because I had to pay both Beau Williford and Doug Bidwell their percentages. I may have been off the dole, but it wasn't by much. I had been given a sponsored Vauxhall Nova and, although we had lost our house in Mitchell Street and had to live with Mandy's mother for a time, the news of my upcoming world title fight had meant that we had been able to secure another mortgage for a terraced house in Station Road, Stanley. Better than living with the mother-in-law, but hardly the kind of thing you imagine for the Champion of the World.

The life-changing phone call I refer to came about, indirectly, as a result of an interview I had given to Ian Darke, the BBC Radio boxing correspondent. He was scheduled to provide radio commentary for the fight and came up to the North East to talk to me in the build up to the contest. We just hit if off immediately. I found him interesting, knowledgeable and fun and thought he asked exactly the right questions.

In the days after the fight I had people coming up to me asking if I had heard the commentary. I told them that I had watched the fight back, assuming they meant the commentary of Reg Gutteridge and Jim Watt on ITV, but it turned out that most of them were talking about Ian's commentary for BBC Radio. So many people were raving about it to me that I contacted the BBC to get hold of a copy. After listening to it I could understand what all the fuss had been about. Ian's commentary was extraordinary and the whole broadcast had captured the atmosphere perfectly. To me, it was one of the great occasions in BBC Radio boxing history. Indeed, Darkey includes that night in his list of the greatest occasions he has experienced during his long career covering the sport.

Clearly that night and our previous meeting had made an impression on Ian, because not long after that I got a phone call off a woman called Emily McMahon. Emily announced that she worked for a company called Sky who had a sporting channel known as Eurosport that was aiming to get into boxing. They had their first ever fight night broadcast coming up. The bill was to feature Olympic gold medallist Lennox Lewis, who had just returned to the UK after a dozen years in Canada to sign with Frank

Maloney. He was being touted as the next big thing and was scheduled to fight an African called Proud Kilimanjaro. Emily asked if I would like to commentate on the evening.

I was stunned. I had never thought of myself in that role, but Emily informed me that they had just hired Ian Darke to be their commentator and were looking for someone to sit alongside him and be his ringside partner. Ian had told them about our recent interview and that he thought I was one of the most passionate fighters he'd ever spoken to. I think I was also the only current UK-based world champion so they were keen to have me on the show.

Despite my initial shock I regained my composure quickly enough to ask, 'What are you paying?' Emily told me it would be £500. £500 sounded awesome to me! I loved boxing, it was my life, and there I was being offered £500 to sit and watch a couple of fights at ringside and talk about them. I did have some brief prior experience as it happens. Around 1986, Tyne-Tees started a show called *Fight Night* and I'd done a bit of co-commentary with Reg Gutteridge for that. I remember covering Billy Hardy a couple of times as my career had gone hand in hand with Billy's to that point. So I had experience, but I still never thought of myself as a commentator.

I have always been someone who wants new experiences and who lives to take chances. If an opportunity comes up to do something different and I think it would be a great experience, I do it. People can tell me that it may not bring me any money, or that it's not relevant to my career at that stage, or that it might get in the way of my achieving something else, but I just think, 'Bollocks! It sounds like an adventure, so I'm gonna give it a go!' There was also the fact that I was being given the chance to work with Ian and I couldn't wait to meet him again having got on so well previously. So, despite the fact that I was only a month away from defending my title, I agreed there and then and headed off to London to prepare.

I knew Proud Kilimanjaro because I had sparred with him when I was a young heavyweight. He was a big, lumbering Zimbabwean who had been African Heavyweight Champion but never quite top class. He came over to fight Lennox and the night before the fight he was denied a licence to box because he refused to share the results of a compulsory AIDS test. The card went ahead, but the main bout of the evening was off. My commentating career had got off to a great start!

Despite the evening marking my Sky debut, I have to say that the whole card was entirely forgettable. Today I haven't a clue who was on the bill that night, but I thoroughly enjoyed the experience and particularly working with Ian with whom my rapport was instant.

I have no idea who we were actually broadcasting to, mind you. Not a soul over here seemed to have Sky TV. Certainly a few friends of mine were puzzled when I told them what I had done. The general consensus was 'you want to get yourself with BBC or ITV. Don't waste your time with that satellite rubbish.' However, I had the advantage of my trips to stay with Beau in America. Beau, in common with many Americans, had a dish in his garden the size of something from NASA. I asked him what on earth it was and he explained about satellite TV. He showed me the hundred or so channels that he had and I couldn't believe my eyes. We had only recently seen the arrival of a fourth channel in the UK at the time.

So, when people over here were warning me to avoid wasting my time with Sky and telling me there was no way that people would be sticking big round things on their roof, I told them straight. 'I've been to America. When people over here get to see life with a hundred channels they are going to love it. This is the future.'

At the same time as my Sky debut I was in training for the first defence of my title, against a tough South African, Siza Makathini. I was beginning to think there was something up when that fight was made because Makathini was a tough opponent. I thought after having just won the title I would get the chance to make a voluntary defence and earn a few quid for a relatively easy fight. Instead I discovered that I was to be fighting one of the top contenders, a man who had knocked out British heavyweight Paul Lister in one round, who just happened to be promoted by Cedric Kushner who was also South African by birth – Cedric having moved to the USA later in life. Something struck me as not quite right.

With the distractions that were going on around me I fell into the trap that so many fighters do after they win a title – I lost my hunger. I had achieved my dream that night in Stanley and my mind was no longer focused exclusively on the fight as it had been for Lumumba. Makathini, on the other hand, was extremely fired up. This was his first world title opportunity and for the first few rounds he gave me a hard time.

The fight was again live on ITV and took place in a marquee in Eston, Middlesbrough. Beau had instructed me to use my boxing skills as he figured that Makathini would come at me from the start, which he did. As the fight went on Beau kept repeating the same thing over and over. 'Box him – use your skills. Stick with trying to box.' I tried to jab away at him but he was just rolling under my jab and punching to my body, often low. I basically got the living crap kicked out of me for several rounds. I was boxing, boxing and boxing exactly as Beau ordered, but all the time I was thinking that the guy was killing me. He was just rolling under everything and working me over. Then, at the end of the fifth round, he landed a big right on my ear which perforated my eardrum. I went back to my corner with my hand on the side of my head and my ear ringing unbelievably painfully. I think everybody in the place was certain I was about to be stopped during the next round. Including me!

Although Beau kept up his demands that I continue to try to out-jab him I felt that the strategy wasn't working. It was ironic that I had often had to put up with Doug telling me to try to knock an opponent out when I should have been boxing and now I had Beau telling me to box when I should have been trying to knock him out. I was sitting on my stool with my ear ringing and everything went into a bit of a blur. I could hear Beau screaming instructions but I was no longer taking anything in. It felt almost as though I had gone into a trance and everything was suddenly in slow motion. All I remember thinking was if I'm gonna lose my title; if I'm gonna get knocked out, fuck it – I'm going down fighting.

The bell rang for the sixth round and I just stood there and effectively said to Makathini, 'Come on then – have some of this. Let's see how you like it.' I started throwing punches. I must have thrown about three hundred! I pushed him back against the ropes and battered him repeatedly. All of a sudden the fight changed. I discovered that he couldn't fight on the back foot; he struggled when somebody took it to him. I had unlocked his secret courtesy of my usual sheer stubbornness by simply standing there and saying, 'Come on then – let's have a fight!'

From then on I was on top and winning the fight, but I was almost going through the motions, hoping to win on points. Beau always did the talking in the corner; the cutman, Johnny, never said a word, but then, out of the blue, he grabbed me by the hair quite painfully, turned my head around so I was looking directly at him, and said slowly and deliberately, 'Knock… this… fucker… out!' It was a wake-up call. The guy never said a word as a rule, so when he did it made me stop and pay attention and I found myself thinking, 'Yeah. Why am I not doing that?'

The eleventh round began and I walked over to Makathini and just kept hitting him until he fell down. The fight was over and I was still Champion of the World.

# 13

'I remember picking Glenn up in Vegas and partying till we dropped. Let's just say we had to leave early – but what happens in Vegas stays in Vegas! We had such a fantastic time that night – one of the happiest times of my life and memories that will stay with me till my grave.'

Lloyd Honeyghan, former undisputed
World Welterweight Champion

My problems with Mandy were still ongoing, but we did make an attempt to get things sorted. I told her I was going to finish boxing soon and that I would then try to settle down and be part of a family. In order to show our commitment to this future we decided to have another baby.

My son Joe was born in October 1990. I had fought a world title bout in March of that year. Not having sex in the build up to a fight has never really concerned me and I certainly never adhered to any of that rubbish!

As I prepared for my second title defence I was getting to a point where making the weight was becoming a real struggle. I had failed to make the weight for both the Lumumba and Makathini fights at the first time of asking and had to go away to work off a pound or so quickly before weighing in again. Although both Alan and Neil played an important part in me becoming champion, neither of them had any experience with nutrition or anything like that and they were all I had around me. We were just making it up as we went along. We cared about each other but we didn't understand any of the business or the fitness sides at all. I knew pasta was supposed to be good, but to me pasta meant lots of cheese, because that's how I liked it. I didn't know it should have been tomato based, I hadn't a clue. Pasta was pasta to me. Weight was therefore becoming a problem. Back then the cruiserweight limit was 13 stone 8 pounds, although nowadays it has been raised by ten pounds, from 190 to 200, which would have helped me immensely in my career.

I would also always tend to have a bit of a blow out after a fight. I was a little like Ricky Hatton in that sense. I would purposely get myself trashed after a fight and would feel terrible, but I felt it would give me somewhere to start training from. It would only be over the weekend though – I wasn't like Ricky where it could go on for weeks! Mind you, he did usually have up to twelve weeks to train it off before a fight and that didn't happen in my career.

My second defence was to be against an American, Jeff Lampkin. Cedric invited me to New York to be at ringside for the George Foreman v Gerry Cooney fight, with the idea being to negotiate a deal for my next defence while

I was there. I love New York and was excited by the prospect of being ringside for the big fight and I jumped at the chance.

Cedric took me out for lunch and I was expecting to be treated to a swanky restaurant. I had never been to a decent restaurant as a child, so when I was introduced to fine dining I took to it like a duck to water and developed a love of good food in top restaurants. I guess it's the same with my love of good clothes and nice suits. It probably stems from never having anything like that while growing up.

We went to Broadway, so I was expecting something special. Then Cedric took me through a door, past huge chunks of meat hanging from the ceiling, into a bar area where there were tables with chequered tablecloths and I remember thinking to myself, 'I'm World Champion and the stingy, tight-arsed sod has brought me to a pub!' To make matters worse he then recommended that I try the burger!

While we were waiting for our food the lunchtime rush arrived and it was all smartly dressed businessman and beautiful women. I couldn't understand why all these well-dressed, obviously wealthy people would be heading for a dingy pub for lunch… and then my burger arrived. Let me tell you that whatever experiences you may have had with burgers, they were nothing like this. This was not a burger. This was melt-in-your-mouth food heaven. It was absolutely amazing. The meat hanging near the doors was being aged ready to be used in the burgers and they are just divine, the greatest burgers on earth. The walls were adorned with pictures of famous clientele such

as Woody Allen. It was clearly a place where the reputation of the food outweighed the initial impression of
simple pub grub.

I've been back to New York numerous times and had
never found the place again until a couple of years ago. I
took a girl out for dinner in Victor's Café, a Cuban restaurant on Broadway, West 52nd Street, where Roberto Duran used to stay. As we left I looked next door and there
it was – my pub! In the previous twenty years I had been
to the Cuban restaurant several times but had never once
noticed that it was right next door! It's called Gallagher's
Steakhouse and it looked exactly the same as it had done
all those years before, even down to the meat hanging
up in public view. If you're ever on Broadway I seriously
recommend giving it a try.

The night of the Foreman-Cooney fight was brilliant.
It was great to be ringside at a big fight and introduced as
a world champion. I was a Stanley lad in Atlantic City and
people were coming up to me and asking for autographs
and taking pictures. The guest list for that fight was extraordinary. It included Muhammad Ali, Larry Holmes,
Joe Frazier, Sugar Ray Leonard, Rocky Graziano, Evander
Holyfield, Alexis Arguello, the Mayor of New York… and
Glenn McCrory. Mine was the only name on the list I
didn't recognise!

I enjoyed the evening and had a couple of beers and
a glass of wine after the fight when Beau came over and
told me we were going to speak to Cedric about my next
defence. John Spensley, from Middlesbrough, was also involved, as Cedric needed a British-registered promoter to
work with in order to put fights on in the UK.

I told Beau I wanted to wait until the next day as it was around midnight, I was out enjoying myself and had already had a few drinks, but Beau was insistent. I was very unhappy having to talk about business under those circumstances but I was ushered in to see Cedric against my protests and I pretty much knew I was about to be shafted. They told me that I would have to fight in two months' time against Jeff Lampkin, another top challenger and another fighter who was also signed up with Cedric Kushner.

I had picked up $20,000 for my fight with Makathini and was being offered $40,000 for Lampkin. It was the highest purse I had been offered in my career to that point, but it was nothing in comparison to the sort of money being earned by so many others. I was insistent that I didn't want to make another mandatory defence so soon for such little money. I wanted a voluntary defence and the chance to earn some extra cash for less risk, as is the right of champions. I was also concerned by the fact that Lampkin was another Cedric Kushner-promoted opponent.

As I have stated previously, I regarded Cedric as a businessman who was out to look after his own interests first and foremost. What annoyed me about that particular discussion was the behaviour of Beau Williford. He was my manager and, as such, his job was to stand up for my interests. He should have been saying to Cedric, 'Glenn is the champion. We're not talking to you tonight after a few drinks. We will talk to you about what we want to do with the title when it's convenient.' Instead Beau was sitting next to Cedric and was backing him all the way as they ganged up on me. John Spensley was the joint promoter, but he was the only one trying to help me at all. I liked John, he was a fun guy who liked a laugh and a drink, but it was not his job to back me up. It was my manager's.

I was on a loser from the start. In the end the deal to fight Lampkin was signed and the contest scheduled for 22 March at Gateshead Leisure Centre, the site of my first ever defeat as a pro. Perhaps that should have served as a warning.

In early 1990 I attended an evening where I was presented with the Sports Personality of Newcastle Award. There are four Newcastle-based sports awards and I am the only person to have won them all. That evening was during my preparations for the Lampkin fight, preparations which were dominated by my need to lose weight. Due to my lack of nutritional advice, pretty much all I was doing to shed the pounds was to not eat or drink and continue to train through it. I would also sit in a heated room wrapped in a quilt after training to sweat away even more of the excess. It was not a routine designed to keep an athlete at the peak of fitness.

I remember John Gibson from the *Chronicle* telling me later that a few of the journalists in attendance were scared for my life when they saw me collect my award that evening. I was so emaciated from trying to make the weight and you can see from the pictures taken that evening that I looked terrible.

There was another fight happening thousands of miles away during my preparations which demotivated me still further. Sky had invested heavily to obtain the rights to show Mike Tyson's fights as he was the biggest draw in boxing by far, and we were hoping he was going to help us pick up more and more subscribers. On the night of 10 February 1990 I was in the Sky studio in London, alongside Gary Mason and Lennox Lewis, as we prepared to give our opinions on Tyson's defence against his hopelessly outclassed challenger, James 'Buster' Douglas. To be honest, despite being in training for a world title defence, I was disappointed not to be in Japan with Ian Darke to cover the fight from ringside. Instead Colin Hart had made the trip.

The three of us in the studio; Gary, Lennox and I, were all potentially in line to fight Tyson one day. Gary was the undefeated British Heavyweight Champion having won almost all his fights inside the distance. Lennox was Olympic Champion and an unbeaten professional, only months away from becoming European Champion. I was the current World Cruiserweight Champion who was known for having performed well against Tyson in sparring. All three of us had a potential claim to fight him, which would have been such a fantastic opportunity, especially as he was starting to come off the rails by then. We were all gobsmacked and gutted when Tyson got beaten that night. Our dreams of being the man to eventually beat Tyson had evaporated. That aim was the only thing that could have kept me going. The payday, the big one, had flown out of the window in Tokyo. I know I said it was never about the money, but the amounts involved for fighting Tyson were something else.

Come the night of the fight with Lampkin, for the only time in my career I went into a fight not even caring. Deep down I knew I was going to get beaten, I knew they had taken my title away. All through training I felt like I was dying. Lampkin himself wasn't anybody to be scared of. I wasn't worried about him in the least. Lampkin had lost to Lumumba, who was still the most dangerous cruiserweight out there, but I knew the Glenn McCrory who was going to step into the ring against Jeff Lampkin was not the same as the one who had hammered Patrick Lumumba. As well as the debilitating effects of my attempts to lose weight I also felt that the whole business was just too unpleasant to be involved in. I felt that, because Lampkin was American, Cedric figured it would be so much easier to deal with him than some guy all the way over in County Durham. There was nothing for him or Beau up here – no decent venues, thousands of miles away from their American homes. I just wasn't meant to be champion. I wrote a letter to Mandy during the training camp to tell her that I was retiring after the fight. I was finished with boxing due to what had been done to me. I had had enough of being used.

To show how far out of it I was during my training, only three days before the fight I went and got fitted for a suit. I've never worn it once in my life. Within a week I was a stone heavier! I was doing daft things, not thinking, which is down to dehydration. Ironically it was the only title fight I had where I came in under the weight limit! I concentrated so much on my weight that I was actually half a pound below the limit when I stepped onto the scales. I felt half dead and people were asking me if I was okay. It really was a disaster waiting to happen.

The fight was Sky's first UK-based world title fight and their co-commentator was in the ring. Lennox Lewis was on my undercard that night. To be honest, if it had been a long fight I could have been killed. If it had turned into a struggle I may well have died that night. Luckily God was looking after me and I got hit with a body shot in the third round. I struggled to breathe. I had never been hurt with a shot like that before, I could always take a shot to the body. I had worked so hard throughout my career that I could have been hit with tree trunks, but I was so weak in that fight that one good blow under the ribs and I was finished. The referee counted me out still on my knees as I gasped for air. Lampkin somersaulted across the ring in celebration. The North East's only boxing world champion had lost his title.

I remember walking out of the venue later that evening and looking through a window to see Beau Williford sitting with Jeff Lampkin, laughing and whooping it up. I just thought 'you bastard' and made my way home.

Beau had genuinely upset me. To top it off he hadn't paid me on the night so I phoned him at his hotel later and asked about my money. He promised he would sort it the following day. The next morning I phoned up and left a message with reception as they said they hadn't seen him yet. I heard nothing so I rang back several times and left messages on each occasion. Still no return call arrived and by now I was starting to worry – I needed the money. Then, after yet another call to the hotel, I was informed that he had checked out that evening. I panicked because I feared I was about to be robbed.

One thing I have always been able to rely on is the number of friends I have made throughout the region. I've always had lots of people to turn to and who will look after me in difficult times. I took advantage of that now as I phoned Newcastle Airport and spoke to a friend of mine in security. I explained what had happened and that I feared my manager was about to get on a plane to London without paying me. They checked the flight lists and sure enough his name was there. Word was put out to find him and hold him until I got my money. He duly wrote out a cheque for whatever amount I was owed after his cut and flew back to the States. That was the end of my relationship with Beau Williford.

The only other time I heard from him after that night was shortly after I had signed to fight Lennox Lewis a couple of years later. I had sorted everything out myself when I got a call from a solicitor telling me I was still under contract to Beau and he wanted 33% of any purse I got from the Lewis fight. I sent a pretty blunt message back to Beau telling him why I didn't think pursuing that would be a very good idea. He dropped the case and I never heard from him again.

Despite much of what I have said about him, it may surprise you to learn that I liked Doug Bidwell. He didn't treat me well, but I don't know full details of his business deals and how hard it was for him or anything like that. I didn't have any money while I was with him, nor did he have much of a clue about training boxers, but it sums up me and the sort of person I am that I still liked him anyway. He was a character and a good person to be around. Beau Williford, on the other hand, was someone who I thought was looking after me. He was one of those that would appear to be being nice to you, your parents and family, but would be manipulating the situation all the time. He was one of those people that would trip himself up occasionally. I remember him saying something to my pal, James Tillis, then saying the opposite to me. I was thinking, 'but I was with you when you told him something different!' I suppose it was just another in a long list of bad relationship choices I have made in my life.

After losing to Lampkin I was good on my word to Mandy and retired. I was just twenty-five years old. I couldn't sit and be idle, however. Firstly, we couldn't afford it. I had just had the best year of my life financially, but now my career was over I had to find another way to earn a living. Secondly, I cannot just do nothing. I am someone who has to be active and having adventures. I decided to buy a pub.

My Uncle Jim, the former boxer, had run a pub in Consett for a while and I would pop in after a fight from time to time. It was a town which was starting to show signs of life again after getting over the shock of the closure of the steelworks and it had become a bustling town centre with loads of pubs which on a night time was a really cool place to go. It seemed to be a potential goldmine, the places were regularly jammed.

Mandy was always very careful with money when she could be – another way in which we were like chalk and cheese. She was always looking after the pennies whereas I was the exact opposite. Joe had just been born and the last thing she wanted was me in a pub. What did I know about pubs? I just thought I would love to buy one, as you did when you were an ex-sportsman back in those days. I didn't know anything about running them, but I figured that I was a relatively well-known boxer and people would want to come in and see me. I therefore went out and bought The Wheatsheaf pub which my uncle had managed. It had been run into the ground and closed by the time I purchased it, but that enabled me to get it for a reduced price. It cost me a hundred grand, which was a lot of money at the time, but I put all my money from the recent fights into it, managed to get a mortgage agreed for the rest and negotiated a good deal with Scottish and Newcastle Breweries. And there I was, a publican! I renamed it McCrory's in the hope of cashing in on my name but, with typical timing, Britain was hit by a recession. All of a sudden my money was tied up in a pub in the midst of an economic disaster.

The crunch came when I was hit, out of the blue, with a huge tax bill. I don't fully understand such things, but there was a two-year delay in certain payments being demanded and that is how the Inland Revenue were able to drop a bombshell on me of an apparent outstanding tax debt of £90,000. That was more money than I had earned in my whole career. To this day I have absolutely no idea how they arrived at that figure. When I contacted them they told me that, according to the figures they had been given, that was how much I owed and, unless I could produce receipts for everything, including training camps, that was what I would have to pay. Beau had taken care of all that side of things so I had nothing whatsoever to give them. I was so wet behind the ears that I never even thought about hiring an accountant to do some investigations for me. I just knew I couldn't get hold of any receipts, or evidence that might tell them anything useful, so I was stuck with it.

The pub was struggling in the recession and work with Sky was still an irregular thing. Mandy was past herself with worry about what was going to happen. I realised there was only one way I could try to raise that kind of money. I would have to go back to what I was good at and what I knew best. I would have to return to the ring.

# 14

'Glenn has treated me like family.
He is my English brother who I love as my own.'
Cesar Aceituno, LA gun dealer

The first decision I made after choosing to fight again was to manage myself. My past experiences had shown me that paying a hefty percentage of my purse to someone else for doing very little to actually help was not something I wished to repeat, especially in the desperate circumstances I was now in.

I knew I would get next to nothing for a comeback fight at a low level, so I had to work out what my aim was and how I was going to achieve it within the year or so I had in which to pay the Inland Revenue. I realised quite quickly that there was only one way I was ever going to get near to £90,000 and that was by fighting Lennox Lewis. He was making great progress up the rankings and was the hottest new thing in British boxing. What he wanted at that stage of his career were names. I had a name. From the start my intention was to get a fight with Lennox as quickly as possible, so I had to return as a heavyweight.

I quickly managed to arrange a fight in Thornaby-on-Tees in which I knocked out a big, seventeen-and-a-half stone opponent with a left hook in the second round. That got my career back up and running so people would know I was back on the scene. All I had to do now was work out how to get a fight with Lennox. As luck would have it I was scheduled to attend a boxing writers' dinner and my plan started to hatch as I travelled south.

At the dinner, at the Savoy Hotel, I shared a table with some of the great old journalists from London that I had known for years. As luck would have it, who was on the table next to us but Lennox Lewis? You have to remember that at the time I was nowhere. I'd had one meaningless fight as a heavyweight after a year off. I wasn't in any ratings, I was nothing. I had to do something special in order to drum up any sort of interest in a fight between me and Lennox Lewis. I thought back to my hero, Muhammad Ali, and how he had managed to persuade Sonny Liston to fight him. I had to be brave.

I had a couple of brandies to assist with my courage and I went over to Lennox. I started by saying hello and asking if he was okay. He was very polite as always, he's a lovely man – a real gent. Suddenly I changed tack. 'Good to see your career is going well. It's just a shame you can't fight.' Lennox looked at me quizzically. 'What?'

I replied, 'Who have you fought Lennox? Just nobodies and bums. Why don't you take on someone who can fight?' He had just beaten previously undefeated British

Champion Gary Mason and former WBA World Champion Mike Weaver in his previous two contests so I was on pretty dodgy ground, but I stuck with it. 'Why don't you take on somebody younger instead of all these old men like Weaver. And you're Canadian! I saw you in the Olympics waving your little Canadian flag in the ring, now you're over here wrapping yourself in the Union Jack. You don't deserve to be here. I'll tell you what – why not come into the car park? Let's fight here and now.'

By now all the journalists' ears had pricked up. All the cameras were turned towards us and Lennox was looking incredulous and saying, 'What? Excuse me?!' I continued with my theme. 'Come on, fight somebody young and tough. Let's go to the car park – I'll show you fighting.' I think he had got it by then. He was laughing at me but then, all of a sudden, we both stood up. A hush descended across the room and the cameras were clicking away madly when he said to me, 'I'll fight you anytime, anywhere.' I knew then it was working. I nearly had what I had come for. I was with Dave Gregory that night, a mate of mine who wanted to get into boxing. I allowed him to act as my manager to help him get into the sport and he gave me a look as if to say, 'You've got it!' When a photographer asked, 'Can we get you nose-to-nose?' I knew it was in the bag.

At that point I thought it was time for me and Dave to make a swift exit, just in case Lennox actually accepted my offer and headed for the car park! It seemed best to just get out of there, so we headed to a London club to celebrate. Within days I had a phone call from Roger Levitt to say Lennox wanted to fight me. Suddenly I was ranked number one challenger in Europe. I smiled and thought to myself, 'You did it son!'

Shortly afterwards, Frank Maloney called. I knew Frank and he had really fallen on his feet with Lennox Lewis. Frank obviously had an idea of what I had been paid in my career up till then and he offered me £25,000 to fight Lewis. For the only time in my life I stood firm. I said simply, 'Absolutely not a prayer Frank. The fight is worth far more than that.' He was working with Roger Levitt at the time so I told him I wanted to speak to the organ grinder not the monkey.

A week later he came back and said, 'I've spoken to Roger – we'll give you £40,000. We know that's more than you have ever been paid before and you're not the champion here. That's all we can offer.' I replied, 'No way whatsoever.'

Later still he was back again, offered £60,000 and threatened to look for another opponent if I didn't accept. Again I held firm and refused to blink. I knew that the press were onto the fight and buying into some of the stuff I had said at the dinner, how it was going to be a proper fight for Lennox, how he had fought nobody and so on. I knew they would go higher. Eventually Roger Levitt himself came on the phone. He was as nice as pie, asked how I was and asked after Mandy and the kids, and offered to take us out to dinner to discuss it. Mandy and I travelled down to London and were taken for a lovely meal during which Roger turned to me and asked, 'How much do you want Glenn?' I said, '£90,000 and not a penny less.' He thought about it for a moment then shook my hand and announced, 'You've got your fight.'

That was the only time that Mandy and I were really happy about a deal during my whole career. We were ecstatic after a great meal and having made the deal for the fight that could save our bacon.

The initial delight was swiftly followed by the realisation that I was about to take on a genuine heavyweight who could really fight. I didn't want to be a fighter anymore, this was the first and only time in my life I had ever agreed to do it just for the money. After a year in a pub having fun with my pals, serving beer and helping them to drink it, I thought there was a danger I was going to get killed if I wasn't prepared. I had no money for training camps or anything like that. Why not do something different?' I tried to come up with something a bit special.

I've always had a feeling of affinity with the army. My dad, uncle and granddad were all soldiers. I decided to call Catterick Garrison and spoke to a PTI there called Mick Tarmey who was working with the Green Howards. I told him I was about to fight Lennox Lewis and I needed to get myself into condition. I asked if he would be prepared for me to train with them for a few weeks. He said they'd love to have me.

To this day I'm proud of our boys and girls in the forces. Living and training with them in preparation for Lennox was a great experience. They took me in and treated me as one of their own for about five weeks. I ran with them, did the obstacle course and also some sparring with guys I had known for years such as Dave Garside and Paul Lister.

Unfortunately it's a fact that army PTIs like to take you to hell and back and I've always had problems with my knees. After the first session I could barely walk as I'd done too much too soon, so my running was hampered.

I was also trying to make myself bigger to match Lennox, or at least not to be completely dwarfed by him, and that caused me the same problem as the old days. With increased size came reduced speed.

For the fight itself I weighed in at my heaviest ever, but the truth is that I went to the weigh-in wearing a full tracksuit with dozens of coins in my pockets and ankle weights on underneath. It was just to prevent me looking stupid when my stats were compared to those of Lennox. I was a lot lighter than the official weights suggest, but I was still nowhere near the shape or condition I was in when I fought Lumumba. I would love to have fought Lennox in that condition, to see how I would have got on as the guy who won a world title. I think the Glenn McCrory who fought Lumumba could have held his own with Lennox or Evander Holyfield. I'm not saying I would have beaten them, but I would have put up a good show. Unfortunately this Glenn McCrory was the guy from the pub!

The Green Howards played me into the ring that night, but it's about the only good memory I have of the evening. I had Jimmy Tibbs alongside Alan in my corner as I felt I needed his experience. However, despite Jimmy's presence, I went into the fight still knowing I was going to lose.

Lennox is a great guy for whom I have loads of respect and in the years to follow I would party with him on numerous occasions. He still hugs me whenever we meet, but Lennox is a fighting man and I had insulted him, so in the ring it was payback time. I knew it was going to be painful, but the Lennox Lewis who turned up to fight me was a Lennox Lewis that no one had seen before. He came at me like a man possessed and I don't know if, in his whole career, he ever attacked someone with as much venom as he did me that night. I know he was wary of my left hook, I had knocked heavyweights out with it in the past, so he decided that he'd have to jump on me from the start. And something I didn't think about beforehand was the size of the ring. One thing I could do was move, I was always fairly quick on my feet, so I needed a big ring. This was the smallest ring you have ever seen for a European Heavyweight title fight. Lennox could take two paces from his corner and be hitting me in mine! He was hitting me round the back of the head and whacking me all over. I'd been hit as hard before – Tyson hit harder than Lennox I would say – but the one thing I remember about fighting Lennox Lewis was how unbelievably strong he was. He lifted me off my feet and threw me around like a rag doll. He didn't knock me out cold, I was on my feet, but he kept whacking me round the side of the head with massive right hands. He was too big and strong. Fair enough – I will take my beating like a man. I tried my best but at the end of the day he was Lennox Lewis, destined to be one of the best heavyweights of all time. I would still like to have fought him as me from two years earlier, but that wasn't to be. The fight was over halfway through the second round.

With the money from the Lewis fight I paid the tax man and I had nothing left for myself. I faced the future with hopes of making the pub profitable, pursuing my acting ambitions and continuing with my commentary career all vying for priority. I had plenty to be getting on with and a lot of hard work to look forward to but then, slowly but surely, the grim realisation of what I had just done came to haunt me.

I found myself thinking back to the whole Lennox Lewis situation and asking myself what I had done. I am someone who loves boxing. I may have long since fallen out of love with the business side of the game, but the sport itself was my life. Yet I had just prostituted myself. Although I would have loved to have been paid vast sums of money for the fights where I believe I should have been well rewarded, money had never been a driving force in my life before. I lived for experiences and, looking back at the Lennox Lewis fight, I felt I had let myself down. I knew I wasn't going to win before I started and I did it purely for financial reward and that just wasn't me. After a period of reflection and internal wrangling I knew what I had to do.

I had to reinvent Glenn McCrory the boxer one more time. And I would have to do it properly – as a cruiser-weight.

# 15

'Who would spend a fortune paying to have tattoos removed because they were one of his regrets then, one drunken night, get the words "El Loco" plastered all over his stomach – ten times the size of the ones he had just removed? Who would move two non-English-speaking Cuban amateur boxing coaches that he barely knew into his home for six months without checking it would be okay with his wife first? That's Glenn!'
Declan Johnson, Sky Sports Boxing Producer

I had recently got to know a guy called Steve Black who was something of a fitness guru. I got in touch with him and he said he would be happy to help get me in shape. He felt I would be able to get back to the cruiserweight limit easily enough, providing I followed the right training plan and nutritional advice.

I wasn't bothered about winning the world title. I just wanted to get rid of the stain of the Lewis fight. I knew that I couldn't finish boxing with that as my final memory. I couldn't live with myself for having done that just for money. I needed to come back, do it right and leave with my head held high.

As Alan had retired, I decided to ask my brother Gary to train me. There's always been an uneasy relationship between Gary and me. We've both been through an awful lot. We've both had our own personal problems throughout our lives and tempers have been frayed for all sorts of reasons. His son, Greg, for whom I was godfather, tragically died of cancer at the age of only sixteen, after having fought off the disease twice previously in his short life. But he's my brother, I love him, and at that point in my life I chose to make him my trainer to hopefully bring us closer together.

Back in 1992 there was a lot going on in my crazy life. Joe was little. Mandy and I were still together and running the pub but things were not great between us, and my announcement of another comeback didn't help matters. Whenever I was at home for any length of time we would end up having arguments. If I was away I would have a few days of peace. When I returned, it would usually be pretty good for a couple of days until real life kicked back in and we would be off again. She said she wanted a normal relationship, me being at home with the pub and the family, but then she didn't seem to like me all that much when I was actually there.

It got to the point where, again, I found myself wondering how I could escape. My favourite place on earth is New York, but I have always been one for romance and so running a close second is Paris. I love the place. I knew a couple of boxing promoters over there and I found myself thinking how nice it would be to be a professional boxer in one of my favourite cities in the world, miles away from home. I can never do anything the predictable, boring way. This was just the latest in a long line of new experiences to try. I got in touch with the promoters in question, the Acaries brothers, Louis and Michel, and put my plan to them. They thought it was a great idea. I found them to be really nice people and Paris is a wonderful city with fabulous food and wine, so I decided it was time to leave the pub in the hands of a manager and head to France.

Louis Acaries had been a good fighter in his day, a two-weight European Champion. Michel was a typically debonair Frenchman. I stayed on the West Bank, trained in Paris and I loved it. I had a coach I knew simply as 'Frenchie' and we'd go running in the morning after which we would go to a café for him to have a brandy and me a coffee. I just thought, 'This is the life!'

I was sparring with some good fighters and struck up a relationship with a Ghanaian, Ike Quartey, who was in the same camp and was on his way to becoming an excellent World Welterweight Champion. The two of us got on really well.

I loved the whole French experience. They were so respectful to me because I had been world champion. I took to wearing shorts in the red, white and blue of the French Tricolore for my fights over there by way of a thank you for how well they had taken to a foreign fighter.

My actual comeback fight was something of a farce. It was in Paris against a guy called Mohamed Bouchiche. I thought I beat him comfortably but it went the distance and the referee scored it a draw. I was an Englishman fighting a Frenchman in Paris and I'm sure the ref thought

Bouchiche was with the Acaries who were at ringside. I know this game so well. I've been everything – a prospect, a journeyman, a champion. Nothing really surprises me anymore. The ref got bollocked by the Acaries after the fight because it was obvious to everyone that I had won it, but I'm sure he had thought the Acaries were looking after the Frenchman and not me. The brothers went mad and were swearing and yelling at him but I told them it didn't matter. At least it wasn't a loss.

For the next few months I was backwards and forwards between England and Paris because, although I had family and other commitments over here, I just had to keep going back, I loved it so much.

My next fight was in Avoriaz, a lovely Alpine ski resort. I stayed in a hotel with a little restaurant and a big Saint Bernard dog although I can't ski so I never went out on the slopes. I stopped Ric Lainhart in the second round of the fight itself and then headed back home.

When I went over to work with the Acaries, I didn't set out with the intention of being in the ring for another five years. I came back to boxing to both make peace with, and prove something to, myself. How many fighters from the North East had won a world title? Only me. How many could then come back a couple of years later and get back to the same point? That was the target I set for myself. The only thing that concerned me about making my comeback was that I could end up back on the conveyor belt and I hated that. I had been so badly abused and ripped off that I had grown to despise the business side of boxing. I love the sport but I hate the money side and always did. It's why I always wanted a good manager, someone to really look after me in a business sense, yet for some reason that's one thing I don't feel I ever had. The Acaries brothers could perhaps have been those people, but circumstances were about to pull me in a different direction.

Frank Maloney called and asked if I wanted to have a fight in Las Vegas. He had managed to arrange for Lennox Lewis to fight former champion Tony Tucker for the vacant WBC Heavyweight Championship and I was going to be there as part of the Sky coverage. Frank was putting on a show a couple of days earlier showcasing a few British fighters and he thought that, as I was going to be there anyway, maybe I would like to be on the bill. I figured that I may as well take the opportunity to have a fight while I was out there so I readily agreed.

I was scheduled to appear live on Sky Sports as part of their commentary team for one of the biggest British fights ever on the Saturday night and I was fighting in a ten rounder just two days earlier. I told you before, I like a bit of drama! I can't remember who I was originally meant to be fighting, but he pulled out for some reason and so, yet again, I ended up fighting a heavyweight in the form of Mark Young, just a journeyman, but someone who had been in with Tyson and Foreman among others.

I won the bout on points and then, literally days later, I received a call from Cedric Kushner telling me that he could get me a fight for the IBF Cruiserweight title against current champion Al Cole. This was the opportunity I had been looking for. I just wanted to get my pride back by showing the world – and myself – that I could fight at world championship level again and not let myself down. I knew – win, lose or draw – that it was going be my last fight. I was done with the business, it had messed me up. All I wanted to do was sleep at night after the Lennox fight and Cedric was handing me my chance. I was only to be paid around £25,000, but it wasn't about the money this time. It was about the chance to regain self-esteem.

I spoke to Louis and Michel Acaries to explain the position. They could have said they wanted to get involved and take a percentage but they were really good guys who said they understood what I was doing and why. They didn't want a penny, they were just happy for me. I haven't been in touch with either of them for several years and I don't know what they are doing now but, to me, Louis and Michel Acaries were the best people I have ever been involved with in boxing. They were a cut above. They just looked after me and showed true class. Even today I can still get into restaurants and nightclubs in Paris by saying, 'Glenn McCrory, Champion du Monde, Louis et Michel Acaries.' Great people.

The world was changing and suddenly I had the opportunity to be a flag bearer at a momentous time in history. The Berlin Wall had been torn down and with it the communism which had shaped the geography of Eastern Europe. The whole landscape was dramatically changing, not just politics. Europe was opening up; the great divides on the map were no more. The Cold War was over, or so everyone hoped.

Boundaries were giving way to openness and the face of a major world city was changing, becoming more welcoming to the west and its ideas. Moscow, the bedrock of communism, suddenly flung open its doors to capitalism and was flooded with new ideas.

One of them was that the city should stage its first ever professional world title fight. Like in Cuba, only amateur boxing had been allowed within the Soviet Union but now, blinkers off, Moscow wished to embrace the rest of the sporting world. Of course, they had no Russian challengers and so they had to look abroad for the two contestants.

The fight was to be at cruiserweight and someone had to be found to take on American Alfred Cole. Someone of acceptable stature, so why not a former world champion at the weight – and a Brit too, which wasn't so bad. So Cedric Kushner got me and, frankly, I was proud to be creating a little bit of history.

That wasn't lost on the media at home and my old mate John Gibson of the *Evening Chronicle* quickly climbed aboard the McCrory bandwagon, as did Tyne-Tees Television who were to film a documentary about the groundbreaking trip entitled *From Russia With Gloves*. Ian Lennox was the producer and he's still a friend today.

What lay ahead was akin to the Wild West or the days when Al Capone ruled the streets of Chicago. Capitalism brought with it the mafia in the shape of a load of exiled Russian crime bosses returning home to exploit the new riches on offer. A Chechen hardcase became our guide and mentor and when I reported for the usual pre-fight weigh-in my party were politely asked to park any guns we were carrying by the door upon entering. I kid you not. This was an experience and a half.

When in London I had met an old Chechen boxer called Albert who had been trained by Angelo Dundee. I mentioned that I was to fight in Moscow and he said he was returning home. He would meet me when I arrived, which I thought was really nice of him. He duly met us off the plane and drove us away in a couple of swanky BMWs, which seemed strange given everyone else in Russia appeared to be in a Lada. We were certainly getting well looked after. I was to find out why. Albert was actually the head of the Chechen Mafia! His dad had died and he had been brought back from London to run it. I thought he was just a half-decent boxer and here he was, the bloody Godfather!

Albert opened doors only he could to a life of glitz and glamour which would have cost an ordinary Moscow citizen a month's wages. He happily picked up any tab for us, although I suspect he wasn't charged by most places. I couldn't take part in the pre-fight nights out, but others in my party could.

The other side of life in Russia back then was very different to the treatment we had been receiving. People were begging in the streets, literally sitting in the gutter with maybe four cigarettes or a couple of apples, just desperately trying to sell one. At our hotel there was a buffet breakfast and I wasn't eating much as I was on a strict diet to ensure I made the weight. I remember one morning I piled my plate high, went outside and started feeding a couple of kids who were hanging about. Well, I almost caused a riot. Before long there were twenty, maybe thirty, kids there. They were grabbing and screaming and hitting each other and all of a sudden what had been intended as a nice gesture had turned into a free for all. It was painful to watch and I had to get out of there as quickly as I could.

The fight with Al Cole took place in front of a large crowd in the old Olympic indoor stadium. I made the weight okay and was in fantastic shape, which goes to show how it was merely bad conditioning that had caused my weight issues previously. The fight went pretty well. He was big and tall, it was amazing how he made the cruiserweight limit because he was massive. He came at me and I was countering him with left hooks and felt very comfortable, but then we clashed heads. It was an accident but I caught the top of his head smack-bang on my nose. I was a bit groggy, but the referee didn't seem to realise what had happened and told us to box on. At this, Cole jumped on me. He didn't hit me all that hard, but I went down to my knee to get a breather and to wait for my eyes to clear. He came at me again as soon as I got up and I did the same again. As I had been down twice in the round, it would be scored 10-7 against me. After that he ran. He would come at me, score with a couple of jabs, then get back to running to ensure he kept out of trouble and earned the points decision.

I had lost on points to a very good IBF Champion. Twice I had been to the top of the world. That was enough for me. I tried. If I could have found a way to win I would have, but something inside me had died.

All the bad things that had happened to me over the years: being on the dole, having my house taken off me, no one looking after my interests despite being paid to do so – it had come close to breaking me. I love this sport, but I've experienced things not many world champions have had to put up with. There was no way I was prepared to go through any of it again. It had done me in at such a young age. I was ending my second comeback and I was still only twenty-eight. I knew it was over and back in my dressing room I felt pretty emotional. It was all captured by the Tyne-Tees cameras for their documentary. I had tears in my eyes as I told them and the world, 'That's it. I can't do this again. I can't give so much of myself. It's over.'

Boxing has been my life – I adore it. It's almost a microcosm of life. Often, in one fight, you can get to see so much of what life is all about: the heartache, the pain, the struggle and the joy. Other sports offer their own special moments but, for me, no sport comes close to boxing in terms of both the drama it gives its audience and in what it demands of its participants. Kids die following their dreams in this sport. When I fought Patrick Lumumba I was prepared to give my life to win my belt – that's real passion when you want something so badly that you're prepared to die to achieve it.

But, at the same time, it is that very drama of putting your life on the line that sometimes causes me problems. You see so many kids who lose a world title and announce 'I'm not finished yet, I'm still young' but they're not seeing life from the bigger picture. I've been there. I was getting knocked out at twenty-one yet I still believed I could be something and went on to spar with Tyson and win the world title so, yes, I know you can come back from a demoralising loss, but it's going to be tough.

Throughout history there have been many fighters that have continued far beyond their best-before date. What is it they are hoping to achieve? Only they will know for certain but, each time they climb back in the ring, they are risking their reputation, their health, and even their life – for what reason?

I know I was never a great champion, although nobody can ever take away the fact that I was Champion of the World. I know I could have been so much better if only I had spent my career with better guidance and facilities. I look at what Manny Steward did with Dennis Andries and think about what I could have achieved with that kind of support and expertise, not only in the ring, but financially too.

When I started with Consett ABC as a boy, my goal was to be the best. I wanted to be better than Ali, better than Joe Louis, better than Sugar Ray Leonard. I set off as a kid not just to be a world champion but to be the greatest ever. I wanted to eclipse Sugar Ray Robinson. I wanted to be the number one pound-for-pound fighter of all time. I don't need anyone to tell me that I came nowhere close but, for one day in Stanley, I flew. In this life we all want to accomplish amazing things, but there's a point when you have to decide when enough's enough. For me, enough was winning the world title. Yes, I would have loved to have made some money. I would love to have thought that after all my hard work I could sit down in a nice house in the sunshine and just cook and be happy, but life's not like that. I was satisfied that I had achieved something special and that was enough for me. From the moment I woke up on that first morning as world champion the game never held the same interest or excitement for me again.

I think back to my brother and I realise that he, too, would have had all of those dreams as a boy. He would have wanted to fly – to soar for a day. He would have wanted to be a world champion, but he didn't get the chance to achieve any of those ambitions. But he did get to live twice as long as the experts thought he would. He got to make his own momentous journey by just doing the ordinary things in life. I'm sure David would have loved to have simply been able to walk and to do the normal things that the rest of us take for granted. I sat and watched my brother die slowly, day by day, so whatever is thrown at me is nothing in comparison.

As I hung up my gloves for the last time, I did so knowing that I'd proven that the night against Lennox was a disaster purely because I had only done it for the money. At last I felt that I had regained my dignity. I could finally walk away for good.

# 16

'When I was growing up, Dad always taught me to stay sharp, keep my chin down and my guard up. It was only later I found out he was talking about women not boxing!'
Joe McCrory

Finally leaving the fighting behind meant I was free to devote more time to pursuing my dream: film stardom! As a child all my heroes were either boxers or actors and either career would have been great for me. I couldn't just choose one and stick with it. I had to have a crack at both!

Although the commentating with Sky had begun while I was still World Champion, I had no idea how big that was going to become. I thought that now I was a boxing champion with a bit of a name, maybe that could be the launch pad to Hollywood. One of the things that had been said to me regularly was that I was unmarked for a boxer. I didn't look like most people's idea of a fighter. Mike Tyson used to call me Pretty Boy from time to time.

I would often receive comments to the effect that I should be in the movies, something that was at the back of my mind.

I had dabbled in bits and pieces throughout the 1980s, as it happens. I did something for the BBC in 1982, a health and fitness piece I believe, and got £6 for the privilege. I appeared on Tyne-Tees' *Northern Life* show a couple of times and got a bit of a taste for it and so, around 1983 it would have been, I applied for an Equity card. I had been paid a few quid and had official contracts for making appearances on the local news. If you were getting paid for media work you could apply for an Equity card, so I told them what I had done, making a few appearances up if I'm honest, and became a member of the actor's union.

My first real break came while I was embarking on one of my comebacks in the ring. I already knew Tim Healy and his wife, Denise Welch, both of whom were well-known actors, and they were about to appear in a play by Alan Plater called *Going Home*, which was set in a pub and contained the role of a doorman. I got the part and performed across the North East during a short run of a few weeks, which I thoroughly enjoyed. I also had the experience of appearing as the Wizard in *The Wizard of Oz* at the Tyne Theatre.

It may sound improbable, but I genuinely wanted to go as far as I could with my acting career and Hollywood was definitely on the radar. My reluctance to accept what most people would see as more realistic expectations meant that I was all set to have a go at making it big. I had already tried out for the part of Ivan Drago in *Rocky IV* a few years earlier, but I had been far too young. I was only about twenty and would have been scarcely believable as a fearsome heavyweight champion, as witnessed by the fact that all the real heavyweights I was fighting at the time were beating me up! Crazy as my dreams may have seemed, you need to remember you're dealing with somebody who had been told all his life that he had no chance of being World Champion. People saying 'you've got no chance of getting to Hollywood' was no different. It may have seemed like a pipe dream, but then so had the boxing and look what happened there.

There was a year between my fight with Lennox Lewis and my comeback in Paris and during those twelve months I really pushed ahead with my new career. I signed up with a couple who ran a London-based theatrical agency, Scott and Denise Marshall, and landed the part of Newton in *Press Gang*, quite a popular show at the time starring Julia Sawalha. I also had a bit part in an episode of *Casualty*. Around the same time I almost achieved my aims of appearing in a Hollywood movie – I changed a letter and settled for Bollywood instead. I played a character called Dave Brubeck in a film entitled *The Princess from Kathmandu*, which was released in 1992.

Things were put on hold for a short time while I completed my boxing career but, having fought for the final time in July 1993, I sought to get back into it as soon as I could. I appeared in a few advertisements, one for Asda and a particularly good one for Iveco trucks in which they compared me to a truck and cut from the vehicle to me punching the bag and skipping. It was a great-looking commercial which also got me a couple of nice days in Spain for filming. I made one or two minor stage appearances too, all of which were with the aim of leading to bigger and better things.

I remember receiving a phone call one day from Denise Marshall. Denise was funny in that she always had a way of making me feel as though she didn't think I was up to the job. This one particular time she rang and in her posh London accent announced, 'Glenn, I don't know what to make of this, but the Royal Shakespeare Company seem to want you.' The RSC had been in touch to offer me a contract for eight months. It would have involved working in Stratford-upon-Avon before embarking on a nationwide tour.

I had just quit boxing and was back at home and working in the pub on a much more regular basis. Would anyone like to guess Mandy's reaction to the suggestion that I disappear for eight months? Needless to say, the idea of joining the RSC was quickly shelved.

I did start getting back into TV work at around that time. I was offered another part in *Casualty*, that of a security foreman on a building site with a hard hat and donkey jacket and sporting a goatee beard, which I used to grow to make me look older and less like a pretty boy for some of these roles. As an ex-boxer, people seemed to assume I was going to be some gnarled old bruiser. I would turn up all fresh-faced and it didn't always fit the bill. Most of the TV stuff I did saw me with a beard simply because it made me look that little bit rougher.

The *Casualty* storyline involved a group of protestors, including one of the doctors, who were attempting to stop me and my team from knocking something down. One of them got in the way of the tractor I was driving, another jumped on it and I tried to push her off. During this my character swallowed his chewing gum and started choking. The protesting doctor then saved my life with the Heimlich manoeuvre.

I filmed that episode at the same time as Ray Winstone and Jamie Foreman were there filming another episode to be shown later in the series. I know Ray quite well; he's a great guy who is very into boxing. I loved the whole acting life and things were going well.

I went on to play the part of 'Mad' Hamish in the ITV wrestling comedy *Rumble*. An actor called Len Trusty, who has been a mate of mine ever since, played one of the other characters. Lesley Joseph from *Birds of a Feather* and Brian Glover played a husband and wife combination who ran a wrestling team, Brian also being the trainer who looked after us. Brian was great; the two of us were really tight. I went to see him whenever he came up to the region and we became quite friendly, but sadly he died not long afterwards.

We also had wrestling legends like Mick McManus coming in as guests, although they were knocking on a bit by then. We took the wrestling part seriously and learned to do it properly. We did all our own stunts, to the point of standing on each other's shoulders, somersaulting off the ropes, doing headstands and all of that. It was great fun and a really good idea, but the timing was wrong. It was just before WWE really took off over here. It also wasn't helped by the fact that it seemed as though the director and the producer didn't see eye to eye on where it was going. They had different ideas on the sort of show it should be. What started out as a semi-serious comedy-drama became a farce. It just grew sillier and sillier until, by the time they finished, it ended up being put out on kid's TV. It should have been so much better than that. Brian Glover and Lesley Joseph were top actors and big names. It should have been a light-hearted drama based around a group of wrestlers, but they kept trying to put more and more comedy into it until it just became ridiculous. There was one episode in which they were trying to raise money for the team. Lesley had us stripping as part of the fundraising show, which ended with Len and me being chased down the corridors by a group of women. There's a fine line between being funny and pathetic and *Rumble,* sadly, crossed it. It only ran for one series, which was such a shame, but hardly a surprise.

The same year I appeared in an episode of *Space Precinct*, another that could have been really good. I was auditioned by the show's creator, the legendary Gerry Anderson, the man behind *Thunderbirds*. I was only in it once but was the main character for the episode in question, the fabulously named Thunder Cole.

Things were going pretty well. I had really high hopes and thought it could genuinely be a successful career for me. It was certainly my main source of income during the mid-nineties. It could have been even better – I was an actor's whim away from a part in a major Hollywood movie.

I was sent to audition for the 1995 movie *Judge Dredd* starring Sylvester Stallone. I met director Danny Cannon, who later directed the *CSI* series, but who was making his way in Hollywood at the time. This film was a major breakthrough for him. I had only been speaking to Danny for about five minutes when he told me I had got the part.

I was absolutely delighted. This could have represented my big break – a Hollywood movie alongside Sylvester Stallone. Rocky himself! It was a fantastic opportunity. I was sent to see the wardrobe man to be measured up for my guard's costume. He took one look at me and simply said, 'Hmmm.'

He looked me up and down again and asked, 'And you're one of the guards who will be standing next to Sly, yes? How tall are you, exactly?' Well when you're asked that you don't know whether to say 5 foot 8 or 6 foot 6, whether to stand tall or crouch down. He measured me up, sighed and said, 'Sly doesn't normally have anyone over 5 foot 10 in his movies.' After I went home, I waited for confirmation of when I was needed in Hollywood. And I waited and I waited. Eventually I got a call from my agent to say, 'Glenn – bad news I'm afraid.' Bloody Rocky eh?

Being a guard in *Judge Dredd* was one thing, but I was shortly to receive a call from my agent which could have led to life being completely different. Denise again approached the subject with her uncanny ability to put me down. 'We've got a funny one here Glenn. They want to see you for a big role. Hmmm, I don't know if I can see it myself – it's James Bond.' Thanks a lot for the vote of confidence! She went further and added, 'Can you imagine it though? A Geordie Bond!' Yes, you're right. It would be just as daft as a Scottish one wouldn't it?

All joking aside, all of a sudden here was a role that could utterly change my life. I knew that the biggest strike against me was that I wasn't really old enough. I was only about thirty and Bond should really be in his forties.

This thought was going through my mind as I travelled by train to meet the producers. I was both nervous and excited when I opened the paper to be faced with an article headed 'Brosnan for Bond'. I was furious. I thought, 'What am I doing spending my own money going all the way to London by train for a role that's already gone?'

On my arrival I went into the office a bit pissed off. I sat down with the producer, Barbara Broccoli, and started the conversation by asking, 'What am I down here for? I'm wasting my money for a role that's gone. It was all over the paper today.'

She assured me that the role hadn't gone and that they still had a few people to see. Looking back I think it was pretty clear that they had Pierce Brosnan pinpointed, but wanted to try a couple of wildcards before making a final decision.

Of course, as we know, Brosnan did get the role, but in case the Bond people are reading this, can I just say that I am now a little older so on the off-chance that Daniel Craig wants to call it a day, I think the time could be right for a Geordie Bond at last. 'Sod the vodka Martini – I'll have a bag of crisps and divven't spill me pint pet!'

Back on TV I appeared in an episode of a TV series called *Ellington* with Chris Ellison from *The Bill*. A mate of mine, former boxer and rugby league player Adam Fogerty, who later forged quite a decent career as an actor and was in *Snatch* among other things, was there too. We were to play two brothers.

There was a classically trained actor called Tom Gregson who was to play our dad and I remember spotting a potential problem. I went to him and pointed out that the three of us who were supposedly in the same family had Scouse, Yorkshire and Geordie accents! I asked what the proper, serious, classically trained actor thought we should do and he simply looked at me and said, 'Well I'm from Liverpool and I don't know where you're from but I'm playing a fucking Scouser.' That left little room for discussion so me and Foggy had to practise our Scouse accents on the morning before we started shooting. After our first scene the director yelled, 'Cut!' pointed at the three us in turn, leaving me till last, and said as he did so, 'Scouser, Scouser... Northern Irish! Any reason why you're from Northern Ireland, Glenn?' I suggested that maybe I had moved there, but he said if that was the case then I needed to move back. He gave me some time to speak with Tom to get the accent sorted and luckily enough I think I managed okay after that. The proof is on film I suppose!

Around that time I appeared in an episode of *Crocodile Shoes* with Jimmy Nail, having also made a brief appearance in his earlier series, *Spender*. Jimmy and I knew of each other but weren't friends like Tim Healy and I were. He was fine with me and we got on okay, but he was in his pomp then and seemed to think of himself as the North East's big shot and number one hard-man actor. He would fire people if he didn't like the way they'd ironed his shirt and stuff like that, just a little bit full of himself, but I have to admit he was always fine with me. I got on much better with Sammy Johnson, who played Spender's sidekick, Stick. Sammy was great and we became quite friendly. Sadly he died a few years ago in Spain. There is an event held in Newcastle every two years called 'Sunday for

Sammy' in his memory. It's quite a big thing up here, the acting and music profession on Tyneside come together to raise money to help young people get into the arts. Jimmy, Tim Healy, Denise Welch and many more all get involved. I appeared myself in a comedy role one year and have played parts on several occasions, including playing a Newcastle fan – that one wasn't too taxing!

Another northern-based part I played was that of a doorman on the Tuxedo Princess in a very successful BBC drama called *Our Friends in the North*. The Tuxedo Princess was a floating nightclub, moored on the Tyne in Newcastle, which was known to all Tynesiders as 'The Boat'. One of the main characters was a drunken tramp played by Daniel Craig. Daniel was lovely. He knew his boxing, was a great laugh and I got on terrifically with him. In my episode his character had to try to get on the boat and I had to grab him and throw him off. It's ironic that he's now James Bond and yet there I was, all suavely dressed, throwing him off the boat. More proof that the Bond producers cast the wrong man maybe? Okay, perhaps not.

While my acting career had been building, Sky had also picked up their boxing coverage substantially. I had been given a decent contract with more regular work and in those days they had a smaller team, so they had me involved in everything. I would be doing commentary, studio punditry, interviewing – the works. I was really learning the ropes, travelling around the country and sometimes the world. Then I was offered a regular part in a new show to be filmed in Newcastle called *Quayside*.

I was to play a bouncer yet again, but this time as a regular character. The show was being produced by a guy called Matthew Robinson who also produced and directed *Eastenders* and *Byker Grove* – another show in which I once made a brief appearance. *Quayside* itself was a really good idea, a soap opera set on Tyneside was a great idea to my mind, but they put us on opposite *Eastenders*, which was madness. You're not going to establish any new soap opera by placing it in direct opposition to that. Soon after that Matthew was offered a role as executive producer on *Eastenders* so, reading between the lines, it seemed to me that the series was really a bargaining tool for him to get a good offer from *Eastenders* all along. If it wasn't then it certainly worked out that way.

Owing to my contract with Sky and the requirements for filming *Quayside* I ended up working seven days a week for six solid weeks. You can imagine how that went down at home. Matthew was great and arranged the whole filming schedule around my days off, so all the scenes involving me could be shot together on the few days I was available, but clearly something had to give. I still had dreams of being a successful actor. I had been successful in the ring, but I hadn't got anything to show for that success. I had lots of great things to put on my CV, but nothing to get me out of a terraced house in Stanley. Landing that one big role could offer that bright future, but there was no way I could keep up the level of work involved in trying to continue with both Sky and acting while enjoying any sort of family life whatsoever.

I was offered another RSC contract, but it wasn't even worth asking Mandy how she felt about that. She didn't like me going away acting any more than she had while I was boxing. Also, with more Sky work now coming in, that too took me away from home. She was still quite insecure. I remember once coming back from a trip to the USA, being in bed sleeping off jet lag, when she woke me up with a women's shoe in her hand to state accusingly, 'This was in your case.' I told her not to be so stupid as nobody could have put a shoe in my case. She then begrudgingly admitted that she was just testing me to see if I panicked. There were clearly a lot of insecure thoughts going through her mind at the time, plus she was still bringing up two young children. She gave me an ultimatum and told me something had to give. I couldn't keep both careers and a family. She was right.

It was a case of sitting down and deciding which way to go. It was an awful decision to have to make because the acting was really starting to take off and I wanted Hollywood. I had a dream that I hadn't finished chasing and I didn't want to close the door, but it was the case that one had to go and, although acting had been my main source of income for a couple of years, I recognised, deep down, that boxing is what I knew best. Plus I had now been given a proper contract by Sky and it was therefore a more regular and reliable income than acting could ever be.

Looking back, although I would love to have pursued my acting career for longer, it has obviously been the right decision. I have had many great experiences through my work with Sky and I hope to have many more.

However, my thespian dreams have recently been rekindled. In 2015, I was interviewed for a radio talk show with Danny Kelly called *My Sporting Life*. During the ninety-minute chat I talked about my passion for acting. I received an unexpected call from theatre director Adam Morley a couple of days later. He told me he had heard the broadcast, thought that my sheer exuberance had really come across, and asked if I would like a role in a play he was doing. I said I was interested, expecting a chance to get back into acting via a small role, and asked for further details. He advised he was working on a Conor McPherson adaptation of *The Birds*, the Daphne Du Maurier novel, which had been turned into a movie by Alfred Hitchcock.

Adam gave me a brief outline of the plot and I listened carefully to the story involving a man and two women before asking, slightly puzzled, where my role would fit in. His reply was that I was to be the lead! If this wasn't enough of a surprise I asked him where and when it was to be staged and he said it was scheduled to run for four weeks in the Leicester Square Theatre in the West End! That hit me like a stiff left jab straight on the nose.

I feared it may be too big a step. Almost all my previous acting experience had been on television. The length of the script I would have to learn would present a problem – I struggle to remember a shopping list. I thanked him for his offer but left it at that, I didn't think it was quite right for me. Adam told me that I would be helped and supported all the way and asked me to consider it thoroughly before making a final decision.

After coming off the phone, I started to think again. Yes, it would be difficult, but all my life I have had to fight to achieve anything. Nobody had ever really offered me something like this on a plate before. I also pride myself on tackling challenges head on. I figured that, even if it turned out that I couldn't do it, at least nobody was going to be trying to knock me out! I decided that being able to add 'starred in a West End play' to my CV was something I could not turn down. I rang Adam back and told him I was in. The month in London was a fantastic experience. My two fellow actors, Emma Taylor and Alice Marshall, were great and helped throughout. The acting bug had bitten again.

Around the same time I went to see *Hadaway Harry*, a one-man play by Ed Waugh telling the life story of world champion rower Harry Clasper. I thought it was brilliant and couldn't believe how actor Jamie Brown had managed to carry it off on his own with so many quick costume changes and in such a dynamic story.

I subsequently spoke to Ed and we discussed my West End appearance. He asked if I was planning on doing anything else with Adam Morley. I told him we had discussed the Carrying David story but that we didn't have a writer as yet. I enquired whether he would be interested to which he replied, 'I've been waiting for you to ask me for fifteen years!' Ten days later I was sent a script which made me cry on the train as I read it for the first time.

I told him we had to do it and we quickly agreed it should be performed in Stanley in May 2016. It was to be another one-man play. I asked Ed who he was going to cast. His reply took me aback: 'You of course. You've just done a play in London and who knows you and David better than you? All you have to do is learn the words, lose two stone, take the beard off and dye your hair!'

He was right; who knows how I felt throughout David's struggles better than me? There is an awful lot of dialogue for me to learn but I won't duck the task. By sheer coincidence the play has come about at the same time as this book is due to hit the shelves and by the time you read this I will have sunk or swum. But at last my desire to tell David's story is coming to fruition.

# 17

'No one has done more for boxing in the North East than my old mate Glenn McCrory. He is highly knowledgeable, gives back to the sport and regularly raises money for charities up and down the country. One of boxing's good guys who I'm proud to call a friend.'
Ricky Hatton, former World Light-Welterweight
and Welterweight Champion

David was twenty-three when he saw me become world champion. That moment when our eyes met and no words needed to be spoken has lived with me ever since. It's the picture I want to remember most because his was a life of happiness and heartache.

No matter how tough anything got in my life, I would walk through the door of my parents' house and be inspired by David's courage and yet, at the same time, find it so terribly painful to see.

I have never met anyone with such a force of will, with such spirit. He had already surprised the doctors who had thought he would not see beyond his early teens. As time went on he was fighting every day for his very existence.

It had been a gradual but inevitable decline from hitting his teens, when we had started to notice how much his feet were turning in and how he was struggling to walk. You couldn't tell the difference from day to day, but it would slowly dawn that he was struggling to pick up things or move about like he had a few months earlier.

The family dealt with the situation the best way it could. Each of us were affected in our own way by David's condition and decline but we all had to just get on with it. There is an inevitability about life in a spiralling crisis.

My family are good people and when a difficult situation arises we just cope. We often resorted to the typically British method of using humour to help get through difficult circumstances. David always had a great sense of humour and never wanted people to feel sorry for him so we used to try to make him laugh. So often in this country we make a joke out of a bad situation. I think it's a product of the working-class culture – just crack a joke and get on with it. So with David we would make jokes about things, poke fun, or say 'pick it up man' if he dropped something, and he used to laugh. We would get him to do things for himself for as long as he still could. That was what he wanted, the chance to retain some independence for as long as was possible.

David's condition got to the point where, owing to the failure of his throat muscles, there was a chance he would choke with virtually every meal. We were literally keeping him alive on an almost daily basis. The amount of times one of us would have to pick him up, turn him upside down and bang him on the back was unbelievable and extremely traumatic for all of us and obviously for David in particular. None of us could bear the idea of him dying by choking while he was in sheer panic. It was absolutely horrific.

There are many things in my life that have left a scar, but seeing David suffer went way beyond everything else. It reached a point where I would sometimes go to bed and pray for him to die. To find yourself praying for someone you love to die is an awful place to be. I was tormented by whether or not I was being selfish in asking for him to be taken, or if it was more selfish to help him stay alive for more suffering. It is a position I would not wish on anyone.

But David was a fighter. He happened to have this dreadful condition, but otherwise he was an incredibly normal kid with regular ideas and a seriously bad temper at times. There is a wonderful line by Dylan Thomas: 'Do not go gentle into that good night, Old age should burn and rage at close of day; Rage, rage against the dying of the light.' And did David rage? Hell he raged!

By the end, though, he was just sitting on the floor. He couldn't walk, couldn't talk, couldn't feed himself or do anything that he used to be able to do. He'd still try to move and speak; he never gave up trying, but he had reached the stage where he was pretty much like a baby again. He wore an adult nappy and had to be spoon-fed as he had lost control of everything. His neck muscles could no longer support his head and he was unable to hold a cup or do anything at all for himself. To be there to watch your brother die slowly in front of you and not being able to do anything about it is the most frustrating and anguished feeling you could possibly imagine.

And then, in February 1996, the end finally came. I was at home in Station Road when I got a phone call early in the morning from my mother telling me to get there right away as they couldn't wake David. I ran in. The pain of seeing my dad shaking David and trying to give him the kiss of life while crying his eyes out because he was obviously gone was unbearable.

David was just a month short of his thirtieth birthday when he died. He had lasted well over a decade longer than had been expected. His funeral was one of the most painful and extraordinary experiences I have ever known.

Father Hickey conducted the service in St Teresa's in Annfield Plain. I couldn't let the occasion go by without somebody saying something and so I struggled with my emotions and stood up to try to explain what he had meant to me, which was one of the hardest things I have ever had to do in my life. Then 'Wind Beneath My Wings' was played, which had been David's favourite song, and the emotion became overwhelming.

After the service everyone got into their cars and headed to Burnhope Cemetery, where many of my relatives are buried. It is way out in the sticks and one of the highest points in County Durham. As we made our way up there the snow came down in what I can only describe as a blizzard. You get a fair bit of snow in Consett and Stanley, but this was as bad as I have ever known it. As we attempted this journey of a little over three miles the snow was so bad that car after car stopped, turned round and returned to Annfield Plain because it was becoming almost impossible. Obviously we had to get through and by the time we arrived everything was white. I got out of the car to feel the wind bite into my face so hard that I wanted to cry. It's hard to put it into words just how bad it was. It was only David's close family who had made it and we were all standing there at the graveside having to cover the children with our coats because the conditions were so horrendous while poor Father Hickey tried to conduct the service.

I wanted to just yell 'stop!' at one point. David's life had been so hard and he was not getting it any easier in death. But then the coffin was lowered into the ground and almost immediately it began to ease. A minute or so later, the sun came out. We were all looking at each other in bewilderment. It was as if David's hardship carried on until he was finally in the ground at rest and then it was over.

The feeling of pure loss and pain was greater than I had ever imagined. I thought that it would be a relief when he finally passed away. In a way it was, in that he no longer had to suffer, but then there was a massive void where David had been. So much of what I had done had been geared around him. I didn't realise how much I needed him, how much my focus was him and how much I fed off him and got strength from him until he had gone.

By the morning after his funeral, the snow had gone too. David, however, I will be carrying forever.

As well as the pain of David's decline, I was also experiencing the ultimate demise of my marriage. We were arguing as much as ever and, to me, there's no argument that's ever good. Some women I've been with over the years seem to like a bit of a scene and the odd argument, but I hate it. What makes it worse is arguing in front of the children, which was happening from time to time. I hated that even more. The thing with Mandy and I, though, was that often the making up again afterwards was great. We were a passionate couple and it wasn't always bad between us. There was a spark that was always there – how else could we have lasted as long as we did, with all the negative feelings that there had been between us?

At times the whole marriage would seem to come down to Mandy telling me to get out of the house. I would be kicked out regularly after stupid arguments which, to be honest, could have been avoided. It became something of a running joke in Mitchell Street that the neighbours would all say 'I see Glenn's been kicked out again' as I was seen clutching a bag in one hand and my posters under my arm as I walked to my parents' house, followed by 'I see Glenn and Mandy are back together' a few days later as I was spotted carrying the same items in the other direction!

Where I didn't help is that if someone reacts badly to something I do I will tend to behave even worse next time. If Mandy told me off for being out drinking and not coming in until one a.m., then the next time I would stay out until two. It was just me saying, 'Don't tell me what time to come in.' I've always had that stupid stubborn reaction to people telling me what to do ever since I went to school. It's the way I've always been and it definitely didn't help things with Mandy.

The problem, ultimately, was that we wanted completely different things. Mandy wanted a normal and settled home life, but the humdrum nature of reality is just not me. I'm terrible if I'm bored. That's when I go off the rails, drink and do stupid things. I have always had so many things going on in my life, travelling here and there and having adventures, shooting for targets and chasing dreams, that I simply cannot handle being idle. I have a problem with keeping myself mentally stimulated and productive when there's nothing happening.

Having said that, for the first time in my life, I have recently started to feel as though I need to settle down with my family. Maybe I am growing up at last, but obviously I wasn't ready for it with Mandy. I was little more than a kid when we married and I hadn't had the opportunity to work out for myself what it was that I wanted from life. I was just thrust into an environment of having to look after a family and pay bills when I was still so young. I'm sure that affected both of us.

The ironic thing was that this marriage which had been so explosive for so long, often because of problems with money, finally disintegrated when we actually seemed to be finding our feet at last. It had been really hard having a wife, two young kids and no money. What made things even tougher for me was the lack of understanding of my situation from the outside. There's nothing worse than driving a crappy old car when you're a world champion because people are thinking, 'What's he done with his money? Where's he hiding his millions?' They just assumed I had to be rich and didn't have any idea how tough life actually was. But, by the mid-nineties, there was light at the end of the tunnel. Although Mandy never really enjoyed the pub it had started to turn the corner after a struggle running it in the early days. I was now getting more acting work and more regular work with Sky as they increased their influence in the UK market. I had a nice car at last and we had recently bought a plot of land in Shield Row, Stanley in order to build a new house of our own, which we partly financed by selling the pub.

Unfortunately, for Mandy the previous few years had taken their toll. My being away and our arguing had got her to a point where I believe she was looking for a way out. If one half of a couple is resolutely following a deter-mined course that the other half doesn't want then it just can't work – and that was us.

It all came to a head after I had been to London for a Sky Christmas party. Immediately after the meal I flew straight home. On the return flight I found myself sitting next to the actor Robson Green. I knew Robson so we chatted all the way home. After we landed we continued talking and were joined by a stewardess I also knew. We didn't chat for long, no more than an hour, but it meant I was a little late getting home. My phone had been off while I was on the plane and I hadn't remembered to turn it on again when I got off, so when Mandy called to ask where I was she couldn't get through. As soon as I got back she began asking me where I had been and who I had been with and it was just like the bad old days. She asked me if I was seeing anybody and, in all honesty, I wasn't. That night, however, I was tired and suddenly realised that I was fed up of arguing all the time and that I just didn't want to be with her any more. When she asked me if I was seeing somebody I decided to say yes.

I knew I was giving her what she wanted. I was giving her the key to be free. She wanted to be out but had no clear cut reason to make that move. I was giving her the excuse she needed. I will be honest and say that if I had stopped to think it out more clearly, I probably wouldn't have said it. It certainly turned out to be a bloody expensive answer!

Next time I returned home, all my stuff was outside in bin bags. We were now in the house we had built in Shield Row but, luckily, we still had the house in Station Road, which was on the market at the time, so I went there. There was no real attempt to reconcile. I think there may have been one window of opportunity had I wanted to take it. She came round to suggest we go for a bite to eat and a talk but I didn't turn up. I think I was afraid that I would end up returning to something I knew we were both better off being out of.

The divorce was very unpleasant and nasty. It must have been the Christmas of 1997 when we split, the divorce being finalised in 1999. Joe was only about eight and still wanted his dad around but Tori would have been thirteen and it affected her more and caused a sizeable change in our relationship which thankfully we sorted over the years. I'm hugely proud of both of them and love them dearly.

Although Mandy and I had been through a lot, and it had been obvious for a long time that it would be best for both of us to make a new start, the truth is that I still cared for her and, when the inevitable break up happened, the pain was unbelievable. I suffered badly and the process of getting over it and moving on with my life took years. I found myself partly relying on the memories of David to help me remember that life is always worth fighting for, which helped give me a sense that the future would be more positive. There would, however, be many dark days ahead.

The end of the nineties and the start of the new millennium was a very difficult time for me. There have been many times when things could have really got on top of me, but the period after David died and then Mandy left was the hardest. To be honest, I just lost the plot.

David died in 1996 and my marriage ended around Christmas 1997, although the divorce wasn't finalised until 1999. Since splitting with Mandy all I did for a while, as far as other people would see it, was party. To be honest though it wasn't really partying, it was self-destruction. It wasn't fun, it was sheer pain. It was a period where I just wanted to drink and seem like I was having fun to disguise the fact that I felt like I wanted to die. I wanted to join my brother. I wished that it had been me instead of him.

I have experienced deaths from an early age. My Uncle Bill had died of cancer, aged forty-two, when I was only ten. I carried both grandfathers' coffins before I was fourteen, I lost good friends when I was still a teenager, I lost a nephew. When you've watched as many people die as I have, you start to wonder what life and death is all about. Living in that community and coming, as I did, from a big family, death was so commonplace that it was almost taken for granted. I'm a Christian and I believe in the next life – in Heaven – so I would have been happy to have been taken back then. My brother is there, my nephew, my best friend, my grandparents, uncles and, most recently, my father.

Almost twenty years to the day since David passed away, I woke during the night and checked my phone to find missed calls from members of my family. I knew what was coming. My dad had been suffering from emphysema and suffered a collapsed lung five years previously. Although he had been unwell for a while, his death was still something of a shock. Only a week or so earlier his doctor had told him he was stable and no longer needed extra oxygen. However he caught a bug and never recovered. He passed away on 5 February 2016.

I immediately went round to see him and say my goodbyes before he was taken away. He was such a great and loving man. He had been there for me throughout my life – he picked me up, calmed me down, encouraged me, consoled me and supported me through thick and thin. He was my hero. The two weeks leading up to his funeral was a very difficult period but I was pleased to get the chance to give a eulogy at the church in Annfield Plain.

My father is the latest in a line of so many special people I have lost. Am I scared of going to join them? No, I'm not. We're all born and we all die and that's the truth of it. I certainly don't fear death.

If my thinking around the late nineties seems confused and contradictory it can perhaps best be explained by the fact that, in 2001, I was diagnosed by a doctor as suffering long-term clinical depression. It is only when I remember this that I can make any sense of my decisions and behaviour in that period.

Even in my darkest days I try to view my glass as being half full. Despite the pain I have felt at times, I believe in life and love and achieving great things. I know that, no matter how bad things get for me, there is always somebody like David, somebody who is worse off than I am. Somebody combating greater hardships and more difficult challenges than I have ever faced in my life. To try to always look on the bright side is just one of the many important lessons I learnt from my brother. Around the time I was going through my painful separation from Mandy, an event occurred which brought home to me in a dreadful way the need to make the most of the life you have.

My great-granddad had come from County Tyrone in Northern Ireland. In August 1998 a terrorist bomb exploded in Omagh town centre, killing twenty-nine people, injuring over two hundred and tearing the heart out of a small community. I had taken my parents to Florida for a family holiday, the first time they had been to the States, when we heard the news. I remember everyone being shocked and upset. It seemed really poignant and it hit all of us quite hard, a feeling which was only heightened when I later discovered that one of the victims shared my father's name, Brian McCrory, and was of a similar age. It was very much a case of there but for the grace of God...

As things turned out, as the people of Omagh were trying to rebuild their lives, the headmaster of a local school got in touch with me in order to try to arrange a charity event to raise money for the victims and to help the town move on. He was a boxing fan, involved with the local

Omagh Boxing Club, and he asked me whether I could help in some way as they were in such a state of disarray in the aftermath of the tragedy. The town centre had been decimated and they just needed to raise both money and awareness of their predicament. I told him I would be delighted to assist in any way I could.

All sorts of people helped out. The boxing community is great for rallying round in times of need. I helped to arrange Frank Bruno's involvement, spoke to the British Boxing Board of Control to see if they could offer some support and also got in touch with Barry McGuigan, who is 'Mr Boxing' over there. He immediately came on board and once he got involved he became the leading light, as indeed he should have been, being Ireland's greatest boxing hero. Eventually many events took place to help the people of Omagh, including a visit from Take That among others, but I remain very proud that I was the person that set the ball rolling.

Later on I took a boxing team over there and it was great to see the people and the places where my great-grandfather had grown up and my granddad was born. I'm sure I must have many relatives over there. The name McCrory is very common in that region, indeed Pat McCrory was President of the Ulster Boxing Council for over twenty years.

As a Catholic kid with the name McCrory, growing up in seventies and eighties England was slightly strange at times. There were regular bomb attacks and even more hoax threats. I remember regularly going to the pictures in the newly opened Metro Centre in Gateshead and hearing an announcement telling us to evacuate the building as there was a bomb threat. It seemed to happen every couple of weeks. So I got looked at a bit warily from time to time with such an obviously Irish name.

As far as a sense of identity goes, I have always struggled to know where I belong in the world. Although I was born in England, as were my parents, I never felt myself to be totally English. I've always thought it weird that a family can come to the UK from, say, China or India, and there may have been three or four generations born here since, and yet they are still referred to as Chinese or Indian in terms of their background and culture. In the same way I have always felt slightly Irish, in that they were my family's roots, but then again not entirely, as my parents had never really discussed that part of my heritage at all.

I am proud to have been born in England, and particularly of being from the North East, but I am proud of my Irish roots too. In America they make much more of a thing about Irishness, despite there having often been several generations born in the States since their ancestors first arrived. In England that seems not to happen. I don't know how much of that is to do with the centuries of trouble between the two countries, but it all helped to emphasise my feelings of not quite belonging as a kid.

I suspect that this all contributed to my desire to be planted as close to the heart of somewhere as I could be once I was free to choose. I love the North East of England and I'm massively proud of Annfield Plain and Stanley. I would say that, first and foremost, I'm a Stanley lad, but the whole region means a lot to me. I've certainly always loved Newcastle upon Tyne and so, as soon as I could, I set up home near the city centre. To me it is at the heart of the region and has everything I could want nearby, but I will I admit I have always felt drawn to Ireland.

# 18

'Glenn and I covered hundreds of fights and had thousands more laughs as we chronicled the careers of Mike Tyson, Lennox Lewis, Chris Eubank, Prince Naseem Hamed, Joe Calzaghe and many more. Occasionally wild and chaotic and fond of a night out, life on the road with Glenn is rarely dull and as one die-hard fan once told me – it isn't really a big fight if Glenn's not working on it.'
Ian Darke, Sky Sports Boxing commentator

Somewhere else that feels like home is Sky Television. Sky has been the one constant factor in my life for over a quarter of a century. It has touched and overlapped with everything I have been through, including births, deaths, marriage and divorce.

In a way, my whole battle to become Champion of the World was a story about how somebody achieved something against the odds. That built the rocket as it were. The rocket then launched as Glenn McCrory: Boxing Pundit.

All the experiences that made me, all the defeats and the pain, helped created a sports analyst. I can talk about being a prospect, a journeyman and a champion. I can talk about knocking people out and being knocked out myself. I have experience of it all. Most world champions were never journeymen or had to survive with no money. They didn't lose five out of six fights and have to prepare for bouts with no proper gym or trainer. There's a little category that I think I'm in all by myself. I was one of a kind. That, fundamentally, is what has made me the commentator I am today.

My career with Sky could be a volume of books by itself. I've covered virtually every world-class fighter since 1989. You can name any champion over that period and there's a good chance that not only have I seen them fight live, but that I have seen most of their career. More than the fights, however, Sky Television has been the story of a family. It started with Ian Darke, whose recommendation brought me into the family to begin with, and with whom I have travelled all over the world covering so many incredible fights.

Ian is the person with whom I have worked most closely over those years and our relationship has always been great. I remember, shortly after David died, we were on our way to London for a show and I was struggling. Ian picked me up to take me to the venue and as we got closer I told him I couldn't do it. Ian tried to encourage me by telling me I could do anything if I put my mind to it and that David would have wanted me to carry on. I really didn't think I could when, all of a sudden, the song 'Wind Beneath My Wings' came on the radio. David's favourite song. I was in floods of tears and Ian held me for a while, but I took it as a sign and we went in and did the show.

In addition to Ian there's been Adam Smith, Paul Dempsey, Bob Mee, Declan Johnson, Jim Watt, big Charles Lawrence, Ed Robinson, Mike Allen and the whole Sky boxing team. I have had such wonderful times and amazing experiences in the last quarter of a century. There are so many great people who have been a part of that and I can only apologise to any I have missed out.

I am being entirely honest when I say that, in terms of my career, Sky TV has been the best thing that has ever happened to me. If you cut me in half, the word 'Sky' would be running right through me. I am Sky TV to my core. I have always been a loyal person, but I have often found to my cost that you can be loyal to somebody but not have that loyalty returned to you. With Sky it has worked both ways. I've been loyal to Sky because they took a chance on me, they backed me, they went with me when I was untried and untested and they've continued to hire me for a quarter of a century. Yes, we've had our ups and downs and certain individuals have been harder to get along with than others, but you're always going to have that in life. Above all, however, they've given me the opportunity to live my dream, to visit places, experience things and enjoy a wonderful journey. I have met, and even become friends with, people regarded as living legends thanks to my job with Sky.

There was a brief moment when Ian and I worried that we may be about to be cast aside, or at least relegated in importance, as Sky grew in popularity. We had covered Mike Tyson when he beat Frank Bruno to regain his world title but then we missed out on his second defence, his first meeting with Evander Holyfield. I had been with Sky since day one and I had been either at ringside, or in the studio, for all of Mike Tyson's fights since. But, after winning the rights to show Premier League football, Sky really began to take off. The bubble was growing bigger and bigger and Sky decided to hire Reg Gutteridge and Jim Watt. They were the most well-known boxing commentary partnership in Britain due to their years together with ITV covering the likes of Nigel Benn and Chris Eubank for those fight fans who didn't have satellite dishes.

On the day of Tyson's defence against Holyfield, Ian and I found ourselves sent to Manchester to cover Steve Collins-Nigel Benn II, which was taking place the same night. It was a massive night for Sky boxing, a huge double-header and one of their pinnacle points. Now, in all fairness, me and Darkey were doing the big fight as far as British audiences were concerned. The majority of the UK boxing audience was interested in watching Benn. It was a great bill, with Naseem Hamed and Ronald 'Winky' Wright defending world titles and other past or future champions such as Carl Thompson and Herbie Hide also appearing, but Ian and I always had a view as to what the real picture was in world terms and there was no doubt to us that Tyson-Holyfield meant an awful lot more, even though many people thought Holyfield had no chance at all. As it turned out Holyfield beat Tyson, and Darkey and I were not out in the cold as we had feared. The boss took us to one side and told us that, owing to Reg's failing health, he was not to become a Sky regular. From fearing that we were about to be edged out by the big ITV boys, all of a sudden we were number one again.

We were sent to cover the inevitable Holyfield-Tyson rematch in Las Vegas where we stayed in the MGM Grand Hotel. I remember on one occasion being late and, seeing Ian in the distance, I rushed through the foyer trying to catch his attention by shouting 'Darkey! Darkey!' at the top of my voice. I became uncomfortably aware of an entire room full of people turning to stare at me. I suddenly realised that Ian and I were the only white faces in the place! As quick as a flash I changed my calls to 'Ian! Ian Darke!'

That fight was to prove the low point of my time covering Iron Mike. It was another occasion where he seemed to be surrounded by all the dirtbags in the world. Darkey will tell you that I seem to have a special instinct for smelling trouble. Maybe it's because I'm a street kid from rough fighting territory but, whatever the reason, I smelled bad vibes on that trip. The same thing had happened when I covered Riddick Bowe against Andrew Golota in Madison Square Garden. I walked into that venue and told Ian I had a bad feeling. The night ended in a riot. I can smell when hate is in the air because there's just some strange energy. I went into the Holyfield-Tyson rematch and didn't enjoy it because the Tyson people were basically not very nice.

When Evander came in with his gospel music blaring, he seemed oblivious to everything. I thought then that Tyson was in trouble. Once the fight started he turned into a delinquent hooligan. He got out the only way he could without getting knocked out. He twice bit Holyfield's ear – the second time taking a huge chunk out of it – and was rightly disqualified on one of boxing's darkest nights.

I've known Evander ever since I became a potential challenger for his title. I've interviewed him, been to his house, spent time with him when he visited Newcastle and have even been out dancing with him. I've got a long history with Evander – a legend of the ring. He knew that the whole secret to beating Tyson was not to be scared of him. That's what beat him. Evander Holyfield wasn't scared of Mike Tyson so Tyson couldn't bully him. From that point on there was only going to be one winner.

Holyfield-Tyson II may have represented a low point, but I am more often asked to name the greatest fight I have ever commentated on. I've been lucky enough to see some fantastic fights over the years, but without doubt the greatest I have covered to date was the first of the three bouts between Erik Morales and Marco Antonio Barrera, which took place in February 2000. Although it was a unification bout, Morales being the WBC Champion and Barrera holding the WBO belt in the super-bantamweight division, it was, from Sky's point of view, a low key event in the Mandalay Bay Resort, Las Vegas. To be honest, Darkey and I were wondering what on earth we were doing there. We didn't really see who would be interested in a fight between a couple of, at the time, not well-known Mexicans in Nevada. Still, we didn't complain because it meant a few days in Vegas so we were happy to go along for the ride.

I spent time in both fighters' dressing rooms at some point and they seemed to genuinely dislike each other.

They wouldn't sign anything together as a rule, but I managed to use my status as an ex-world champion to persuade both to sign my T-shirt. It may very well be the only one with both signatures that exists and I've still got it. They may have disliked each other, but to me they were both great. I've met Barrera since and he's a lovely guy. Morales was more of a working-class street kid and when we went to do an interview with him in his dressing room at the weigh-in the day before the fight, it remains the only time in such circumstances that Darkey and I have been offered beers. Morales' father and uncle were busily handing the bottles out and that's just the sort of thing I would have done. I loved the whole attitude and atmosphere within the camp and I remain a big fan of Erik Morales. He was a total warrior in the ring, this young lad from Tijuana, and he's probably my favourite ever Mexican fighter.

The fight was amazing and if you listen to the Sky coverage you will notice I'm struggling for words as it wears on. It was an incredible battle, rightly named *The Ring* Fight of the Year. To be honest I thought Barrera won but it was Morales who was awarded the verdict. It was a typical Vegas decision, but it had been a truly great fight and in a way I didn't really care who won, because these two warriors had just served up something that will live with me for the rest of my life. Ironically, in the rematch I felt Morales had done enough, but this time Barrera was the official winner. The third meeting ended in a majority decision for Barrera, giving him a 2-1 edge in the series, but it was a rare occasion when it may have been better to have called it a draw. Neither fighter deserved to lose that trilogy.

As well as Tyson, I was in the studio for the whole of Lennox Lewis' career – or at least the bit where I wasn't getting beaten in the ring! I was there for De La Hoya v Chavez, which was a massive 'passing of the torch' moment, and subsequently covered De La Hoya's entire career too. The same with great British fighters such as Ricky Hatton and Joe Calzaghe.

I have had the pleasure of meeting some legendary people through my involvement in the sport: the 'Sugar Rays' Robinson and Leonard, Mike Tyson, Larry Holmes, Muhammad Ali and Don King. Willie Pastrano, Joe 'Old Bones' Brown and Emile Griffith, who came to see me fight and who flirted with me the whole time, but in such a funny way. He kept trying to get me into the showers – it was hilarious! I thought the world of Emile Griffith. I've met famous boxing writers like Harry Mullan and Budd Schulberg and been to dinner with Bert Randolph Sugar. I feel truly blessed to have been around so many of the greats. I can call some of the most well-known people in the sport my friends. The ones I tend to like in particular are the normal kids – the ones that have their feet on the floor. Men like Carl Froch, Ricky Hatton, Duke McKenzie, Steve Collins and Richie Woodhall; who are all great people. I love Chris Eubank – behind all the bollocks is a really nice guy. Chris once paid for my room during a trip to South Africa. I thought that was such a nice, classy gesture. I made up for it in champagne when I went to see him in Brighton though! I have got wonderful stories involving Lloyd Honeyghan in Las Vegas and I have had many amazing nights with the great press guys; those men who have seen me grow up and make the transition from young fighter to friend and colleague: Jeff Powell, Colin Hart, John Rawling, Bob Mee – you name them.

I also feel honoured to have witnessed some of the greatest warriors and most incredible nights in boxing history. Who knows if a fight like Barrera-Morales will ever happen again? The same goes for Gatti-Ruelas, Riddick Bowe and Evander Holyfield's three-fight series and great occasions like Lewis-Tyson. I feel privileged to have been there to witness them all at first hand.

To be part of this family; this band of brothers we call boxers, is an honour. I love them all – from the Peter Buckleys of this world, the man whose 256 defeats is the most of any pro fighter in British boxing history; those fighters who go and ply their trade for a few hundred quid as the journeymen; right up to the world champions. I have loved and respected almost all the boxers I have covered during my Sky career. I regard them as brothers. There's something different about us that makes us fighting men and when we're together it's the best family in the world. It doesn't matter if you fought each other, even almost killed each other, generally you all love each other.

It's an unbelievable brotherhood and most of us would go out of our way to help a fellow fighter, but there are always a few exceptions. I can honestly say that there have only been two fighters I have genuinely disliked covering over the whole period I have been with Sky: Mike Tyson, for reasons I have already mentioned; and Naseem Hamed, because I thought he took brash confidence to the lengths of disrespect.

I remember first meeting Hamed when he was a teenager. His trainer, Brendan Ingle, had brought him out to Atlantic City for the George Foreman-Gerry Cooney fight as he was regarded even then as a tremendous prospect and I think Brendan wanted to give him a taste of what could be in store. This was in January 1990 when Hamed was only fifteen and I was World Cruiserweight Champion. I can still remember him coming up to me and basically asking: 'Yeah, so who are you mister?' I just wanted to say, 'I'm the Champion of the World son.' So me and Naseem didn't get off on a good footing. I just felt he had no respect.

He came unstuck when he fought Marco Antonio Barrera. What I hated about the Barrera fight was the way Hamed approached it, again showing no respect. Barrera was a typically tough, honest to goodness, Mexican fighter. You got no bullshit, no added frills and spills, just a straightforward 'I'm here to fight' attitude from Barrera. Hamed tried to intimidate Barrera on fight night by doing his old trick of bringing half of Sheffield into the ring with him. He had already kept Barrera waiting while sorting an apparent issue with one of his gloves and was now hoping to intimidate his opponent by crowding out the ring. All the time I was sitting there thinking, 'why don't you just fight him?'

Since Muhammad Ali retired, I have generally disliked anyone who has tried to copy the sense of arrogance that Ali carried off with such humour and style. There's only one time I've enjoyed it and that was with Chris Eubank, because Chris did it with his tongue so firmly in his cheek I thought it was fantastic. Naseem Hamed never made me feel that way. If ever I've wanted to smash someone in the mouth when Darkey was interviewing them, it was him. He would always seem to have a go at Darkey at ringside. He never showed Ian any respect. On one occasion I was virtually prepared to lose my job over him. He had been so arrogant with Ian that I was sitting alongside him thinking that if he said just one disrespectful thing to me that I was going to forget my professionalism and just smack him in the mouth. I swear to God, if he had crossed the line that night I would have knocked him clean out and waved goodbye to my broadcasting career!

Ironically, that fate did befall a friend of mine when covering a Hamed fight for German television. Ralf Rocchigiani had been a fellow World Cruiserweight Champion, although the two of us never met in the ring. He was summarising the Naseem Hamed-Kevin Kelley fight in Madison Square Garden for German TV. It was a terrific scrap with both fighters getting knocked down. I was covering the bout for Sky and Ralf was sitting just along from us when Kelley knocked Hamed to the canvas. Quick as a flash Ralf leapt to his feet and shouted, live on German television, the German equivalent of 'Go on son! Knock the fucker out!' It was his last broadcast for that channel!

I can't deny that Naseem Hamed had bags of talent in the ring. It was simply his lack of respect both to his opponents and others connected with the sport that led me to feel so negatively about him for his entire career.

It was on the trip to cover the Hamed-Kelley fight that I managed to embarrass myself in front of a crowd of music lovers at a famous New York jazz club.

Darkey and I had met a couple of pals who invited us to join them to watch the legendary Dizzy Gillespie All-Star Band perform at the Blue Note. The red wine was soon flowing freely and we were having a great night. The music was amazing and I found myself really getting into it. After a few more wines and several vodka tonics I was feeling seriously musical so when the trumpeter came to the microphone and asked if anyone in the audience wanted to get up on stage and play, I felt I couldn't let the opportunity pass. I was caught up in the moment – maybe caught up in the alcohol might be nearer the mark – but for some reason I thought that I could just get up and play and maybe do something great musically.

As soon as I put my hand up to volunteer, I could see Darkey and the guys we were with staring at me as if to ask 'do you know what you're doing?' but I stood up and made my way to the stage fully convinced that if you believed in it enough you could play. It was my old attitude coming out – if you believe in yourself enough you can make it happen. So it was that I joined the band on stage, the trumpeter put a new mouthpiece in for me, gave me a big introduction then moved away leaving me with the microphone to myself. I stepped forward, took a deep breath and blew. There was barely any audible response at all. Reality was slowly dawning on me but I gave it another go. There was the same terrible, pitiful outcome. In England people would have found the whole situation funny. They would have laughed at me and maybe thought, 'well at least he was brave enough to have a go.' Not in the Blue Note Jazz Club. I had the trumpet snatched back from me and had to make the long walk of shame back to my table with every face in the room glaring at me. As I reached my seat Darkey said simply, 'I think we had better go.'

I learned a valuable lesson. The Blue Note Jazz Club is not a good place to take the piss. At least I can say that I have been up on stage with the Dizzy Gillespie All-Star Band. I would be able to say that I played with them too if only I had managed to make any kind of noise!

I may regard Sky TV as being something of a family but, without doubt, my closest family in boxing are the journalists. The thing I love more than anything is great writing and literature – right from the days when Tommy Gardiner introduced me to his old boxing books and ignited my literary fire. I had no education but I love words – even though I can't spell them – so I have always tended to love writers and literary people. I've got a fascination with them the same way as writers seem to have a fascination with fighters.

Working with Sky, I cross the boundaries between the worlds of boxing, broadcasting and reporting. I tend to spend most of my time away in the company of 'the journos'. Over the years, guys such as Colin Hart, Paul Hayward, Jeff Powell, Sri Sen, Kevin Garside, Walter Bartleman, Harry Mullan and John Rawling, for whom I was best man at his wedding, and many more have been, more than anybody, my boxing family. In America I have been proud to befriend such legendary boxing writers as Mike Marley and the late Bert Randolph Sugar among many others. I've got stories I could tell involving each and every one of these fabulous people. There are many great sports, but for a truly great sports writer there is only one and that's boxing. We, the fighters, give the writer everything. We give them our souls – we live, we die. The other sports are just that – sports. Boxing is life and death.

In Annfield Plain we fell inside the catchment area of the *Newcastle Evening Chronicle*, the *Newcastle Journal*, the *Northern Echo* and the *Stanley News*. When you get into any sport as a young lad, you obviously want to be in the paper and I was no different. Even back then I held sports journalists in high esteem as they seemed to hold my future in their hands. Their pen could make me. I remember meeting Jeff Brown from the *Journal* who now presents the BBC Look North programme. There were other good writers too. In particular, there was John Gibson.

John is someone I regard as a truly great writer and he has since become my greatest friend. He is boxing and football correspondent for the *Chronicle* and a man who seems to have been named North East Sports Writer of the Year about fifty-five times!

It is my belief that every great fighter is connected to a great writer and every great writer has a favourite fighter. It's a wonderful coming together of personalities and has been true throughout the ages. It was certainly the case with me and Gibbo up here in the North East. I would live my life through how Gibbo wrote about my career from when I was a promising amateur kid of about fifteen. I was trying to get to speak to him in those days because he was, and still is, the man to talk to in North East boxing if you wanted to have your achievements reported. From the start I thought he was a smashing bloke, a grey-haired, hard-drinking lunatic, which was right up my street. That was Errol Flynn-style living to me. John was always lovely to me when I was young and I really appreciated it. We've been the best of friends ever since. We have been having lunch together regularly for over thirty years since the days when he would meet me at the back of the *Chronicle* offices before he'd chain smoke his way through ten fags over dinner, which I hated. I'm pleased to say he has now managed to quit.

Later, Gibbo would often live through me. He shared my glory nights in the ring and captured those occasions brilliantly in prose. He has also had opportunities opened up to him simply through being my friend. He has been able to meet and write about such legends as Mike Tyson and current champions like Carl Froch thanks to my friendship with those fighters.

Gibbo is one of life's wild men, but he's also one of life's steady men and that's why we get on so well. I'm the same. He's got a side to him which is a little bit crazy and has caused him to go out and do great things. Like me he is driven by a wish to have adventures and it's led him to attend Olympic Games and World Cups all over the planet and chat with the likes of Diego Maradona and Pele among many others. He's something of a legend at Newcastle United, was best man at Malcolm MacDonald's wedding, and I really looked up to him as a kid.

We had a link very early on when my name started appearing in his columns. It would just say 'Glenn McCrory won on points' as one of about fifteen results in the amateur boxing reports, but it was a start. It soon moved to 'Glenn McCrory and Billy Hardy have won Junior ABA titles', 'Glenn McCrory and Billy Hardy are in the Young England squad', 'Glenn McCrory and Billy Hardy have turned professional' and so on. I was a promising young fighter on the way up and I would occasionally have the Chief Sports Writer ring me. As a kid that was monumental! When you're sixteen or seventeen and a top sports writer like John Gibson wants to talk to you, it makes you feel fantastic.

Over the years we've grown from that early professional relationship, in which I was trying to get his attention, to his being with me throughout my career. He was the only member of the press I would allow in my dressing room for my title fights. He was like family by then, and he's become my best friend.

He is definitely an enigma though. He is a top journalist – in my opinion the greatest sports writer that ever has, or will, come out of these parts – but he's one of those one in a million characters who doesn't have a mobile phone! How he conducts his business as a journalist in the twenty-first century without one is beyond me. He is also somebody who can hold his own in any company. I could take him down to Stanley Working Men's Club and he would swear and curse worse than anyone in there. I could then take him to meet the Duchess of Northumberland and he'd be the best-behaved person around. He's like me in that respect – we can control ourselves on whatever level is necessary. We can be as mad as can be or as good as gold. We've always looked after each other and have travelled together to some of the most incredible places on earth to enjoy some of the greatest laughs you can imagine.

This book was originally planned over ten years ago. I wanted Gibbo to work with me as my ghostwriter. John has ghostwritten over twenty books in his career and with him having spent so much time around me we thought it would be straightforward. We headed to Casablanca in order to get away from it all and begin work on my life story. We ended up in Sam's bar, enjoyed a week of complete mayhem and came home with about six hours of drunken, unintelligible, incoherent tapes. We later went to Paris, Shanghai, New York, Las Vegas, you name it – and we never managed to write a single solitary word! We did, however, live through a great many more stories.

# 19

'Travelling with Glenn for twenty years has been like careering
around on a perpetual ghost train at a funfair. At every turn you
bump into something that's half nightmare, half crazy-comedy.
An unmissable ride.'
Bob Mee, Boxing historian, analyst and author

In November 2001 I travelled to San Francisco to cover
the Floyd Mayweather-Jesus Chavez fight. One of the
great things about my job is that I get to cover some great
fights in some legendary boxing locations such as Las
Vegas and New York. But I have also had the chance to
visit other fabulous places like San Francisco and Fresno
in California and Grand Rapids in Michigan courtesy of
Floyd Mayweather. Back in about 2000, unbelievable as
it may seem now, Floyd Mayweather was struggling to
get fights in Vegas and the like as he wasn't deemed exciting enough to be a big enough draw. San Francisco is a
wonderful city with its spectacular hills, famous trams and

Alcatraz, but it hasn't been known as a fight town for quite some time. I was pretty excited to get the chance to visit and having arrived I arranged to meet up with my friend Cesar Aceituno, from Los Angeles, who was in town for the fight with a pal.

I've got friends from all over the world in all walks of life. The lifestyle I've led means that I've always been surrounded by tough guys; I know the best and worst of society. Cesar was a Mexican from California and had been a former member of the notorious Vineland Gang in west LA, where life is often not worth a dime. Cesar and his brother Fernando had both turned their lives around and were real bad boys made good. Cesar and I got on like a house on fire and he had been over to England to stay with me. On this particular night in San Francisco we went for a meal together and we were joined by a friend of his friend, a local girl called Miranda, who had come to show us a little bit of the city.

Miranda and I hit it off pretty well. She seemed very friendly and told me how she would love to travel and that she would love to be in television one day, so we talked about the sort of things I was doing, which included an upcoming trip to Rio to shoot a pilot for a TV documentary I was planning about great party cities.

She kept in touch after I returned home and after several phone calls she asked if she could come to Rio with me to work on the pilot project. I agreed and she ended up coming over to England and staying with me for a little while before we set off for Rio and had a really good time. Sadly, nothing came of the documentary idea but

Miranda had enjoyed herself working as a would-be presenter and we had a fun trip.

Soon after that we officially became an item, which was difficult at first because of the distance, but she quickly came over to join me in England and our relationship could begin properly. At times it was great fun but at others it was very difficult. I was still struggling massively with the loss of my brother, the break up of my marriage and not living with my kids all the time any more. It was around this time that I had been diagnosed as suffering from depression and, although I have always tried to keep myself upbeat and see my glass as being half full, there were times back then when it seemed like I was walking in the clouds, not really dealing with life down on planet earth. My relationship with Miranda was growing while all this was going on and as a result we went through extremes of really good times and very bleak periods with many arguments. Miranda was adapting to life in a new country, thousands of miles from home. She was trying to find her way in life, hoping to forge a new career and explore what her new life had to offer, but this was at a time when I probably needed a bit more steady support and, looking back, I suppose we were just seeing things from different angles. It was definitely one of those relationships that was either good or bad. When it was good it was very good and when it was bad it was awful.

My first marriage had been quite traumatic because Mandy had not wanted me to box in the first place. I had signed bad deals with managers, was struggling for money and felt that I was not being handled properly. Then, when I got home, I felt I had little support there and it caused terrible arguments. It had been very volatile at times and I'm sure that must have left scars. I think by the time Miranda came along I was looking for something settled and somebody to love me. In that I don't believe I'm different from anybody else. We're surely all looking to be loved and cared for; we're all hoping to find the right partner, have kids and be part of a loving family. Everybody wants that don't they? Miranda was also someone who would enthuse about many of my ideas and push for me to do stuff whereas Mandy hadn't, so it felt like I was finally getting the support I had craved. Despite the nature of our relationship we tried to make things work. We got married at Bothal Castle in Northumberland and rented a house nearby.

It was a hasty decision. Life always has its ups and downs and it certainly did with Miranda and me. As well as the fact that we were ultimately looking for different things, I was also very insecure because I found it very hard to trust anybody and would go into relationships wondering how long it would take for me to get hurt. That's not a great way to begin a new relationship and I found that because I was waiting for it to happen it often did, as I was effectively looking for it.

I had been hit very hard in regard to maintenance payments after my first marriage. I felt that Mandy had taken me to the cleaners. I was scared that it could happen again if marriage to Miranda didn't work out, but the self-destructive part of me almost pushed me into tempting fate. It felt as though I wanted to put myself in a situation where I could end up being hurt, just to prove that I was right.

I accept that at times I must have been very difficult to live with. The marriage was probably doomed from the start. Needless to say I think we both contributed rights and wrongs to the situation and there is nothing to be gained from going into details. Along the way we had a lovely, gorgeous little girl called Maya but the marriage crumbled shortly after. Then the thing that I thought was going to happen happened. I was taken straight to court for huge maintenance payments and the divorce was finalised in 2011. In recent times there has been a quite unsavoury court case which I do not wish to relive here, but ultimately Maya has been a really positive outcome of our turbulent relationship for which I am truly thankful.

In 2014 there was to be another major upheaval in my personal life when Miranda returned to live in America with Maya. The decision came out of the blue as Miranda had never mentioned it before coming to ask me to sign Maya's passport and tell me tearfully that she had no family in England and wanted to go home. From the initial conversation to their leaving the UK took a matter of weeks around the Easter holidays. Naturally I am upset to not be able to spend time with my little girl on a regular basis, but we talk via Skype and she has loved showing me her new home.

To be honest I would have been more upset if she had moved to a busy and potentially dangerous city, but they have moved to a lovely small town in California's wine district, not far north of San Francisco. It should prove to be a wonderful place to live and I'm sure she will love growing up in such beautiful surroundings. I want what's best for all my children and I am happy for Maya to have all the benefits of her new home. I also look forward to making a fuss of her whenever she comes to visit.

# 20

'Man, Glenn left a trail of carnage and madness.
It was like the Wild West!'
Len Trusty, actor and friend

I'm an ideas man. That's my forte. I love being creative and like to think of myself as being artistic, which is something I get from my mother who writes poetry and songs. With my constant need to be active I am forever coming up with new plans and schemes, which, as a dreamer, I then go out and try to make happen.

So it was that John Gibson and I often found ourselves discussing potential ways we could work together creatively after my boxing career was over. One that kept coming back was the desire to make TV programmes. I've always loved the idea of creating drama and telling stories and really fancied setting up my own production company. I had experience of working in television and with John's expertise as a writer we figured we would make a great team. It helps that almost every time I see Gibbo we come up with a new idea. We must have had hundreds.

I remember going to meet John for lunch one day and taking Cesar Aceituno along. After lunch we were chatting about boxing when I remembered having seen pictures of John with Sonny Liston, the 1960s Heavyweight Champion. I asked him about his memories of Sonny and he started telling stories of how he had interviewed Liston in Las Vegas and later witnessed him slap his wife in the hotel foyer, plus the time Sonny had ridden a white horse through the streets of Newcastle. I asked what he thought of Liston and John reckoned he used to be the meanest man on the planet.

I reminded John that I had spent time with and around Mike Tyson at the time he was destroying everybody and asked whether he genuinely thought Sonny was meaner than Mike. He said he did and I disagreed. After a while I stopped and said, 'You know what – wouldn't that be a great show?' At this Cesar jumped in. 'That would be fantastic! It's amazing! You're two friends from Newcastle. He's been with Liston and you've been with Tyson. How many friends have spent time with those two? It's unbelievable!' Maybe the enthusiasm of a third party was what we needed to hear. I immediately got in touch with Graeme Thompson, then boss of Tyne-Tees Television, to pitch our idea. Back then Tyne-Tees was great. It was in the days when regional television was still being made and I can recall going to record a piece for a sports show and passing Jools Holland in the corridor as they were busy filming *The Tube* in another studio.

I put the idea to Graeme and he loved it. He said he would try and get us a budget, which he duly did. It was a fairly small sum but it was enough to get us to Las Vegas. I pulled in some of the people I worked with at Sky, including director Mike Allen, who has worked with me since 1989.

The trip to Vegas didn't go entirely according to plan. John recalled having met Sonny Liston at the Thunderbird Hotel and that it had been the place to be in Las Vegas back in the sixties. As well as being Liston's training camp for several of his big fights it had also played host to many other famous people, including President Kennedy and many of the great entertainers of the time. I thought it would link nicely to the programme we were making if we were to stay at the same hotel that Liston had used, so we booked our rooms and turned up expecting something special.

We arrived in the middle of the night and, to be quite frank, a brothel would have looked better. It was an absolute hole. John entered his room and almost melted. The temperature was 110 degrees and not only was there no air conditioning, there wasn't even a ceiling fan. The bath had no plug and was chipped to bits. John came storming out stating, 'This is not the Thunderbird Hotel!' I told him it was. John was adamant, insisting, 'Glenn – there is no way in the fucking world JFK stayed here. Sonny Liston didn't stay here. Frank Sinatra and Dean Martin did not stay here. It's a shithole!'

We had been travelling all day and it was now the early hours so I said we should just stay the night and sort out somewhere else in the morning. I clearly hadn't grasped the full extent of John's feelings because his response is un-printable! The gist of it was that there was no way he was going to sleep in a room in that heat, with no bath and then go and do some filming in the morning. We decided to leave. We managed to find another hotel which was absolutely brilliant, although the person tasked with find-ing our new accommodation had also arranged to book himself into the penthouse suite while the rest of us all had to share standard rooms, the crafty sod!

We put together a half-hour documentary called *The Meanest Men on the Planet* for a budget of something like fifteen grand. The show was broadcast on Tyne-Tees in August 2003 and it won a TV award from Northern Film and Media. One programme made, one award won. We didn't mess around!

The award gave me a little bit of money to enable me to make another documentary. Next time around I decided I was going to produce and direct it myself. Now I knew nothing about producing or directing, but it's just the way I am that I have to give these things a go. You've got to get out there and try.

The second show came about in extraordinary circum-stances following a chance meeting in Memphis where I was covering the Lennox Lewis-Mike Tyson showdown in June 2002. That trip was one of the more memorable of the hundreds I have made during my career. Mem-phis itself was incredible. I did the Elvis tour and walked along the famous Beale Street. I'm sure it is busy most of the time, but on the weekend of one of the biggest sporting occasions in years it was unbelievable. The entire street was jam-packed with people literally arm to arm the whole way.

I had travelled with a guy called Chris Payne. I've known Chris since around the time I fought Lennox Lewis and he's become a great friend. He runs his own building company and is a huge boxing fan, often attending major fights all over the world. Chris is the only guy in my life who has ever really paid for me to go places and do things. I've looked after so many people in my time, whether I could afford to or not, but Chris is the only one that has ever asked me if I wanted anything, or has simply told me, 'You need a holiday – I'm taking you away.' A great guy.

Chris and I were enjoying what Memphis had to offer when we bumped into a couple of Scottish guys, one of whom was a singer called Raymond Blondell, the other his manager, Jim. We got on well and they invited us to their hotel where they were working with Jerry Lee Lewis. I couldn't refuse that offer as Jerry Lee Lewis is a hero of mine. Not only do I love his music, but he was another wild man in the mould of Harry Greb and Errol Flynn. All my heroes seem to be wild men – they are my brothers! Chris and I went along and not only were we introduced to 'The Killer' but we spent time with him in his dressing room and even ended up on stage with him at one point. I remember the comedian Frank Skinner being sat in the second row and I'm pretty sure at least one or the other of Ant and Dec was there as well. They were over there for Lewis-Tyson and were taking the opportunity to watch a rock 'n' roll legend while they had the chance.

After Jerry's show I ended up back in his dressing room. While I was there I asked him where he had enjoyed his favourite ever performance. To be honest, I already knew the answer because I'd read it in his autobiography. In that he had said quite clearly that it was at Newcastle City Hall in 1962. When he confirmed this in his dressing room, I told him that Newcastle was where I was from and asked if he would ever come back to play the venue again. He told me he'd love to and we left it at that. I swapped numbers with Jim and Raymond and went to cover the fight.

I commentated on Lewis knocking out Tyson to really bring the curtain down on the end of an era. After a night out enjoying some great Memphis music, Darkey and I set off for home. We flew to Chicago to be greeted by terrible stormy weather. We were scheduled to travel with British Airways – Sky always look after us and use either BA or Virgin Atlantic. I would like to say here and now that both those airlines have been wonderful to me and I love all who are connected with them. I would also like to add that I will happily take any upgrades they may have available at any time in the future!

Having checked in at Chicago, there was an announcement that all scheduled flights from that airport had been cancelled because of the weather. I really didn't fancy spending another night away; it had been a tiring trip. One of the things I have become great at over the years is knowing how to blag. I have an ability to get people to look after me, mainly by just being nice to them. My Granddad Joe's favourite phrase was always 'it's nice to be nice'. He was a grumpy old fella mind you, but he was always saying 'it's nice to be nice' for some reason! I know that if people are nasty then others will generally not want to do anything for them so I always make a point of being extremely polite if ever I want good service.

On that particular occasion there were people queuing up at the British Airways desk to be very unpleasant to the poor staff that worked there. They were giving them a hard time and threatening to sue – the works. I decided it would be nice to be nice and asked politely what they could do to get me home. At first the girl on the desk said nothing could be done, so I gave her a bit of a sob story about wanting to go home to my new American girlfriend who I missed terribly and who was waiting for me and all that. I have been a paid actor you know! I told her that if there was anything she could do I would be very grateful. All this time Ian was standing in the background asking what I was doing and generally being a pain in the arse. My relationship with Ian is great. I love him to bits and we've had a great time over the years, but I have found that almost every time I have tried to blag something he would usually burst in and ruin it. Honestly, he was like Mr Bean the way he would come in and announce, 'Hello. My name's Ian Darke.' They would just give a look as if to say, 'we really don't care – now why don't you go away?' It might be funny, but it wouldn't help us in an upgrade situation.

Right now I was stranded in Chicago in a thunderstorm. I was very tired and just wanted to go home. I was in the middle of my nice, polite approach when Ian strolled up and said, 'Hello. I'm…' I turned and snapped, 'Ian – just for once why don't you shut up. We are not together. You're going to London – I'm going to Newcastle. All the flights are cancelled, it's a bad situation and I don't want you screwing this up. Now piss off and leave me alone!' I was really angry at him for the only time ever and he hadn't really done anything wrong, but I knew he was just about to blow it for me again. He mumbled 'okay' and went off to sulk somewhere.

A little while later I get a nod from the girl, went over and she whispered, 'You're sorted. We're going to get you home. You're going to a hotel for three hours. We'll take you there and bring you back. You will then get on the first flight to New York and we've managed to get you on Concorde from there.' I couldn't believe my ears. I was going to fly on Concorde! I then paused for a moment, swallowed hard, smiled sweetly and asked her, 'Is there any chance I can take my friend, Ian Darke?'

Ian and I were taken to the hotel where we had a wash and got changed. They then took us back to the airport, flew us to New York where we boarded Concorde and we were back in the UK in a couple of hours with the whole airline staff having been fabulous to us the whole time. It was amazing. The past couple of days had seen me meet Jerry Lee Lewis in his dressing room, be ringside to commentate on one of the biggest fights of the decade and then fly home on Concorde. What a trip!

In February 2004, I received a call from one of the Scotsmen who I met in Memphis. Jerry was in the UK and about to embark on his tour. They told me he was about to play in Gleneagles and wondered if I could come to see him. Of course I jumped at the chance and I took the opportunity to ask him again whether he would come and play Newcastle. He said he'd love to so I called Gibbo and told him, 'I think we may have a second show, John!'

Newcastle was not part of the itinerary for the tour and he was already here. I tend to fly by the seat of my pants, but when I decide to do something I either get it done myself or I manage to find someone who can do it for me, even when it seems impossible. I had about ten days to fix everything up. I got in touch with the City Hall and managed to book it at ridiculously short notice through a mixture of charm, contacts and the name Jerry Lee Lewis. I have no idea how I managed to get tickets ready and available in that time but somehow I did and on the night it was sold out. I truly believe you can do anything if you really want to.

I went with Gibbo to see Graeme Thompson at Tyne-Tees about my idea to film the build up to the concert and footage of the show itself. He just said, 'Great – do it!' I knew nothing of producing or directing, but I was determined that I was going to do both. I approached the people at Sky and managed to persuade them to provide a full outside broadcast unit, which cost a lot of money and ultimately left me out of pocket on the venture. But then, as I've mentioned before, money has never been what it's about for me. All I wanted was to be able to put 'Producer – Jerry Lee Lewis' on my CV!

We booked Jerry in at the Copthorne Hotel on the Quayside in Newcastle, which was managed by Stephen Deakin, a bit of a legend in Newcastle, who went out of his way to help us. We were all there ready to film, but we ran into something of a problem. Jerry wouldn't come out of his room. For days he was in there, living like some kind of recluse. I just wanted to get hold of him and explain that it was a different world now. Elvis was dead and he would be safe to walk around Newcastle city centre because nobody would know who he was anymore! There I was in the awkward predicament of having nothing at all on tape because the man we were there to film was holed up in his room. In the end we had to go with footage filmed in the car on the way to the venue and at the City Hall itself. It hadn't been what I had planned exactly but it worked out pretty well because the show was amazing. He came on stage, did his thing, blew everybody away and walked off with no encore whatsoever. He was a megastar and he knew it.

I finished up with the honour of having put Jerry Lee Lewis on at the City Hall and being the producer/director of a half-hour documentary and concert film called *Great Balls of Fire, Pet* which was broadcast in June 2004. Tyne-Tees loved the show as much as they had *The Meanest Men on the Planet* and wanted to know what I had lined up next. That gave me and Gibbo the green light to begin work on project number three. I tend to be the ideas man and John's role is to help open up my imagination. He helps me think creatively.

With the television documentaries coming along I had decided to set up my own production company, which I called No Place Films in honour of the village of No Place near Stanley. I am friendly with Tom Harvey, who was the boss of Northern Film and Media, and he arranged for me to attend a day's event in which you could pitch programme ideas to a TV executive. That's when I put forward my idea for *Looking for a Legend*.

Having done some work on Sonny Liston for *The Meanest Men on the Planet*, I had started thinking about other great sportsmen who could have been legendary but for some reason or other things didn't quite work out that way. I suppose I always had a feeling that I never received the credit I deserved for being the only North East boxer to ever win a world title because I hadn't had the benefit of working with someone like Frank Warren. I figured that if I hadn't got the glory that I felt I should then there must be many others in the same boat. Who else didn't have the backing, or was around at the wrong time and missed out on the status they should have enjoyed?

The guys running the course thought the idea was a dream. I came up with all sorts of suggestions for legends that didn't get their just desserts for one reason or another. The one that most interested Tyne-Tees was Hughie Gallacher, one of the greatest centre forwards of all time, scoring over four hundred goals during his career. He loved the drink and had something of a hard life after his playing days were over, culminating in his suicide at the age of fifty-four.

We stuck with the idea of calling the programme *Looking for a Legend* and hoped it would be the start of a series. I produced and directed again while John helped with the script. Both Alan Shearer and Sir Bobby Robson were involved and I felt we ended up with a terrific show.

In all honesty I am really proud of all three shows that I made. I am sure that if people were to see them again now they would be knocked out by the standard of them all. The sporting documentaries were fascinating and when you take one of the kings of rock 'n' roll and you bring him to Newcastle to film him preparing and performing, it's just incredible.

I would love to have done more but the whole process was changing. I was in the wrong place at the wrong time. Regional programming, whereby a local independent TV company like Tyne-Tees could make their own shows to be broadcast in their own region, was coming to an end. These days everything is planned nationally. If John and I had been there ten years earlier we would probably have been given free rein to make many other programmes. Unfortunately it was not to be, although I have so many great ideas just waiting to be made and continue to have more on a regular basis. Maybe a TV executive reading this might like to get in touch because I'm always available for negotiations!

I was also a whisker away from having a script of mine turned into a major Hollywood movie. I had written a screenplay about a group of Geordies travelling to Las Vegas for a stag do on the weekend of the Lennox Lewis and Evander Holyfield fight, which I called *In For A Penny*. I had the promise of financial backing from a group in London and travelled to Los Angeles to discuss details with no less than Warner Brothers who were keen to proceed. We had got to the stage of having top actors hired and studio time booked when the financers pulled out, leaving me around £50,000 down. The idea was shelved and I never heard from them again. I was gutted at the time, but imagine how I felt a few years later when *The Hangover* appeared with a story not too dissimilar to mine. It became a box office smash. Timing is everything!

When it comes to creating shows, plays, films or whatever, my number one desire is that I get to tell David's story one day. I have come very close to doing so on several occasions in the past. My brother helped to make me, although there are times when I'm not sure how much credit he would like to take for that. I have always wanted to repay him by telling the world how inspirational he had been.

The idea to make a movie originally started thanks to Jeff Powell, the sports writer from the *Daily Mail*. Jeff is a great friend who I've known for a long time. I was telling him one day about a movie I wanted to make based on the life of one of my heroes, the 1920s Middleweight Champion, Harry Greb. It was the book *Give Him to the Angels* by James R Fair which had sparked my initial interest in boxing literature all those years before and I felt that the life of the incredible fighter it had portrayed was possibly the greatest story never told. I had long wanted to break into the world of film making and Jeff informed me that he had a friend who was one of the top guys in Warner Brothers' London offices so he would see if he could arrange for me to meet him.

I drew up a one-page synopsis and went with Jeff to the St James' Club in London to meet his friend, Julian Senior. Julian had worked with Marlon Brando as an executive producer on *Apocalypse Now*, so we're talking about a serious industry figure here.

It went well and I was invited to pitch my idea back in the Warner Brothers office itself. I explained why I wanted to make the movie and what a great story it would be when Julian stunned me by saying he thought it sounded fine, but that he was more interested in my story. He told me he was a bit of a fan and knew things about my life which he thought would make a great film. Now I had never spoken to the guy before and I don't know exactly what he knew about me but I found myself travelling home on the train somewhat blown away.

Being honest, my initial reaction was that I felt that I may have just been fobbed off, but then I started to wonder what my story really was. By the time I arrived home I had realised that my story was that of Carrying David. I had no idea as to what form that story might take exactly, but I knew that was the pivotal factor in my life – the greatest thing I ever did was to carry my handicapped brother. My ultimate highs and lows and my most extreme feelings of both joy and sadness were all centred on my brother. God had given me something very special. To begin with he had given me a talent which enabled me to achieve boxing success at the highest level, but he had also given me an insight into somebody who was handicapped – a chance to be aware of those things we would normally take for granted. He gave me David to make me realise I was nothing really. Who was really special – him or me? As far as I was concerned there was only one answer – and it wasn't me.

Shortly after returning home I spoke to a guy called Arthur McKenzie, a great writer from the North East. Arthur was keen on doing some writing with me and he suggested trying to make the Carrying David story into a play. We managed to hire Dave Whitaker to play David. Dave was an excellent actor who has appeared on Broadway in *The Pitmen Painters*. To be honest, Dave was a little too good at times. He did a fantastic job of playing my brother, but it was possibly too much. It was all still very raw at that stage and was almost too painful to watch at times.

We were offered the chance to perform the play at the newly opened Gala Theatre in Durham, but I will admit that I had already begun to feel a little unhappy while work was developing as to how I was being portrayed, in particular in terms of my relationship with David. Arthur was using artistic licence to write the play as he thought it would work best and was looking at the difference between the rich and famous boxer and his handicapped brother. In the play I had a Rolex watch and was coming across as arrogant and uncaring. My character was behaving as though he was focused solely on himself and his selfish behaviour marked him out as the bad boy. The truth is that David and I loved each other and I would have gladly swapped places with him at any stage. This did not sit well with me, but there was to be one specific incident which was to scupper the whole venture.

Arthur had been very excited when we secured the services of director Teddy Kendal from the Paul McCartney Theatre in Liverpool. It was seemingly quite a coup and everybody had high hopes. Unfortunately, I was unable to be there for the final round of auditions so my sister Kelly went along in my place to cast her eye over proceedings. At one point she mentioned to Teddy that David's favourite song had been 'Wind Beneath My Wings' to which his response had been to look down his nose and say 'commercial garbage'.

That evening, Kelly called to tell me how the day had gone. She's a lovely girl and hates to make a fuss about anything but that incident had upset her and so she told me what had been said. Maybe the whole thing was just too close and raw, but I hadn't felt particularly comfortable with how things were going for a while so when Kelly told me that I decided there and then to pull the plug. It had cost a lot of money – I'd invested ten grand in it personally, but it was proving too painful and it just wasn't the right time, or the right people. At the end of the day I don't care what anybody else thinks of that song, the fact is that it was David's favourite and that's that. I still struggle with it if I hear it today. 'I can fly higher than an eagle, but you are the wind beneath my wings.' To me that summed up David's and my entire relationship – each of us taking it in turns to be the wind beneath the other's wings as we soared in our own different ways. For the director to make such a dismissive comment to my sister gave me an insight into what he really thought about the play. He was only interested in making a piece of theatre and not telling the story of my brother. I liked both Dave Whitaker and Arthur McKenzie – they seemed like really nice people – but there was no way I could let it continue if it wasn't going to do justice to David.

A while later I found myself at the Cannes Film Festival. I had been invited to go along to talk to a couple of people at around the time I was making the documentaries and looking to set up my production company. Who in their right mind would turn down an invitation to attend the Cannes Film Festival? While I was out there I was introduced to a guy called Ed Atkinson. Ed was involved in the financial side of the film industry and he told me that he had heard about the story of my relationship with David and wanted to know if there was a possible film in it. That was getting on for ten years ago and we're still just talking about it. Several people have looked at the idea: at one point the actor Tom Hardy was sounded out about playing me and he went as far as to going into training with the late Dean Powell, who worked as a trainer for Frank Warren at the time. Nothing came of that; but I believe it was for a reason. The timing hasn't been right as yet but I am convinced that the story will be told and will become a film, a musical and a stage play; starting with Ed Waugh's one-man play. That will be my greatest achievement. People know my story – I have been in the public eye and lived my life with my heart on my sleeve. My successes and failures, my highs and my lows, they are all there to be seen; but David's story remains untold and I am determined to put that right.

# 21

'I have known Glenn for many years and what an amazing character he is. The whole Calzaghe family have loved to be in his company and I am proud to know him.'
Enzo Calzaghe, boxing trainer

Although I have experienced some troubled times, I would be lying if I was to suggest that I didn't have some fun times along the way. I remember one particularly riotous trip to Rio with one of my greatest friends, Len Trusty, who I had met when we had both starred in the ill-fated *Rumble* back in the nineties.

I was in the middle of a bleak period and my attitude at such times tends to be to try to escape by doing the daftest, most fun thing I can think of. On this occasion I called Len and asked him if he'd like to fly to Rio for a week-long party.

The two of us were accompanied by a pal of ours called Tony, a music producer from the Caribbean. I was asleep on the plane when one of the stewardesses came by. I don't know what happened exactly but somehow a tray fell off her trolley and landed on my head, cutting it quite badly. That was a great start to our trip, with me arriving in Rio with a bleeding head and the aircrew running around in a panic, filling in forms and making sure I was put in a wheelchair until I was checked out as they needed to go through their health and safety procedures seeing as one of their staff had just injured a passenger! I felt terrible when that happened, having my head cut open at the end of a fourteen-hour flight.

The next thing I knew, Tony was attempting to get through passport control when one of the officers started waving his arms and the police dashed in, grabbed him and slapped the handcuffs on! To this day I'm not entirely sure what the story was, but Len and I pieced together that whichever passport he was travelling on he was not supposed to be there. He wasn't arrested as such but they carted him off and he was put straight on a plane home. That was the last Len and I saw of him that trip!

After a rather incident-packed start to our holiday, we had a great time. We stayed in a fabulous apartment and had loads of fun. Sadly, we had little in the way of money – I had to phone home more than once when my credit card was declined. There was one night when Len and I were out, watching parties and girls having fun in one of the greatest cities in the world, and neither of us had a single penny between us. Talk about frustration! Somehow though the two of us still managed to have the most fun you could imagine on that trip. We saw the Brazilian Cup Final in the Maracana Stadium and, with me being single, I fell in love with virtually every thong I saw on Ipanema beach!

Of course, things around me tend to get rather chaotic and I inadvertently caused one of the biggest fights you have ever seen in the legendary Help nightclub on Copacabana Beach. I had spent the previous evening there in the company of one girl and now I was back chatting with another young lady I had met earlier that day. Unfortunately the previous night's acquaintance was in the nightclub again and she came over to cause a bit of hassle when she saw me with someone else. I was amazed, but she clearly seemed to think she had some sort of say in the matter because she started kicking up a stink. She turned to the girl I was with and said something to her in Portuguese. By this stage I was starting to feel rather protective towards my current companion, she was being dragged into this unpleasantness through no fault of her own. I needn't have worried though because, all of a sudden, she threw a right hook and absolutely flattened the girl who had clearly just insulted her! I'd never seen anything like it. The next thing I know another girl was taking a swing at mine and within seconds pretty much everyone in the place seemed to just stand up and whack the person next to them! It was like a scene from a 1920s silent cowboy movie.

Looking back it was one of the funniest things I have ever seen, but at the time it seemed pretty hairy. The whole nightclub had just erupted in a mass brawl so I grabbed the girl I was with, kicked open the fire doors and we ran for it.

Hours later I was back in the apartment when Len came through the door. Len is from a Jamaican family but he is a Londoner who lives in Kent and doesn't sound Jamaican at all. On this occasion however he put on the strongest Jamaican accent you can imagine and, rather than go into details about what happened after I left, said simply, 'Toootal caarnage!' He just laughed and laughed.

Len is great. I was best man at his wedding and I am godfather to his son, Tate. I often see him when I'm down in London and we've been all over together: New York, Paris, Amsterdam and LA, as well as Rio. He's a huge fight fan and has often accompanied me on trips to watch some of the biggest bouts around the world.

I'm often too much for people – whether that is in terms of my personal relationships or simply when out with friends. Len is one of those characters who just takes a step back and laughs his big laugh. He is there to pick up the pieces if they need picking up, but he tends not to get emotionally involved, which is the best way because so many have become burnt out. Len just steps back and laughs and it's probably the only way to survive me. He's the best mate I have from within my own age group and we've certainly had some pretty good times.

I began another foreign adventure soon after it was announced, in July 2005, that the Olympic Games were coming to London in 2012. Most normal people would have thought 'that's great!' and then left it to the organisers and various sports national bodies to get on with the business of doing what needed to be done, but not me. I wanted to do something special for the Olympics. I wanted to try to help Britain's boxers achieve glory.

To be frank, I was embarrassed by the state of British amateur boxing. A teenage Amir Khan had won a silver medal at the Athens Olympics in 2004, but he had been our only representative. To have only one fighter deemed capable of competing across all the various weight divisions was a disgrace. I thought there was a need to change the whole approach to amateur boxing in this country by persuading the black-tie-and-blazer brigade to recognise that we needed to take thing seriously and get professional people involved. I said my piece at the time, but rather than let it rest I decided to open up my own boxing school and gym which became a recognised boxing Centre of Excellence. I negotiated with Newcastle City Council to rent some old school premises at Newbiggin Hall in the city. I managed to sort some sponsorship from Lonsdale to get a couple of rings put up but the company who sub-let the building wanted a percentage of the rates for the whole building, not just the gym. It was madness, far too much money and ultimately unsustainable at that price, but at first the place looked a million dollars. The Amateur Boxing Association, however, weren't impressed with my regular attempts to put a spoke in their wheel and blocked my coaches from becoming involved with the national team. Nevertheless, I am nothing if not persistent and I wanted to pick up expertise from another country to see what we could learn. And there is only one country to turn to for an insight into how to do amateur boxing: Cuba.

The photographer for my wedding to Miranda was a guy called Neil Atkinson and he had spoken about wanting to do something with me professionally, so I told him I was thinking of going to Cuba to see if I could discuss some kind of relationship between their amateur boxing coaches and ours. He said he would love to come along and take a few pictures, so he was in. I also took another friend of mine, a local lawyer called Gwillam Williams.

We set off for Cuba to try to fix up a deal. I landed in the country without having told anybody over there that I was even coming, much less why. I felt that as it is virtually impossible for anyone from the UK to get in touch with the Cuban boxing authorities, then I wouldn't even bother to try. I just figured I would turn up and blag it.

On arrival I tried to locate the Cuban sporting authorities. I find that if you go through the right channels it is sometimes hard to get hold of who you were looking for because you often find that somebody cuts those channels off. I've never gone through the right channels for anything in my life – largely because I usually don't know what the right channels are!

We had taken a load of boxing gloves and gear with us, so I began asking around for the whereabouts of local boxing gyms so that we could give these items away to the kids. We found a gym in Havana and the people who ran it were lovely. Once there, I was able to enquire who the head of Cuban boxing was, who the top trainers were and where I could get hold of them. In a society like Cuba word spreads fast and clearly our visit and gifts were creating some interest, because the first person I got on my phone was Teofilio Stevenson, who suggested we met for dinner. Teofilio Stevenson is, quite simply, the greatest amateur boxer of all time. He won three Olympic Heavyweight gold medals and may well have added a fourth had the Cubans not boycotted the Los Angeles Games in 1984. We went out for a meal together and became firm friends from then until he sadly died in June 2012.

I went on to meet several other Cuban boxing legends on that trip, including Teo's fellow Olympic champions Hector Vinent and Jose Gomez. Gwillam, Neil and I had a great time over there, but we left for home having not had the chance to speak to one single person from either the Cuban government or the boxing authorities.

I realised that wasn't good enough, so I went back out a few months later. Neil couldn't come this time, so me and Gwill took Malcolm Dix and Peter Ratcliffe along, two more long-term friends and bastions of North East sport. This time we were summoned to see the sport's governing body in Havana. We sat down in the offices of some of Cuba's top boxing executives and explained that we were looking for a couple of coaches to come over and help us out. They were very nice and polite but said that although they let coaches go to fellow communist countries, they wouldn't allow them to assist western countries such as Britain. The conversation went on for a while but was getting nowhere so we moved on to more general chat. I was asked if I liked their country and naturally I replied that I did. Someone then asked me how much, so I rolled up my sleeve to reveal a large tattoo of Che Guevara on my right arm and said, 'quite a lot!' At that the head of Cuban boxing literally stood up, walked out of the room and returned with two pieces of paper and said, 'Sign here for two coaches.'

I took the two guys chosen back home with me. Sport England had indicated that they would be happy to sponsor the whole venture but when I got back they told me I had to go through the proper channels first. I explained that I actually had two Cuban Olympic coaches with me right now, but it got me nowhere. I had brought them back for the good of British amateur boxing, but I ended up having to put them up in my own house for a month and I didn't see a single penny from Sport England until years later, by which time it was largely too late.

Over the next couple of years I went back to Cuba several times and met up with Teofilio Stevenson on each occasion. I would never tell him I was coming in advance because word just seemed to go around as soon as I landed. Within hours he would be on the phone and we would go out to dinner. He'd sing, play guitar, drink loads of rum and I'd have a great night with the greatest amateur boxer of all time. I've met Ali, Holmes, Tyson, Leonard, Robinson. Here was another legend to add to the list.

Without a shadow of a doubt, however, the most memorable experience from all my visits to Cuba was when I took Gibbo with me to meet Teofilio in the hope of him being able to get an article for the *Chronicle* out of it. John has been all over the world with me but he's still a bit reluctant to travel unless everything is properly sorted. I had therefore booked tickets with Virgin Airlines and a few nights in the fantastic Saratoga Hotel.

John was a little concerned as to whether he would get what he had come for. He kept saying, 'I'd better get a story out of this.' I told him not to worry, he would get his story, but the way I like to do things is to have some fun first. He seemed to accept this for a while, but he kept on asking when we would meet Teofilio, how we could get in touch with him etc, etc. I told him, 'John – he will ring me. Whenever I get to Cuba, Teofilio rings me. He knows my number and he will want me to take him out and that's the way it's been for a couple of years.'

John still wouldn't settle. 'When's he going to ring? Am I definitely going to get a story? I want a proper sit-down interview with him.'

'John – you're not gonna get a sit down. You don't speak Spanish and his English isn't brilliant. We're just gonna go out, have some fun and you're gonna be in the presence of greatness. You will get a story, trust me.'

'That's no good for me! I need a sit down! I've sat with Maradona, Pele, Bobby Moore…'

'You're in Cuba now, John, and you don't speak Spanish, so you're not sitting with anybody.'

All of a sudden the phone rang. On the other end was Teofilio's unmistakable deep gruff voice, extending the words as he would tend to do: 'Glennnn, my friend. Come and see me now.' It was unheard of to hear from him in the morning, the usual routine was for him to call around six or seven in the evening ready for a night out. By ten he would normally be wrecked on the rum and I would have to take him home. His wife would then help him upstairs. That was how it had always gone in the past and yet now he was ringing me at breakfast time and asking to see me straight away. I told him I'd brought a mate called John with me who would like to do an article about him. He replied, 'Great, great, great. Come and see me now Glenn.' I protested that it wasn't even 9.30 in the morning yet but he was having none of it. I was to go to his house right away.

I told John we were going to Teo's house and he thought that would be great as it might improve his chances of having a proper conversation with him. He was still grumbling though. He wouldn't shut up about getting a sit down and dismissed my suggestion that instead he would get a bit of colour with the straightforward retort, 'Fuck the colour! I haven't come all this way for a bit of colour. I need a proper sit down!'

Teofilio lived in a little house on the coast. We arrived at around ten o'clock and knocked on his door. All of a sudden a big looming shadow came to the door and opened it to reveal Teofilio, this huge man, completely naked but for a small pink towel around his waist. He greeted me with a warm: 'Glennnn – come innn! My brother!' and gave me a big hug. His eyes were completely glazed and all I was thinking was, 'Oh shit. He's completely wrecked!'

I asked him if he was ok and he replied, 'Nooo. Mi mujer vamos. Mi hijo vamos. Final.' *(My wife's gone. My son's gone. For good.)*

'Why Teo?'

'No comprendo.'

'Is it because you are borracho?' *(a drunk)*

'Nooo! Me no borracho!'

This was despite it being ten in the morning; him dressed in nothing but a pink towel and quite clearly smashed!

'Well, I was just bringing mi amigo Gibbo to see you, Teo.'

'Ahh Gibbooo – mi amigooo!'

At this Teofilio gave John a huge bear hug. To this point, however, the man who wanted a 'proper chat' had not spoken one word since the front door had opened.

Teo then broke off to turn to me and say, 'Uno momento Glenn, uno momento.' Off he went upstairs before returning wearing his Cuban tracksuit and with a big bulge in his pants, which I didn't think was because he was glad to see me. I had been with him several times before and I had a nasty feeling I knew what it was.

'Are you ok Teofilio?'

'No problema Glenn. No problemmma! Come to me, come to me.'

Then he put his hand in his pants, withdrew it and brandished the item he was holding proudly, 'This is from Castro – El Comandante – he give me this gun.'

'Ohhh. Well that's... wonderful Teofilio, that's wonderful... We're gonna go now mate, we need to get back.'

'Nooo Glenn, Glenn. You not go! Come into my garden.'

There had still not been a word from John. I turned to look at him and he seemed ever so pale all of a sudden. I said, 'Come on John. It looks like we're going out the back.'

So it was that the three of us walked into Teofilio's back garden with him brandishing this silver 45 magnum in his hand which el Presidente, Fidel Castro, had, in his wisdom, given him as a present. I had seen it before and

Teofilio was my friend and a great guy, but this was a little different to previous meetings.

Nevertheless, John and I followed him into his back garden which consisted of a load of weeds and a hole in the floor which used to be a swimming pool at some point, but which had clearly not seen water in decades. Teofilio sat on a coal bunker which was no longer full of coal but instead held dozens of empty rum bottles.

I told him we had to go, even though we had only been there for about ten minutes. I informed him that we had to be somewhere else, but he was insistent that we stay. 'No no no, Glenn. You with me all day.' I explained that I hadn't got the time because I had other things to do. To be honest I didn't know what they were, but I knew I could find something! But no, he insisted that we stayed.

'Glennnn, Gibbooo. Mi amigo Glennnn.' At which point he took out his gun and stuck it in my face. I said calmly, 'Come on Teo. Let's let this one go mate. I know you're not feeling as good as you should at ten o'clock in the morning, but maybe you should just let this one go.'

'Nooo. Tu amigo Gibbo.' He turned and pointed the gun in John's face instead.

'No Teofilio. John has come a long way to see you. He's old, he's gone very white and I do believe he has just shit his pants. So why don't you just put that gun down and leave Gibbo alone please?'

At this I took his arm and moved the gun back in my direction. I had seen him mess around with his empty gun before, I knew he wasn't being vindictive, merely playing. Only this time his wife and son had just left him and he was drunk at ten o'clock in the morning. He said,

'Glennnn. Mi amigooo!' and fiddled with the gun, where-upon it made a loud clicking sound and he promptly pulled out a full cartridge, replaced it clumsily and started waving it back in our faces. John, of course, had still not uttered a single word.

At this point we both started to think we may be about to die. I tried to focus on something else by suggesting to Teofilio that we went for a bite to eat, to maybe have some lobster. This seemed to do the trick because he smiled and said, 'Yessss. Let's have lobster.' We went back inside, ordered a taxi and he put his gun back in his pants and posed for a photo with us taken by the cab driver. You can clearly see the bulge of the gun in the side of his tracksuit as Gibbo tries to smile!

We climbed into the car with his gun still in his pocket. He said he needed to stop off and see some people. John and I started to wonder whether our chances of getting killed were about to increase again. Once we arrived at the downtown taxi office in question Teofilio turned to us and stated, 'We go upstairs and see my friend.' I suggested it would be better if we just waited outside for him and he shrugged and set off up the steps. As soon as he was through the door I turned to look at John. The same John Gibson who had done nothing but bang on about getting a proper sit-down chat with Teofilio Stevenson from the minute our plane had touched the Havana runway, and yet who had still not spoken one word from the moment we arrived at his front door. He looked back at me and I said, 'Let's go!' We were off! Usain Bolt could not have caught us! We tore down the street, disappeared round the corner and jumped in a taxi. Job done – we were still alive!

On his return to the UK he wrote an article about that day in Havana and won yet another award, despite never mentioning either the gun or Teofilo being drunk – as I have said, the finest sportswriter the North East has ever produced!

Back at home, I trained three undefeated Cuban fighters for a while in addition to having brought the coaches over. I even arranged for the contemporary Cuban dance company to come to England and perform at the Theatre Royal in Newcastle. Their show went on to win an award. They came back in 2012, but I was away in Colombia at the time. My pal Richard, who works at the theatre, told me they were disappointed because they had all wanted to see me. For a while I would have seriously doubted if there was anybody in the west who had a better relationship with Cuba than I had.

After having received some positive publicity for my work with Cuban boxing, I found myself sitting in Newcastle Airport in 2008 when a small and distinguished-looking grey-haired guy came up to me and introduced himself as Dave Harrison. He congratulated me on the work I had been doing with the Cubans and went on to add that he was from Annfield Plain. Dave explained that he originated from New Kyo and that his daughter ran the New Kyo Working Mens' Club. Wherever I am in the world, someone from the North East gets my attention, but anybody from my own village is extra special.

I asked Dave where he was about to jet off to and he told me he was heading for Colombia. He ran his own Tyneside-based company called Team Savant, who supplied specialised security and protective services in hazardous areas and they had operations in Colombia. It sounded like the typical sort of thing an Annfield Plain person would get up to!

Dave returned to what I had been doing in Cuba and wondered whether I would be able to help Colombia out by doing something similar with them. There and then he invited me to fly out to Colombia at some point to look into whether I could set something up.

I've been to Mexico and Cuba and I love exciting places like that. To me they represent an adventure. I have to admit though that Colombia sounded a little too crazy to me. I had heard that it was pretty much the most dangerous place in the world. I had in my head all the stories of kidnapping and drugs and murder. I felt that Europeans who went there stood a fair chance of not coming back. Dave was adamant that this was not the case. According to him it had certainly been extremely hazardous a few years earlier, but the government over there had been fighting and winning a battle to reduce the levels of drug-related crime which had made the place so lawless. He maintained that they were now suffering from years of bad publicity because all across the world people still had the attitude I had just displayed, which is to believe that it is still an incredibly dangerous place.

He asked me again whether I would be prepared to visit and try to arrange something special in respect of their Olympic boxing team. Normally I would relish the chance of a challenge, but even at this point I was a little unsure, despite Dave's assurances that I would be perfectly safe. The thing is that it did tickle my fancy a little. It's just the kind of 'mission impossible' that has always appealed to me. It's another opportunity for an adventure, another chance for a bit of drama. Perhaps a rational person would have asked themselves, 'am I going to make some money and is it potentially dangerous?' The answers would have been 'no' and 'yes' respectively and so they wouldn't have gone. For me, however, that ticks all the boxes!

I found myself reasoning: okay – Dave says it's a wonderful place and he goes there regularly so he must know what he's talking about. Plus he's from Annfield Plain so he's bound to be right! I decided there was no harm in going to have a look so I gave him a call and he invited me to fly out and visit his company over there. In the meantime he contacted the powers that be in the Colombian sports authorities and they swiftly got in touch with me because they knew what I had done with Cuba. They made arrangements for me to fly out and meet the head of Colombian boxing, Oscar Gomez.

I flew to Bogota with Chris Payne as my travelling companion. We were scheduled to meet one of Dave's employees, a guy called John Baycroft from Tynemouth, who just happens to be the most decorated SAS soldier of all time. John turned out to be a lovely guy and the whole trip was brilliant. Bogota is an incredible city with terrific art, great restaurants and fabulous chefs. It was a world apart from my pre-conceived images of kids running about with no shoes on as guys with guns roamed the streets. It was just a perfectly normal, large capital city. Chris and I had great fun and were looked after fantastically well. They put on a boxing show especially for us, showcasing the best of Colombian amateur boxing. It is a fabulous country with some great people so I decided there and then that I would see if I could do something that would work both for them and for the North East of England.

I learned through my experiences in Cuba that if you go through the system a lot of things don't happen. If you get bogged down in red tape then eventually you hit a road block. The trouble is that everything is always linked to money. At the end of the day there is always somebody in charge of the purse strings and if they don't feel as if they are going to see some reward at the end of the process then it's not worth it for them and the whole thing grinds to a halt. For me, it has never been about the money. I'm all about the experience and exciting experiences are worth paying for. If I can do some good for people that's great, if I can help my region at the same time then that's even better. What motivates me is creating something special. Other people can ride on the bandwagon if they like, but they don't have the satisfaction of having created that particular piece of theatre. I look at things with the view that if I created it, then it is my achievement. That is all I want from these ideas and arrangements and I therefore decided to dig into my own pocket to ensure something would happen between Colombian boxing and the North East.

I spoke to David Bunce of Gateshead Council and managed to arrange a working relationship between the council and Colombian boxing. Things had changed a little since I had welcomed the Cubans over. The Glenn McCrory School of Boxing had gone by this point. A problem with grants promised by Sport England had led to a lack of funds and had left me no alternative but to close down. Instead we arranged for the Colombian team to do some training at Gateshead College and then at Birtley Amateur Boxing Club, which is a very accomplished local team.

At this point my job was effectively over and I handed the reins to Gateshead Council. As it happens, both the Colombian Olympic boxing and athletics teams trained in Newcastle ahead of the 2012 Olympic Games. I did it – I pulled it off. I may have handed over the responsibility for all the arrangements to the appropriate authorities because I had no connection with the Olympics in any way, but ultimately I feel it was me that made it happen by going out there and making the necessary connections. I hope that my efforts have benefited both the Colombian athletes and the Newcastle and Gateshead authorities in some way. At least I am able to say that I gave it a go and hopefully made a difference.

One important by-product of my involvement with Colombian boxing is that I have discovered a fabulous country. I've been to Bogota, Santa Marta and Cartagena and found them all to be wonderful places.

My experiences of Colombia have been nothing but positive. I have yet to see one single, solitary argument in all the times I have been to Bogota. I was over there with Chris Payne again in 2012. To kill time one afternoon we popped into a jeweller's shop. John Gibson has had a ring for over thirty years which I absolutely love – so much so that he has apparently left it to me in his will. Much as I want to have it, I don't really want him to die in a hurry, so I am always on the lookout for one like it. It's a gold ring with a large green stone and it just so happened that there was one very similar in this jeweller's shop called Joyeria Coscuez in downtown Bogota.

Over there they mine emeralds so they have all sorts of jewellery featuring that particular stone. The gold ring like John's, however, was priced at 7,000 US dollars! I liked it, but couldn't afford that much and was about to leave when they asked me to look at the silver one instead. It featured the largest emerald they had and was a bargain at only $3,700! I explained that not only did I not have $3,700 but that, in actual fact, I only had $200 left.

The lady in Joyeria Coscuez thought about it for a minute and announced, 'Okay – $2,700.' I decided to play along and said I would pay her $210 for it.

She phoned her husband who owned the mine and came back to offer $2,000. I replied, '$200.' She protested that I had just gone back ten dollars, but I explained that I had to because I certainly couldn't go forward ten! I was just taking the piss really. Eventually I said I would have to leave as we had been in the shop over half an hour. We were a million miles apart and just wasting each other's time.

As I was about to walk out of the door she suddenly shouted, 'I will do it for $500 for you.' As quick as a flash I turned round and said, 'Okay – deal!' before she could change her mind! Now I didn't have $500, so I had to dash off to find Chris and beg him to lend me another $300. He agreed, so I went back to buy this ring, a silver version of Gibbo's which I loved so much, especially with the emerald and my family connection to the Emerald Isle.

The shopkeeper measured my finger and sent the ring off to be re-sized and we had a nice chat in the meantime. She called me up on Google and saw pictures of me with my World Championship belt and meeting the Queen and we were having a really pleasant time when a couple of concerned looking guys came to the door, called her over and started talking in hushed Spanish. I immediately thought, 'Here we go. Here's where the other five grand gets added.' I was just expecting all that usual shit you have to go through whenever you buy anything valuable in a poor country. Instead she came across looking very disappointed and told me I couldn't have the ring after all.

I couldn't believe my ears and assumed it was some sort of scam. I told her that she had to sell it to me as we had done a deal, but she explained that it had been damaged. In trying to resize it they had burnt the edge of the emerald and they didn't have any others of the same size.

I was devastated. I was about to begin moaning and complaining and had just got as far as, 'Look – I've been here for nearly two hours...' when she looked at me and said, 'Here. It's yours.' I obviously looked a bit puzzled because she added, 'Take it – it's a gift.'

I told her I couldn't do that and I would have to pay her something. I offered to leave my $200 dollar deposit with her, but she was insistent that she couldn't accept any money and that it was a gift from them to me. I turned to Chris and said, 'Right – let's go!' I stopped to give both the lovely shopkeeper and her daughter a kiss and off I went wearing a $3,700 ring which I had just been given for nowt! What's more, I consider it to be a lucky ring.

It's a wonderful place, Colombia!

# 22

'When I asked Glenn if he would be interested in being Honorary Colonel to Durham Army Cadet Force he gave me an unconditional yes. For him it was the beginning of an enthusiastic journey into the unknown and that seems to sum up Glenn's life.'
Colonel Chris Tierney

I'm proud of my Irish roots and I'm equally proud of my Englishness. I love Britain, Ireland, England, the North East – everywhere that has shaped me. Being from a family with a long tradition of Army service I am also fiercely proud of our armed forces and the great job they do. In recent years I have been handed roles and titles that have only magnified my levels of pride and have made me feel truly honoured.

In 2010 I was asked to become Deputy Lord Lieutenant of Northumberland. Can you believe it? A Stanley lad being an official representative of the Queen? I will always treasure my certificate and the official letter from

Her Majesty appointing me to the position. I took over the role from Jack Charlton, a good friend of mine and a fellow member of that rare club of North East world champions.

Through that appointment I have come to know the Duke and Duchess of Northumberland and achieved perhaps my proudest moment when I officially met the Queen. I am a big fan of the Royal Family and I was so excited when preparing to meet the Queen I must have been like a little kid at Christmas!

In 2011 I received another great honour, this time courtesy of the British Army. My family have been connected with the Army over the years and it is something I have always had a desire to be involved with. It may sound contradictory given that I have admitted that I hate anybody telling me what to do, but somehow the Army is different! I am happy to be instructed by someone who knows what they are talking about. After all, you don't get to become Champion of the World if you're a total rebel who can't take instruction. I feel that if you sign up for the Army you are effectively volunteering to be told what to do. You go in knowing you are going to have to obey orders and you are therefore far more willing to accept them. Whenever I have spent time around the services I have never had that feeling of people just bossing people about. It has always seemed just a natural acceptance of responsibility and teamwork. At the end of the day there is a saying that someone has 'earned their stripes' and that is why people with stripes have the right to issue orders. They're not just some nobody who thinks they know best, they have earned their position by already doing what they are asking you to do and that earns respect.

I also think that I would have valued the team aspect to Army life. Boxing can be a very solitary sport and I found I enjoyed it far more when I had a little team of people I knew and trusted, such as Alan Walker and my brother Neil, around me. I certainly loved that side of things when I trained with the Green Howards at Catterick before the Lennox Lewis fight.

The Army seems like a big family to me. Whenever I have worked with them I have always made friends and they have then come to see me fight, or visited my pub and displayed that comradeship I love. They give you support and backing and they never ask you to do something that you can't do. And, if you are going to find yourself in potential trouble, they give you a gun!

I travelled to Cyprus a couple of years ago as a guest for an inter-military tournament. I was knackered when I arrived, but they insisted I had a couple of pints in the Officers' Mess before I headed off with the colonel with whom I was staying. I got to bed around one o'clock in need of a good long sleep, only to be woken at six by the colonel yelling, 'Right, time to get up! Breakfast is served!' I was wondering whether he had forgotten that I wasn't actually in the Army but I jumped out of bed anyway because I didn't dare disobey orders on my first morning!

I also appeared in a charity football match in memory of a young soldier from Ashington who had sadly been killed in Afghanistan shortly beforehand. The Army asked me to play for their team against what was pretty much Ashington FC as far as I could make out. We got

hammered about 9-0. I was playing alongside the pa-
dre, a brilliant guy called Alan Hughes. There was also
a guy standing on the touchline in his combat gear who
reminded me of the Colonel in the *Rambo* movies. He
was Colonel Chris Tierney and after the game he politely
asked, 'Glenn – we'd love you to be part of our service.
Would you consider being an honorary colonel?'

Of course I accepted. Leaving aside my family's history
and my respect for the armed forces, it is simply a massive honour. I received letters from the Queen and Major-
General DG Jones inviting me to become an Honorary
Colonel of the Durham Army Cadet Force. I have a full
uniform and I even get saluted! It's amazing. If I go to an
army do of some sort I walk in and everybody salutes –
it's a brilliant feeling. Most of all, I feel honoured that my
country seems to be proud of me. I have been trusted with
important titles and roles. I feel a sense that I have been
accepted, a sense that I belong.

My life today seems to be going pretty well. I am certainly
much more optimistic for the future than I was for much
of the previous decade and more.

In the period from David's death in 1996 to the finalis-
ing of my second divorce in 2011, I had many bleak moments. As well as coping with depression, I also suffered
the ignominy of being declared bankrupt in 2008. Following my divorce settlement with Mandy and a hefty tax
bill I was well in the red. The fortune I lost on the aborted
*Hangover*-style film project only made matters worse. Finally, the spiralling costs of fees for the upkeep of my gym
in the absence of the expected grants made my position

impossible. I could see no way of ever getting out of the debt I was in and eventually I was left with little alternative but to file for bankruptcy.

It should be clear by now that money has never been my god and also that I have never been able to manage it properly. I've always lived well and been to great places, but I have had experiences that would send most people hurtling towards a breakdown. On more than one occasion I have been left standing at a hotel reception desk with a three-grand bill and no money on me and been forced to plead for help via numerous urgent phone calls after my credit card had been rejected again. The people I would call often asked me how I had managed to get hold of a credit card in the first place, but the truth is they were generally taken off me pretty rapidly.

That period of my life was not all bad, however. While with Miranda I created the 'Ten Club' which has been running for nearly a decade now and long may it continue.

I've had various houses over the years and lived all over the place, but when I was with Miranda we rented a house in Bothal, next to Bothal Castle near Morpeth in Northumberland. It was like an absolute fantasy – the most gorgeous little place on God's earth. It's not even a village, merely a handful of houses next to the castle, but it's like something out of a fairytale.

We were a bit daft really, in that we wanted to make it into some sort of palace and ended up spending far too much doing all sorts of stuff to the property that we couldn't take with us because it was rented accommodation. However, one of the things we did buy was a big dining table. I had always wanted a beautiful table because I love cooking and the whole occasion of preparing and serving food. We had such a beautiful dining room that it seemed an ideal opportunity.

As well as loving to prepare food, I also love dressing up for special occasions. Boxers are almost always dandies, often because they had been so poor earlier in their lives. When they get a few quid, one of the first things they tend to do is buy a nice suit. I am no exception. I installed a large, rectangular table, put up some chandeliers and decided that it would be a waste for just the two of us, so I simply had to entertain and that it would have to be in formal attire. I think I felt that, living in the country in the shadow of a castle, I could somehow play at being the gentry for once.

I've been blessed with great friends like Malcolm Dix, head of Sport Newcastle; Peter Ratcliffe, who helped run the Newcastle Eagles' basketball team; Colonel John Astbury; John Gibson from the *Chronicle* and Bob Gladwin, the Chairman of the Variety Club; all of whom have helped to look after me for thirty years. I am also big friends with Jack Charlton, as well as many colleagues from the world of boxing. I thought, with my love of cooking and entertaining, what could be better than to get these people round a table for a gentlemen's dinner? To bring together a group of my friends from all walks of life, sit them round a table and have gentlemanly discussions about the things we love: sport, food and drink, lives and family. I initially thought of it as nothing more than a daft idea which might create a fun night.

I came up with the name Ten Club because I wanted to call it something and there were ten seats around the table so it seemed like a natural name to me. Right from the start I felt that if you were invited then you would be filling one of the ten seats and were therefore a member of the Ten Club for the night.

What started as an idea for a one off, with hopes that it may be repeated if it went okay, has turned into a regular event over the last decade. The table even survived my move from Bothal to my top-floor apartment in Jesmond, Newcastle after which the removal men announced 'never again Glenn!' having lugged it up three flights of stairs! When I installed a baby grand piano in 2012 I had to get my friend Ian Freeman, the former MMA Champion, to help manoeuvre it into the flat as the professional piano movers had been unable to manage it!

The Ten Club evenings tend to happen whenever I want them to. They depend largely on my schedule, but I try to have them if there is a special occasion of some sort, or sometimes if I'm just bored or lonely. We've had them for people's birthdays, the two hundredth anniversary of the Battle of Trafalgar, the Queen's Diamond Jubilee, Burns' Night, St Patrick's Day – generally for any occasion on which you can celebrate and propose a toast. I swiftly changed my initial plan of it being a men-only evening and, on one occasion, it ended up being just me and nine ladies! I thought it would be the worst night ever, but it turned out to be one of the best Ten Club nights I've ever had.

I suppose my enjoyment of the club nights harks back to my love of theatre and putting on a show. It is precisely the sort of evening that used to happen in the days of literary heroes of mine such as Oscar Wilde. I insist on formal wear – men in tuxedos and bow ties and women in evening dress. It has become a much-loved occasion among my friends and associates – people love to get an invite to the Ten Club – and over the years I have hosted the likes of Frank Maloney, Johnny Nelson, Jack Charlton, several of the newsreaders from the North East region and my crew of Malcolm Dix, Peter Ratcliffe, Gibbo and my lawyer, George Lyall, who, being a Scot, turns up in his kilt. It is also a tradition for guests to sign their name on my toilet wall. You should see the list of names and comments in there!

Life for me is about making things special and having good nights. I have also always loved to meet nice people. With the Ten Club I can satisfy all these urges and indulge my love of cooking at the same time.

Mentioning Jack Charlton, he is a great friend who I have known for many years ever since I used to sit at the table as teenager with him, his mother Cissie, and his cousin Jackie Milburn at Malcolm Dix's Newcastle Sports Council annual awards. We had a memorable occasion a couple of years ago when he invited me to join him on a fishing trip on the River Tweed.

I had been fishing with Jack a couple of times before and he has helped teach me a few things as I really don't know what I'm doing. This one particular occasion he invited me and my brother Shaun, a keen angler, to meet him at Ponteland from where we would head to the River Tweed in the countryside a few miles from Berwick, which Jack knew as being a superb spot for catching a few nice fish.

We set off early on a bitterly cold January morning and after a couple of hours' drive Jack pulled in and we wandered down to the riverbank. Shaun climbed down the side of the bank near a bridge, where there was a bit of a drop, then Jack suddenly stopped and stood still. I assumed he meant for me to go around him so I tried to pass on his outside when I lost my footing and went arse over tip straight into the icy waters of the Tweed. It was pretty deep and I became entirely submerged with my hat lifting off my head, before I popped back up, replaced my hat and looked up to see Jack and Shaun both staring at me with a look of total disgust and disdain. Neither of them spoke, they just walked away and began to fish!

I clambered out of the water and wrung myself out as best I could. I suddenly realised that I was soaking wet, freezing cold and miles from anywhere with no change of clothing. I didn't know what to do as I didn't want to spoil Jack's day or let him down, so I simply strode into the water and began fishing. The water was about three-feet deep outside my waders and four-feet deep inside! I spent what must have been two hours standing there absolutely freezing with neither Jack nor Shaun looking at me or mentioning what had just happened.

Eventually I was that cold that I couldn't feel my legs so I called to Jack to tell him I couldn't take it any longer. I felt I was going to die. His response was to call back, 'What took you so long lad? I thought you'd have gone ages ago.'

I took Jack's car and drove a couple of miles to a small shop which sold clothes and went inside, soaked to my skin and shivering, and explained my story to the two ladies who worked there. After they had finished laughing they were lovely and told me to use their shower and warm myself up before I froze to death.

I bought a cheap pair of jeans and some other bits and pieces and drove back to Jack and Shaun. Jack casually stated, 'I was getting a bit worried about you. I have no idea why you went and stood in the water for so long – if I was you I'd have left ages ago.' Well why didn't you tell me that two hours before, you bugger?

I know Jack relishes that story to this day and of course, to top it off, I still never caught a damn thing.

What does the future have in store for Glenn McCrory? To be honest, I feel much more positive today than I did a few years ago. That this is the case is down, by and large, to two unconnected events.

Firstly, there is this book. I have been intending to write it for over ten years now and the fact that I have finally got round to it has given me renewed focus in other areas too. Top of the list is telling David's story. We came so close to having a play about him performed and there have been those discussions about a movie but, for some reason, the timing wasn't right. Now I have written this book and a play is imminent, it seems as though it finally is. I have mulled over my life story and recognised how important David was within it. I can honestly say that I think about him every day. In moments of stress or unhappiness he keeps me going. The story of my life is not just about me

– it is the story of David too. It is the story of how our lives weaved themselves together so that one is impossible to relate on its own. I am now more determined than ever that his story will be told to the widest audience possible.

More than that, my very nature is to aim for the stars. I'm not thinking about merely making a film – I intend to win an Oscar. That is the target I have set. The story will be made into a play and a musical and it will appear on Broadway. My goals are always high – I must aim for the stars. In some way that will provide closure. In writing this book I have started that process – the rest will follow and will be my major focus until everything is complete.

Secondly, recent years have seen a major change in my personal circumstances. Earlier I told the story of how I ended up with an emerald ring for nothing after my trip to Colombia. Soon after returning home, I flew to Northern Ireland for a Paul McCloskey fight at the Kings Hall in Belfast. The next day the whole Sky team jetted to London and I ended up in a bar watching Newcastle United take on Manchester City. All of a sudden a gorgeous girl came over and asked me the score. I told her it was currently a draw and she informed me she was a United fan. I assumed she meant Newcastle, as they were playing at the time, but she turned to me and said, 'I meant Manchester United not Newcastle, you numpty!' I made some light-hearted derogatory comment about Manchester United and she returned to her friends. A moment or two later she came back over to apologise and to say that, in actual fact, Newcastle were her second team. I looked at her and asked if she was single. She said she was and I told her she wasn't anymore! At that she rolled her eyes and made a little noise to suggest the phrase 'in your dreams' was floating around her head. She returned to her friends again and I remained sitting there thinking she had been right – I was a numpty!

Before I left I thought, 'nothing ventured...' and went over to say, 'I think I'd better have my girlfriend's number before I leave.' Incredibly she gave me it! I couldn't believe my luck! It was the first time I had been out wearing my new emerald ring, I had spent the previous night in the Emerald Isle and had now asked an Irish girl out. I have known girls from all over the world but, incredibly, I don't think I had even spoken to an Irish girl before, never mind had any form of relationship with one. Even more incredibly, given my rather cocky opening line, she had given me her number and we spent the next couple of weeks texting each other non-stop.

Nicola is from Donegal in the north-west of the Republic of Ireland. Like mine, her family is an odd mix of bloodlines over many generations but Nicola is fully-fledged Irish with all the history that goes with it. The Irish thing has always been a big thing in my life in that I never really knew where I belonged. I've always had this feeling that if you achieve something in the world you want to stand and state proudly, 'I am from the clan McCrory and this is my history,' yet I have never felt able to do that because I don't really feel I have a history. I was born in North East England and I love where I'm from. I often look at some of the numbnuts out there in this country displaying such dismal behaviour at times that I despair, but I've never known a nation that can come together so amazingly when required. In some ways that is how I am myself I guess. I can be the biggest idiot in the world but tell me to stand up and do my bit and I will. I believe that is something wonderful about this country. I think we all like to think we belong to something and so my Irish heritage has always played a strong part in my life too. I've been a success in my life but the one thing I haven't got is history. Nicola's family has that in abundance.

2014 was also a big year for me. Not only did I hit fifty in September, but it saw the twenty-fifth anniversary of both winning the world title and my first broadcast for Sky. To be at Wembley Stadium with David Haye and Johnny Nelson, giving our considered opinions on Froch-Groves 2, with 80,000 spectators there to witness possibly the biggest British boxing occasion ever, seemed a fitting way to mark my twenty-five years with Sky Sports.

Even more fitting was discovering, on the twenty-fifth anniversary of that incredible night in Stanley when I beat Patrick Lumumba to win the world title, that Nicola and I were to have a baby boy. Little Aidan duly arrived to add to the growing clan. Nicola and I already had a beautiful daughter, Aoife. Her initial due date made me feel that it was another part of God's plan to tie up the loose ends of my life. 2 March was the date we were given: David's birthday. Nicola has another lovely daughter, Caoimhe, from a previous relationship. She too is a welcome addition to the family and a great big sister to Aoife and Aidan. I now have six children I love dearly and always will.

I am so proud of my kids: Victoria, Joe, Maya, Caoimhe, Aoife and little Aidan. I am getting used to changing nappies again – even more so in my new role as Granddad.

Joe's partner, Charlotte, gave birth in December 2013 to my first grandchild, a lovely little girl called Esmae, making Aoife an auntie already and Esmae older than her Uncle Aidan! Soon after that my second gorgeous granddaughter, Annabel Louise, was born to Victoria in May 2014 and then a third arrived with the birth of Joe's second daughter, Isla, in February 2016.

I was also very proud and deeply humbled when, in November 2014, the Variety Club held a dinner in my honour and presented me with a Silver Heart Award – their highest accolade. But although those anniversaries and events are all special in some way to me every day is a blessing. When you've had a brother who lives one day at a time, and you've lived it with him, you then tend to view life like that – something to experience day by day. I've recently lost three friends I knew quite well, all dying not long past fifty, and it's the same when I go to the annual Boxing Writers Dinner, which I've been attending for longer than I care to remember. There's a point in the evening when they refer to 'our friends who can't be with us' before displaying the names of all those connected with the sport who have passed away over the previous twelve months.

I spoke to someone recently who works in mental health and I am aware that I am still having difficulties in some aspects of my life. There are scars from the past that still show from time to time. I have tried to sweep these under the carpet but I now accept that putting your head in the sand is not a long-term solution. Of course I'm glad I won a world title despite all the troubles and the hardships, but I'm also still bitter, resentful and angry that I was treated so badly. I also know that carrying David was a lasting, painful experience. There was a lot of joy in supporting my brother but there was never going to be some great outcome. There was no light at the end of the tunnel. It was an unavoidably downward spiral that was always going to end with his death. Trying to cope with that has left its mark.

Seeing Shaun Curry, my friend as a kid, dying so young doing the sport I love. Losing Tommy Gardiner who was a mentor, who gave me an education by lending me his boxing books and who was the first person to take me away with him and show me new places. These things too have had an impact. And, of course, there are the difficult times I experienced in two marriages. I've been through some dreadful relationship experiences, going all the way back to my teens, so in some ways I accept that I'm something of a nightmare because I've got no relationship training. I probably need to be taken away, re-programmed and then sent out into the world again. All these things have taken their toll and left me with scars that are still not fixed. What the future has in store is impossible to say.

We might like to think that we will drift off into the sunset and sit on a nice beach in Spain with a large glass in our hand, which in my case never empties, but life is rarely like that. You never know what's around the corner and what you might have to face. By carrying David with me at all times I am able to appreciate that every day is a new day with fresh challenges and new experiences to seek out. I believe I am finally ready to settle down and enjoy a calmer few years, but I know that I will always have something inside me making me want to go out and search for more. And in the words of Dante: 'For better waters heading with the wind; My ship of genius now shakes out her sail; And leaves that ocean of despair behind.'

# ACKNOWLEDGEMENTS

It's been my ambition to tell my story – and that of David – for many years now. I'm so happy that it's finally done. A big thank you has to go to Paul Dixon for the hours he has spent listening, prodding and searching. Well done mate. But there are so many others who have played their part in making this journey so amazing.

Truth be told, I've met hundreds of good people who have been nice to me and I would love to mention all of them in this book. I want to acknowledge every single one by name, but I can't, or it would end up like a telephone directory! So, having thought about it, the one thing I want to say is that they will know who they are. People will know if they have been my friend and helped me over the years. They may be looking for a name check but, ultimately, my book is not about that – it's my journey – so they can sod off! Joking aside, they know who they are and I thank them all.

Specifically though, I must mention my parents, whom I adore. Dad, I miss you. Also my sisters Karen and Kelly, along with brothers Gary, David, Neil and Shaun, who must have got sick of hearing my name at times.

Friends – where do I begin? John Gibson, of course, who has been a friend and mentor for most of the way; Chris Payne for looking after his boy. Leonard Trusty, who would laugh as the wheels came off. Davey Moat, Mal Dix, Peter Ratcliffe, Bob Gladwin, Cesar Aceituno, little Billy Hardy, Danny Naylor, Spencer Oliver, David Bourne, Cash Hussein and all the guys who have touched my life and laughed along the way.

Thanks also to Sky TV. One of my greatest achievements is twenty-five years and counting in boxing broadcasting. To Ian Darke, Bob Mee, Adam Smith, Jim Watt, Nick Hawling, Johnny Nelson, Paul Dempsey, Dave Clark, Ed, Charles, JB, Sarah and Sara and everyone who has been with me from cameramen to riggers – thank you – it's been a great journey.

To my fellow boxers – it is only in your company that I am truly at home. To every boxer that ever laced up a glove I am immensely proud to stand amongst you. Thank you.

The journos: Colin Hart, Jeff Powell, Steve Bunce, Gareth A Davies, my great pal John Rawling and all the boxing writers – I've spent a quarter of a century with you talking about the fighters and the writers and I've relished every minute in your company. From Hemingway to Hart. Mine's a red boys!

And thank you to Nicola and to all my wonderful children. Victoria and Joe, I am truly proud of you both. Maya and Aoife; you are my little princesses. Aidan, you are already such a character. Not forgetting my lovely stepdaughter, Caoimhe. And to the latest arrivals: my wonderful granddaughters Esmae, Annabel and Isla. I adore you all.

INNOVATIVE AND EXCITING SPORTS BOOKS

**Chequered Flag**
PUBLISHING

www.chequeredflagpublishing.co.uk